D0207931

United States Policies and the Latin American Economies

United States Policies and the Latin American Economies

Edited by
Werner Baer and Donald V. Coes

PRAEGER

New York
Westport, Connecticut
London

Library of Congress Cataloging-in-Publication Data

United States policies and the Latin American economies / edited by
  Werner Baer and Donald V. Coes.
      p. cm.
    Includes bibliographical references.
    ISBN 0-275-93502-7 (alk. paper)
    1. Latin America—Foreign economic relations—United States.
    2. United States—Foreign economic relations—Latin America.
    3. Latin America—Economic conditions—1982- . I. Baer, Werner,
  1931- . II. Coes, Donald V., 1943- .
  HF1480.55.U5U55   1990
  337.7308—dc20   90-31182

Library of Congress Catalog Card Number: 90-31182
ISBN: 0-275-93502-7

First published in 1990

Praeger Publishers, One Madison Avenue, New York, NY 10010
An imprint of Greenwood Publishing Group, Inc.

Printed in the United States of America

The paper used in this book complies with the
Permanent Paper Standard issued by the National
Information Standards Organization (Z39.48-1984).

10 9 8 7 6 5 4 3 2 1

In Memory of
Bruce Bushey

Contents

Tables   ix

Introduction
    Werner Baer and Donald V. Coes   1

1.   Baker to Brady to Chance? Tinkering with the Latin American Debt Crisis
    David Felix and John Caskey   5

2.   United States Policies and Latin America's Trade and Debt
    Werner Baer and Donald V. Coes   39

3.   Economic Growth and External Debt: Some Analytical Macroeconomic Issues for the "Baker Plan"
    Paul Beckerman   55

4.   Privatization and the State Sector
    William Glade   75

5.   Economic Performance of Public Enterprises in Latin America: Lessons from Argentina and Brazil
    Melissa H. Birch   97

6.   United States Policies and the Labor Sector in Latin America
    Russell E. Smith   121

7.   Debt Servicing and Its Impact on Financial Markets in Latin America
    John H. Welch   137

8.   U.S. Policies and the Prospects for Latin American Economic Integration
    Carlos Alberto Primo Braga   153

Bibliography   169

Author Index   179

Subject Index   183

Contributors   197

Tables

1.1   Market Prices of Highly Indebted LDC Debt, 1987–89   7

1.2   Bank Exposure in Latin America, 1982–87   10

1.3A Size and Distribution of the External Debt of Latin
      America and Its Major Debtor Countries: 1982   11

1.3B Size and Distribution of the External Debt of Latin
      America and Its Major Debtor Countries: 1987   12

1.4   Debt and Net Resource Transfers of Major Latin
      American Debtors, 1980–86   14

1.5   Indices of Real GDP and Consumption per Head and the
      Real Industrial Wage, 1982–88   16

1.6   Real Gross Investment per Worker, 1970 and 1982–88   17

1.7   Annual Percentage Increases in Consumer Prices, 1983–88   18

1.8   New Loans in Relation to External Debt   19

1.9   Foreign Debts and Foreign Assets of Six Major Latin
      American Debtor Countries   21

1.10 Projected Percentage Change in Per Capita Consumption
      Between 1990 and 2000   23

1.11 Projected Annual Net New Lending Requirements   24

1.12 Projected Debt Burden Ratios   26

1.13 Projected Debt Burden Ratios   28

1.14 Internal Debt of Private Sector as Percent of GDP,
      1975–85   30

1.15 Fiscal Deficits and Tax Revenues as Percent of GDP   32

1.16 Interest and Public Investment Shares of Fiscal
      Expenditure, 1970–88   33

1.17 Private Foreign and Domestic Deposits, 1980–85   34

2.1   U.S. Merchandise Trade with Latin America   40

2.2   Latin American Trade and Investment Earning Balances
      with the United States   41

2.3   U.S. and Latin American Trade Shares   42

2.4   Net U.S. Service Trade with Latin America   43

2.5   U.S. Financial Capital Flows to Latin America: Banking
      and Total Net Capital Flows   46

2.6 U.S. Financial Capital Flows to Latin America: Securities
     and Non-Banking   47
2.7 U.S. Direct Investment Balance with Latin America
     (Millions US$)   48
3.1A Debt Stabilizing Real Growth Rates   62
3.1B Debt Stabilizing Real Growth Rates   63
3.2 Domestic Saving in Latin America, 1976–86   64
3.3 Simulation of Economic Growth and External Debt   70
5.1 Distribution of Nonfinancial State Enterprises by Major
     Sector and Sphere of Government in Brazil and Argentina   99
5.2 Indicators of Economic Performance, 1965–83   103
5.3 Enterprises Included and Years Covered   104
5.4 Indices of Output of State-Owned Enterprise   106
5.5 Real Rates of Growth of Public Enterprise Investment
     and Output   107
5.6 Sectoral Allocation of Public Enterprise Investment   108
5.7 State-Owned Enterprise Employment   109
5.8 Capital/Labor Ratios, Selected Years   111
5.9 Capital/Output Ratios   112
5.10 Alternative Capital/Output Ratios: Capital per Unit of
     Physical Output, Argentina   113
5.11 Productivity: Value Added per Employee   114
5.12 Productivity: Physical Output per Worker, Argentina   115
5.13 Real Rate of Return in State-Owned Enterprises   116
7.1 Value Added by the Financial Sector   142
7.2 Average Financial Market Size: 1981–86   142
7.3 Financial Efficiency Index: I   143
7.4 Financial Efficiency Index: II   143
7.5 Average Annual Resource Transfer   148
8.1 Latin America and Caribbean: Exports and Regional
     Integration Programs   154

Introduction

Werner Baer and Donald V. Coes

The United States has not had a cohesive policy toward Latin America since the Kennedy administration's Alliance for Progress. That policy consisted of the commitment of a relatively large amount of U.S. public aid, both bilateral and via multilateral organizations, to the region, conditional on each country producing development plans with substantial socio-economic reforms. The goal of the Alliance for Progress was "growth with equity," or equivalently, economic development.

Unfortunately, the Alliance for Progress did not achieve its goals. As one perceptive observer put it,

in general the institutional structures of these societies showed little change. How could they, when a central premise of the whole effort was that private enterprise, most especially including foreign investors, was the key to national progress? The program lacked any definition of what to do about the many possible conflicts between the concerns of private investors and the goal of structural reform. Private enterprise can be an important key to progress, but if intended reforms are checked whenever they run contrary to the interests of the people responsible for the society's existing institutions, the reforms cannot be expected to change the institutions.[1]

The lack of cohesiveness in U.S. economic policy has manifested itself on a number of fronts. Examination of U.S. positions on individual issues, however, does suggest a kind of implicit policy structure. This consisted of a group of disparate and even politically contradictory positions. Over the 1970s and 1980s, U.S. economic policy toward Latin America included the following positions:

1. Pressure on Latin American economies to liberalize their trade;
2. Advocacy in the 1970s of the private recycling of petrodollars as a solution to the problems created by the oil shocks;
3. With the explosion of the debt crisis in the 1980s, a switch to the position that Latin American economies should adopt adjustment programs that would enable them to service the debt, even if this implied a sharp decline in living standards;

4. Support for a return to democratic regimes and human rights, particularly in countries in which we had few direct security interests;

5. Opposition to the use of tax and credit incentives to diversify Latin American exports, and support instead for more realistic exchange rates;

6. Support, especially in the 1980s, to privatization programs;

7. In the latter 1980s, increasing concern with the environmental impacts of Latin American economic development;

8. Rising concern with Latin American narcotics production and exports to the United States;

9. Resistance to large-scale Latin American labor migration to the United States.

U.S. policy, in short, was far from being a monolithic edifice. This was an obvious result of the various constituencies which, in an open political system like the United States, produce a complex and even tension-ridden foreign policy.

This volume examines a number of these issues. The essays show in detail how the latent tensions among U.S. policy goals have been exacerbated by the economic crises of Latin America in the 1980s.

In their analysis of Latin America's debt crisis, David Felix and John Caskey point out that despite the proprivatization stance, both the banks, and frequently the U.S. government, insisted on socializing the debt, and that ideology often played a role in relationships with debtor countries. They also find that financial liberalization, always pushed by the U.S. government, did not reverse capital flight, but rather encouraged it. Using various alternative projections, they conclude that the resources of the multilateral lending agencies and the lending which commercial creditors are willing to engage in would not be enough to restore adequate growth. They also show that past plans like the Baker Plan required the type of internal adjustments that lowered imports and investments, further compromising long-term growth and modernization. One must conclude that U.S. policy in this area has had rather mixed, if not perverse, results from the point of view of the long-run U.S. interest in Latin America's return to higher real growth.

Werner Baer and Donald Coes examine the contradictory positions of the United States toward Latin America with regard to debt and trade relations. The United States has insisted throughout the 1980s on the continued servicing of the debt. At the same time, because of pressures from various industrial sectors, the U.S. government has demanded that Latin American countries eliminate export incentive programs and liberalize their imports. Although the adverse effects on the trade balance of such reforms could probably be offset by real depreciation, it is still questionable whether the large trade surpluses implied by the continuation of debt servicing would be accepted by import competing sectors in the creditor countries. If so, this leaves substantial debt forgiveness as the only feasible solution.

Paul Beckerman develops a model of an indebted nation that can be used to simulate future real growth and external debt accumulation. Highly indebted developing nations face a difficult macroeconomic trade-off between controlling their external debt and maintaining adequate real growth. Because their external financing flows fell off so sharply over the 1980s and because they have found it difficult to lift their domestic saving rates, they have had to forgo capital formation in order to maintain their heavy debt service. As as result Latin American nations' capital formation has lagged seriously. This implies not only that their growth prospects and debt servicing capacity for the 1990s are more limited than they might otherwise have been, but also that the physical-capital basis of their real export competitiveness has probably eroded. This is why United States policy—which until very recently insisted on the need for Latin American nations to maintain their debt service—has now had to call for a "new deal" on the debt.

William Glade examines privatization, one of the measures recommended as part of adjustment programs. His analysis concentrates on four countries—Argentina, Brazil, Chile and Mexico—where he finds considerable variation in the type of privatization pursued and degrees of success achieved. In Chile, in part for ideological reasons, the government was fully behind the privatization process, which it has generally conducted adroitly. In Brazil the process was allowed to run by itself by letting the development bank (BNDES) privatize firms as opportunities arose. One consequence is that much less privatization has occurred in Brazil than in Chile. In Argentina the process was very slow due to lack of a strong political commitment by the government and also to the erratic macroeconomic policies followed by the state. A similar situation was found in Mexico, though due to adverse general economic circumstances a substantial degree of privatization did take place. Glade's study shows the complexity and range of potential variation in privatization experiences and possibilities while highlighting the critical role of government commitment to the process.

The emphasis on privatization obviously implied favoring a diminishing role of the public sector in Latin America's economies. State enterprises have been increasingly looked upon as inefficient entities whose growth had to be checked and even reversed in order to restructure the region's economies. Melissa Birch's examination of the performance of Argentine and Brazilian public enterprises raises some doubts about such generalizations. She traces the appearance and growth of state enterprises and shows how they often complemented other ownership sectors, especially during the industrialization process. The performance of these firms in Argentina depended on how the governments in power viewed them. When used as instruments for broader national objectives, their financial performance would suffer and they would become a burden to the public purse. In contrast, Brazilian public enterprises performed much better for a longer period of time due to the country's longer period of steady and consistent growth. In periods of economic stagnation, public enterprises often become a drain on public finances and worsen general macroeconomic conditions. Using a relatively robust measure of total return, she concludes that public firms are not necessarily inefficient and that the question of ownership of state enterprise assets is not the real issue, but rather their management as part of the management of the economy as a whole.

Russell Smith examines the impact of direct and indirect U.S. policies on Latin America's labor sector. The sector has to be examined against a background in the 1980s of slow employment growth in the formal sector and the resulting expansion of the informal sector. The redemocratization of the 1980s improved the functioning of the labor relations system and the political participation of unions; also, the process of industrialization increased the sophistication of workers, undermining the older corporatist labor relation systems. Smith shows how U.S. influence on labor relations can only be indirect through the impact of its general economic policies on Latin American economies, its support of open democratic societies in the region, through programs of labor education, workers rights clauses in U.S. trade and investment legislation and in international organizations in which the United States participates.

U.S. policy has emphasized both financial liberalization in Latin America and, at least until very recently, full servicing of the region's debt. John Welch studies the implications of this policy stance in the context of the financial liberalizations that have been attempted to varying degrees in a number of the Latin American economies. He finds that further liberalization is undercut and perhaps not even viable if large resource transfers from the Latin American economies to their creditors continue. These transfers place large strains on domestic financial markets, which must either channel private savings to the indebted public sector, or contend with the consequences of inflation, when domestic markets for public debt are limited.

Latin American regional trade arrangements are the focus of the study by Carlos Primo Braga. Recent U.S. policy has had potentially negative effects in this area, as it has retreated from the global multilateralism of the post-World War II period toward bilateralism. This trend, as exemplified in the recent United States-Canada trade agreement, threatens the trend toward more open trade under way in a number of the Latin American economies, and raises the possibility of trade-diverting regional arrangements, which Braga characterizes as "minilateralism."

NOTE

1. John Sheahan, *Patterns of Development in Latin America*, p. 337.

1

Baker to Brady to Chance? Tinkering with the Latin American Debt Crisis

David Felix and John Caskey

The March 10, 1989 proposal by U.S. Treasury Secretary Nicholas Brady to write off part of the foreign commercial bank debts of the fifteen "highly indebted" LDCs (ten are Latin American) marks an important conceptual shift in the debt crisis containment strategy of the creditor club. It breaks with the public optimism of the crisis managers that the economic restructuring programs they have been pressing on the debtors since 1983 will in time restore the twin goals of economic growth and full debt servicing capability to debtor economies. That optimism, to be sure, had become strained as the time frame for achieving these goals—initially three to four years—kept elongating. But until the Brady announcement, the crisis managers had continued to reject criticism that the twin goals were incompatible, much less that the restructuring programs were fundamentally flawed. By embracing the "Brady Plan" the creditor club is now officially if belatedly conceding the goal incompatibility criticism. Criticisms of the restructuring strategy, however, continue to get the back of the hand. The debtors are still being urged to intensify the liberalization of commodity and financial markets as central components of the economic restructuring effort.

Our chapter assesses whether the debt relief implied by the Brady proposal will suffice to revive economic growth in the major Latin American debtor economies. To allay suspense, our conclusion is pessimistic for two main reasons. The debt relief and renewed lending induced by the proposal are likely to fall well short of the external financing needed to sustain economic growth of the debtor economies, and the proposal's stance on restructuring is probably inappropriate for breaking the domestic financial gridlocks that also impede economic revival in many of the debtors.

In Section I, we summarize the evolution of the creditor crisis containment strategy and of the major Latin American economies since the beginning of the crisis. Section II gives estimates, based on simulation modeling, of the foreign exchange requirements for sustained growth of these countries under alternative assumptions about the state of the world and debt write-offs. Section III explores whether the restructuring policies urged by the creditors have been reducing or augmenting internal barriers to renewed growth in the debtor economies.

I. THE ROAD TO THE BRADY PLAN

The Brady proposal, soon elevated, despite its initial nebulosity, to the Brady "Plan" by the press, is a response to growing threats to the crisis containment efforts emanating from both the creditor and debtor camps. Among the creditors, there is the growing reluctance of commercial banks to participate in the "concerted" lending packages by which the crisis managers have been defusing periodic debt service stoppages and buoying up flagging debtor commitment to the restructuring programs. Among the debtors, there are increasing incidences of payment arrears, food riots, and other indicators that extending the time frame for the restructuring efforts may be reaching political limits. Let us assess each of these threats in more detail.

Phases of the Creditors' Crisis Containment Strategy

The crisis containment strategy has gone through three phases in route to the Brady Plan. In 1982–84 its prime focus was to allay the threat of a global banking crisis. As this threat receded, the main focus after 1984 became geopolitical: to stanch threats of economic and political breakdown in the debtors or their open default and breakaway from market-liberalizing restructuring. Continued participation of the commercial banks in the IMF-crafted concerted lending was judged essential for this. The high point of this phase was the Baker Plan, which called for $20 billion of new commercial bank loans during 1986–88 to "highly-indebted" LDCs willing to adhere to market liberalizing restructuring. This goal fizzled because the banks, having altered their own strategy, were striving to reduce their exposure in the debtor countries. The official creditor club partially covered up the failure by labelling the efforts of banks to exit "the market-based solution." Thus the onset of the third phase.

Initially, the efforts of the bank consortia to negotiate debt adjustments with individual debtor countries using the "menu of options" (debt-equity and debt-debt swaps, buy-backs, exit bonds, etc.) were cheered by the creditor club with a minimal laying on of official hands. The results as regards debt relief, however, also proved minimal. At the end of 1988, the nominal value of Latin America's bank debt swapped for equity was little more than $12 billion (Morgan Guaranty Trust, 1989, p. 7). Of the major Latin American debtors only Chile and Mexico had reduced their overall bank debt. Mexico reduced only modestly, through debt buy-backs by some private firms and a disap-

Table 1.1.
Market Prices of Highly Indebted LDC Debt, 1987–89 (Percent of Face Value)

	March 1987	March 1988	March 1 1989	July 17 1989
Argentina	62–65	26–28	18	19
Brazil	68–70	42–46	28	32
Chile	66–69	58–60	56	65
Mexico	57–59	45–48	34	44
Peru	16–19	5–8	nd	nd
Philippines	72–76	47–49	38	54
Venezuela	72–74	53–55	27	40
Yugoslavia	77–81	44–47	44	54

Note: Brazil 1988 entry is February 1988.
Sources: Calcagno y Martinez (1988), Tabla 19; *The Wall Street Journal*, July 19, 1989.

pointingly weak government debt swap with the banks (*IMF Survey*, July 16, 1989, p. 211).

Although debt-equity swaps remain the preferred option of the U.S. money-center banks, who garner sizeable fees from arranging the swaps, the debtors have lost their initial enthusiasm for that approach. To induce swaps, the central banks of the debtor countries had to allow dollar loans available in the secondary market at substantial discounts (see Table 1.1) to be exchanged for local currency at exchange rates that gave buyers the lion's share of the discount. Repurchasing dollar paper with local currency involved monetary expansion in already inflation-ridden economies. Foreign investments that would have been undertaken in any event received needless exchange rate subsidies that depleted an already inadequate supply of foreign exchange. Investments requiring the subsidy added foreign exchange on net in the short run, but in time the profit outflows were likely to exceed the reduction of interest service from the debt-equity swaps. Politically, subsidizing foreign investors was a hot potato: local businessmen complained of unfair crowding out, nationalists charged *vendepatria*, etc. Whereas in 1985–86 the debtors competed with one another in attracting debt-equity swaps, by 1988 the majority of the programs were in contraction or total suspension.

The Brady Plan now brings official pressure to bear on the banks to grant greater debt relief. The attempt is to strengthen the bargaining power of debtors in negotiations with the banks and to soften bank resistance to loan write-offs by offering creditor club guarantees of their reduced claims.

The March 10 Brady announcement contains two suggestions for strengthening the debtor's negotiating power. The first is that the banks suspend for three years the applicability of the negative pledge and sharing clauses in their loan contracts. In the negative pledge clause, the debtor abjures negotiating separate deals with individual banks, that is, the debtor forswears working the case-by-case approach on the banks. In the sharing clause, members of bank consortia forswear making separate deals. Deals violating the clauses can be challenged in creditor country courts. The second suggestion is that the IMF and World Bank no longer make their loans contingent on the successful completion of parallel negotiations between the debtor and its bank creditors. The two institutions would, in effect, be partly relieved of the duty of arm twisting the debtors on behalf of the banks.

Official financing is also to be used for facilitating write-offs of bank debt. The IMF and the World Bank are to permit part of their structural adjustment loans to be used to help finance debt buy-backs and to guarantee the reduced principal or interest resulting from debt exchange agreements. Other countries with large current account surpluses, notably Japan, are expected to provide much of the requisite financing through contributions to the two multilateral institutions, or bilaterally.

With the debt overhang reduced, the longer-term financing for sustained economic growth of the debtors is to come from renewed voluntary bank lending and from a reversal in capital flight. The *public* emphasis on the need to repatriate the extensive private foreign assets of the debtors is a new development from the creditor side. On the debtor side, reticence about the existence and use of these sizeable assets remains the rule. Moreover, the recent creditor club emphasis is not accompanied by new policy advice on how to achieve repatriation. The debtors are merely to persist in their efforts to liberalize financial markets, ease the tax burden on profits, reduce monetary expansion and fiscal deficits, and maintain "realistic" exchange rates. Revival of voluntary bank lending is also expected to follow soon after successful restructuring.

There is thus a circularity to the Brady Plan. Successful restructuring with growth depends on sustained access to external financing that depends on successful restructuring with growth. The Plan would break into the circle by offering help from the creditor club in extracting debt write-offs from the banks to supplement the modest ongoing lending from the multilateral institutions. This is expected to jump start growth and facilitate attainment of the liberalized markets and monetary-fiscal balance that are to induce the external financing needed to sustain the economic recovery. Whether the circle proves to be benign or vicious depends in the first instance on the response of the banks. Can the Brady Plan induce them to take large write-offs and then resume long-term lending to the defaulting debtors?

Consider the three phases of the creditor club crisis containment strategy. Only in the initial phase did the interests of the banks and the official creditors fully coincide. This was because Mexico's payment suspension in August, 1982 caught the U.S. money-center banks overexposed and overleveraged. The Latin American loans of the nine largest U.S. banks had risen to 2 ¼ times their capital and reserves, while their capital/asset ratio had fallen to a postwar low of 4.6 percent. Provisioning 40 percent reserves against losses on their

Latin American loans—much less than the market discounts on these loans a few years later (see Table 1.1)—would have exposed many of the large banks as insolvent. Nor could they easily augment capital through new share issues. Sensing their fragility, the stock market had already depressed the price/earnings ratios of the money-center banks before the Mexican crisis; after the outbreak it was even less receptive to new bank issues. Moreover, the danger had global dimensions. With the easing of capital controls and banking regulations, foreign banks had greatly increased their deposits in the money-center banks to handle the rapid increase in international capital and trade flows, almost all dollar denominated. The interbank deposits were a ready transmission belt for globalizing a financial panic. Understandably, the money-center banks eagerly participated in the initial lending packages that the U.S. Federal Reserve and the IMF put together to relieve payment stoppages.

Accompanying the emergency lending were comforting statements from bankers—commercial, central and multilateral—and econometric exercises by house economists supporting the thesis that the Latin American debtors were merely illiquid, therefore meriting temporary bailout funding, not insolvent, which would require writing down the debt. Applying the terminology of business accountants to sovereign countries was inappropriate, but the implication of the distinction was clear enough. So was the "damage control" purpose of disseminating the thesis. It offered reassurance to financial markets that the banks were not throwing more good money after bad, and to the debtors that their travail was transitory, with voluntary bank lending returning as the liquidity crisis faded away. It was hoped that the reassurance would at least buy time for the banks to grow out of their insolvency by raising their capital/asset ratios and expanding their non-Latin American assets.

Collaborating in the bailout lending also enabled the banks to strengthen their Latin American claims by getting creditor club help in forcing debtor governments to assume ex post formal responsibility for the foreign liabilities of their private sectors. These made up a large proportion of the total foreign debt in some of the debtor countries: around 30 percent in Argentina and 80 percent in Chile.[1] The private debt had mainly been contracted when the two governments had liberalized their capital markets in order to improve allocating efficiency and strengthen market discipline. To be forced now, in effect, to socialize the foreign liabilities of their private sectors came as a shock to the free market policy planners of the two governments. But for the banks the option of using local contract law to seize collateral from delinquent debtors—to do debt-equity swaps—was unappealing in light of the collapsing asset values in the debtor economies. As shown in Table 1.2, the rise in the total debt during 1982–87 was in all six countries accompanied by a large increase of the publicly guaranteed proportion.

There was a latent conflict between the overexposed money-center banks and the less-exposed banks in the lending syndicates. Were their Latin American loans to go bad, the money-center banks would be insolvent. Hence with

Table 1.2.
Bank Exposure in Latin America, 1982–87

	Nine US Money Center Banks		Other US Banks		Total Latin American Bank Debt ($ billion)
	Amount ($ billion)	Change (percent)	Amount ($ billion)	Change (percent)	
Latin American Loans					
1982	49.9	--	33.0	--	261
1984	54.2	4.2	33.0	0.0	287
1986	51.0	-3.0	27.9	-15.5	289
1987	49.3	-3.3	25.4	-9.9	--
Loans to Argentina, Brazil and Mexico					
1982	32.7	--	22.7	--	171.0
1984	35.6	8.9	22.8	0.4	175.4
1986	34.8	-1.1	19.8	-13.2	187.8
1987	34.7	-0.3	18.1	-8.6	189.2

Source: Calcagno y Martinez (1988), Apendice Estadistico, Tablas 11, 16.

limited liability, deposit insurance, and central bank protection against a liquidity squeeze from depositor runs, they were in a heads-I-win-tails-you-lose situation as regards bailout lending. The gains, were the bailouts to delay open defaults long enough to allow the banks to regain solvency or, were the liquidity thesis to prove correct, would accrue to the banks. The losses, were neither to happen, would be borne by large depositors and bank deposit insurers. Less-exposed banks, on the other hand, would risk some of their equity by participating in bailout lending.[2] The money-center banks and the Fed therefore had to strong-arm many of the less-exposed banks of the syndicates into contributing. Even so there was slippage, some banks selling their Latin American portfolio and exiting from the syndicates. Tables 1.3A and 1.3B show that all of the increased U.S. bank lending to Latin America between 1982 and 1984 came from the money-center bank group.

By 1985 however, most money-center banks had reached or were near solvency again, with rising capital/asset ratios and falling relative Latin American exposure. The profit-loss-risk calculus would now dissuade the money-center banks from further bailout lending, unless debtor progress was validating the liquidity thesis. However, as Table 1.4 shows, the limited progress in the dimensions relevant to the banks was slackening. The ratios of trade surplus to interest paid, which had been moving upward in most of the debtors after 1982, began falling off in many after 1984, while the Debt/GNP and Debt/Export ratios continued rising. All the preceding happened while most

Table 1.3A.
Size and Distribution of the External Debt of Latin America and Its Major Debtor Countries: 1982

	Argentina	Brazil	Chile	Mexico
Total External Debt (Billions US$)	43.6	91.9	17.3	86.1
Percent Publicly Guaranteed [a]	36.4	55.9	30.3	60.2
Percent from Private Lenders [b]	62.0	79.6	75.3	62.9
Percent Short-term, excluding IMF credits	37.9	19.0	19.3	30.4

	Peru	Venezuela	Latin America
Total External Debt (Millions US$)	12.3	32.0	333.2
Percent Publicly Guaranteed [a]	61.9	38.5	53.7
Percent from Private Lenders [b]	55.3	55.4	73.1
Percent Short-term, excluding IMF credits	24.6	45.9	27.5

Note: (a) Includes IMF credits; (b) Short- and Long-term loans. For lack of a breakdown, unidentified short-term debt in the source tables are assumed to be owed to private lenders.
Source: World Bank, *World Debt Tables*, 1988–89, Vols. I and II.

of the major debtors were still relying on new loans to cover part of their interest bill.

Table 1.3 shows that both groups of U.S banks were reducing their loans outstanding to Latin America in 1986 and 1987, the Baker Plan years. To emphasize their change of strategy, the money-center banks announced in 1987 a first-time provisioning of bad loan reserves against their Latin American loans. The slight increase in Latin America's total bank debt after 1984 shown in Tables 1.2 and 1.3 does not mean that non-U.S. banks were filling the vacuum. Much of the increase reflects a rise in the dollar value of non-dollar denominated foreign debt. The share of that debt in the total rose dramatically after 1984 when the dollar began falling relative to the yen and key European currencies and the banks of those countries insisted on refinancing their dollar

Table 1.3B.
Size and Distribution of the External Debt of Latin America and Its Major Debtor Countries: 1987

	Argentina	Brazil	Chile	Mexico
Total External Debt (Billions US$)	56.8	123.9	21.2	107.9
Percent Publicly Guaranteed [a]	89.8	77.2	80.0	81.5
Percent from Private Lenders [b]	77.7	54.2	67.3	81.7
Percent Short-term, excluding IMF credits	4.7	11.2	8.3	5.4

	Peru	Venezuela	Latin America
Total External Debt (Billions US$)	18.1	36.5	442.5
Percent Publicly Guaranteed [a]	81.8	69.1	80.6
Percent from Private Lenders [b]	48.8	86.6	65.2
Percent Short-term, excluding IMF credits	18.2	10.3	9.1

Note: (a) Includes IMF credits; (b) Short- and Long-term loans. For lack of a breakdown, unidentified short-term debt in the source tables are assumed to be owed to private lenders.
Source: World Bank, *World Debt Tables*, 1988–89, Vols. I and II.

Latin American loans with new maturities denominated in their own currencies.[3]

The current withdrawal strategy of the banks is thus at odds with the Brady Plan's expectation that the banks will be a major source of long-term financing of the hoped-for revival of economic growth of the Latin American debtors. The large debt write-offs that the banks are expected to grant on existing debt merely increases the incongruity.

Are the instruments of coercion and inducements in the Brady Plan as unveiled thus far adequate to overcome the incongruity? The ready answer is that they seem inadequate even for obtaining significant write-offs. As regards coercion, the initial suggestion that banks suspend the negative pledge and sharing clauses has now been withdrawn. "It was a mistake," Treasury Under-

Secretary Mulford explained (*The Wall Street Journal,* May 10, 1989). The mistake presumably, was underestimating the political clout of the banks rather than overestimating the strengthened bargaining power of the debtors the suspension might have effected. As for inducements, the financial assistance unveiled thus far for underwriting debt reduction is quite modest. Japan has pledged $10 billion over a five-year period for this purpose. The IMF and World Bank are reputedly budgeting $12 billion each over the next three years for the highly indebted LDCs, of which up to 25 to 30 percent may be made available to underwrite debt reductions. The Bush administration is pressuring West Germany and Taiwan(!), contending that countries with large current account surpluses should be the major underwriters. This contention, which has the added virtue of absolving the United States from putting its own money where its mouth is, is receiving a frosty response from Germany, which pointed out that it was more heavily engaged than the United States in lending to East Europe, a more important region for Germany than is Latin America (*The New York Times,* July 20, 1989). Unless there are very large write-offs of the $290 billion of bank loans outstanding to the highly indebted LDCs, the $20 billion or so of underwriting money currently pledged cannot guarantee a great deal of the remaining debt.

The Mexican agreement, the first tangible product of the Brady Plan, reflects the weakness of the coercion and inducement instruments. Under prolonged pressure from the U.S. government, which viewed the Mexican negotiations as the crucial test case of the Plan, the negotiators agreed in July, 1989, on a menu of debt relief options. Assuming the hundreds of banks involved eventually fulfill their quotas, the outcome, according to U.S. Treasury estimates, will probably be a one-time 5.5 percent reduction of the stock of bank debt and $1.5 billion lowering of annual interest on that stock. However, because of the heavy volume of new lending pledged this year from the IMF, World Bank and Japan, plus the capitalization of interest on debts owed to the Paris Club governments, Mexico's overall debt will probably rise and the net decline of its total annual interest bill will be minimal (*The Wall Street Journal,* July 25, 1989). The first test case of the Brady Plan reduces the bank debt but not the debt overhang.

The Mexican agreement suggests that the Brady Plan is still forced to operate in the earlier crisis containment mode that produced the pattern shown in Table 1.4 (official lending to keep the debtors more or less current on their interest bills to the banks which raises debt and future debt service) while the banks gradually extricate themselves from long-term lending to Latin America.

The agreement also points up a perverse selectivity in the Brady Plan that further weakens its ability to coerce the banks into accepting large write-offs. The banks had reason to be confident that Mexico's current regime would avoid invoking a payment moratorium as a bargaining weapon, since the reattainment of international creditworthiness in order to attract foreign capital

Table 1.4.
Debt and Net Resource Transfers of Major Latin American Debtors, 1980–86

	Argentina	Brazil	Chile	Mexico	Peru	Venezuela
Net Resource Transfer as Percent of GNP[a]						
1980–82	0.2	-1.5	-4.9	-0.8	-0.4	15.1
1983–84	2.3	0.3	0.6	7.4	0.1	36.8
1985–86	2.1	3.5	2.1	6.5	0.6	12.2
1987	0.5	1.5	2.5	3.5	-1.6	7.6
Foreign Debt/GNP						
1980–82	0.65	0.33	0.58	0.40	0.47	0.48
1983–84	0.72	0.52	1.08	0.65	0.66	0.66
1985–86	0.74	0.45	1.42	0.71	0.74	0.72
1987	0.74	0.39	1.24	0.78	0.41	0.95
Foreign Debt/Exports of Goods and Services						
1980–82	3.16	3.30	2.70	2.67	2.48	1.40
1983–84	4.67	3.76	3.96	3.11	3.24	2.03
1985–86	5.09	4.05	4.08	3.77	4.16	2.59
1987	6.61	4.32	3.27	3.63	5.03	2.84
Balance, Goods and Non-Factor Service/Interest Paid on Foreign Debt[b]						
1980–82	-1.09	-0.81	-1.28	-0.66	-0.79	1.77
1983–84	0.11	0.44	-0.09	1.41	-0.17	3.21
1985–86	0.49	0.59	0.00	0.83	-0.45	1.16
1987	-0.16	0.64	0.06	1.36	-8.63	0.77

Notes: (a) (Current Account Balance + net profit transfers + interest paid on foreign debt −
change of international reserves)/GNP, all values converted into current US$. Negative num-
ber represents a resource inflow. (b) Excludes arrears and unpaid capitalized interest.
Sources: World Bank, *World Debt Tables,* 1988–89; Inter-American Development Bank, *Economic and Social Progress in Latin America,* Annual Reports, various years. Statistical Ap-
pendices.

is a central objective of the market liberalizing strategy on which it is staking
its political life. They also knew that Washington was making special efforts,
using the multilateral institutions and even its own resources, to help Mexico
stick with that strategy. Hanging tough in order to collect interest on the full
bank debt could, of course, backfire on the banks were Mexican restructuring
to fail or the regime to fall. There are also the Peruvian and Argentine examples to consider. But the opportunity cost to the banks of taking large write-
offs in exchange for creditor club guarantees is much higher on the loans to
countries like Mexico that meet Brady Plan eligibility requirements for the
guarantees than it is on loans to non-payers like Peru and Argentina, whose
delinquency makes them ineligible for the guarantees.

If, as the Brady Plan proponents seem to believe, rewarding the virtuous will encourage the others to shape up and become eligible, the perverse selection bias in the plan may not prove damaging. That presumes, however, that not shaping up has been primarily from lack of political will and not from flaws in the market-oriented restructuring approach.

Restructuring Efforts and the "Lost Decade"

When Latin Americans refer to the 1980s as their "lost decade" they can easily document their case statistically. When the creditors laud the progress in restructuring, their documentation problems are more difficult. In this section we try briefly to summarize the statistical backing for each perspective.

Table 1.5 provides the statistical underpinnings of the food riots and other manifestations of rising social tensions in most of the debtor countries. It shows, first of all, that the large drop in GDP per capita that afflicted all six countries after 1981 has in four of the six persisted through 1988. Of the other two, Brazil shows a nonmonotonic partial rebound while Chile has overtaken its 1980 level of GDP per capita. As regards the domestic availability of goods, however, 1988 Chile was still short of 1980 due to the large reversal of external resource transfers shown in Table 1.4.

Secondly, Table 1.5 shows that consumption in all six countries declined proportionately no more than, and in some cases less than, the GDP. That is, to effect the net outward resource transfers shown in Table 1.4, the required drop in absorption depressed investment much more than consumption.

Thirdly, real wages have fallen substantially more than consumption per head in at least four of the six countries. Since formal sector employment also slackened, it appears that the decline in consumption in the majority of these countries has been absorbed mainly by the wage-salary classes. To be sure, informal sector employment has risen, but wage competition from that low wage sector can hardly do more than dampen the decline of formal sector wages. Thus accompanying the rising social tensions in many of the debtor countries has been not merely reduced consumption but also grossly inequitable impositions of the reduction.

Table 1.6 documents the massive decline of real investment per worker and gives an important clue to why the time frame for successful restructuring keeps elongating. In 1988 investment per worker remained well below not only the level of 1980–81, but, except for Brazil, below the level of 1970. Restructuring through market liberalization is supposed to produce two types of efficiency benefits. The more important is an improved resource allocation that "getting prices right" is expected to encourage. The less important is the gain in X-efficiency that increasing external competition is expected to generate in existing facilities—enhanced competition is expected to force more effort from the managers and workers of these facilities. Reallocating resources to activities favored by the "correct" set of relative prices requires, however, re-

Table 1.5.
Indices of Real GDP and Consumption per Head and the Real Industrial Wage,
1982–88 (1980 = 100)

	1982	1983	1984	1985	1986	1987	1988
Argentina							
GDP per capita	85.7	87.1	87.9	82.6	85.9	86.2	85.2
Consumption per capita	84.4	85.4	89.3	82.3	87.3	87.9	95.8
Industrial wage	79.3	106.3	135.0	118.5	111.8	103.3	n.a.
Brazil							
GDP per capita	94.5	89.3	92.0	94.8	99.8	101.2	98.7
Consumption per capita	97.6	91.3	92.9	93.1	99.6	100.6	95.8
Industrial wage	99.2	87.9	80.5	82.9	83.1	61.2	n.a.
Chile							
GDP per capita	87.7	85.6	89.5	90.1	93.7	97.4	102.8
Consumption per capita	93.8	89.5	89.1	86.7	88.5	90.4	96.9
Industrial wage	101.0	86.4	86.6	82.4	82.9	83.5	n.a.
Mexico							
GDP per capita	101.0	89.7	90.9	97.6	91.8	91.0	89.8
Consumption per capita	103.9	94.3	95.6	96.3	91.6	90.3	89.6
Industrial wage	87.2	80.4	74.4	73.4	67.6	63.4	n.a.
Peru							
GDP per capita	98.8	90.1	88.7	86.6	93.9	98.7	87.5
Consumption per capita	96.8	90.4	88.7	86.6	97.1	103.7	94.5
Industrial wage	98.0	95.2	85.9	74.7	86.8	94.1	n.a.

Table 1.5.
(continued)

	1982	1983	1984	1985	1986	1987	1988
Venezuela							
GDP per capita	94.6	86.8	85.6	82.3	85.6	85.7	86.2
Consumption per capita	97.7	87.2	81.1	77.9	78.2	76.4	81.8
Industrial wage	93.5	86.8	80.2	80.4	n.a	n.a	n.a

Sources: Inter-American Development Bank, *Economic and Social Progress in Latin America,* 1986 Report, Table II-4, Appendix Table 4; 1988 Report, Tables II-5, A-1, B-3, and Country Profiles; 1989 Report, Tables A-1, B-1, B-3.

directing investment to these activities, and Table 1.6 indicates that there has not been much investment to redirect.

Some proponents of market liberalizing restructuring have taken, therefore, to hyping the X-efficiency gains, since these don't require new investment; for example, privatizing public sector firms is supposed to produce large X-efficiency gains, even when the privatized firm remains a monopoly. Making X-efficiency benefits the chief rationale for market liberalization has, however, the troublesome implication that either the relative prices that had shaped the existing structures of production were not very "incorrect," or that "getting prices right" is not all that important.

Table 1.7 points up another reason why the time frame for restructuring may be bumping against political limits. Inflation in Argentina, Brazil and

Table 1.6.
Real Gross Investment per Worker, 1970 and 1982−88 (1980/81 = 100)

	1970	1982-84	1985	1986	1987	1988
Argentina	87.4	60.7	42.0	49.0	56.3	61.7
Brazil	61.2	68.1	68.5	82.8	82.5	80.6
Chile	88.5	36.5	46.4	51.7	63.6	67.7
Mexico	63.6	62.7	61.0	47.0	47.6	53.7
Peru	54.8	69.2	42.5	52.7	52.3	42.2
Venezuela	104.0	72.7	59.0	61.1	60.2	53.9

Sources: Inter-American Development Bank, *Economic and Social Progess in Latin America,* 1986 Report, Appendix Table 5; 1987 Report, Tables VII-1 and VII-3; 1988 Report, Table B-6; 1989 Report, Table B-4.

Table 1.7.
Annual Percentage Increases in Consumer Prices, 1983–88

	1983	1984	1985	1986	1987	1988
Argentina	343.8	626.7	672.2	90.1	131.3	343.0
Brazil	142.0	196.7	226.9	143.7	231.7	682.3
Chile	27.3	19.9	30.7	19.5	19.9	14.7
Mexico	101.9	65.5	57.7	86.2	131.8	114.2
Peru[a]	111.1	110.2	163.4	77.9	85.8	150.0
Venezuela	6.3	12.2	11.4	11.6	28.1	29.5

Note: (a) 1988 increase first quarter only.
Sources: IDB, *Economic and Social Progress Report,* 1988, Country Profiles; IMF, *International Financial Statistics,* June 1989.

Peru has oscillated during the 1980s in a three-digit range with an upward trend. Mexico's inflation has oscillated between two and three digits and Venezuela's has been accelerating to higher two-digit levels. Only Chile has managed to keep its inflation in the low two-digits. Progress toward hyper-inflation is not evidence of restructuring progress.

Proponents of the restructuring have had, therefore, to seek statistical comfort in selective examples. Chile is being worked as hard now as success story and exemplar as it was in the ill-fated Chicago Boys era. Singled out are Chile's superior performance along most of the dimensions of Tables 1.5 and 1.7, plus the fact that its notable export expansion and the restructuring of its foreign debt and debt servicing enabled Chile since 1986 to lower its extremely high Debt/GDP and Debt/Export ratios. However, on the permanence of the success the jury is still out; take for instance, debt-equity swaps and interest capitalization will give Chile a payment bubble after 1991 that could prove indigestibly large (Ricardo Ffrench-Davis, forthcoming). The return to democracy may unleash popular "catch-up" demands that the Pinochet dictatorship has kept bottled up. In addition, Chile's inequitable distribution of its adjustment burden is passed over silently, as is the evidence in Table 1.4 that as late as 1987 Chile was still covering almost all its interest bill with external financing.

This raises the intriguing question: who provided that financing? Table 1.8 shows that during 1983–86, it was the multilateral institutions; Chile's share of their total lending to Latin America during the four years was 111 percent higher than Chile's share of the Latin American debt. If special optimism about Chile's prospects motivated the lending concentration it was not shared by the commercial banks; Chile's share of their lending to Latin America during 1983-86 was a niggardly 18 percent of its share of the Latin American debt. The absence of bilateral government lending to Chile in this period, so

Table 1.8.
New Loans in Relation to External Debt

	Argentina	Brazil	Chile	Mexico
IMF	1.56	1.07	1.90	1.11
IBRD	0.40	1.47	2.27	0.87
IDB	1.98	0.29	3.42	0.12
All Multilateral	0.99	0.95	2.46	0.75
Bilateral	0.85	1.17	-0.08	0.37
All Official	0.95	1.02	1.65	0.63
Private Loans	0.82	1.04	0.18	1.46

	Peru	Venezuela	Six Major Debtors
IMF	0.16	0.00	1.05
IBRD	0.40	-0.08	0.95
IDB	1.35	0.74	0.79
All Multilateral	0.58	0.19	0.75
Bilateral	1.16	-0.07	0.66
All Official	0.76	0.12	0.82
Private Loans	0.27	0.64	1.05

Note: Entry is country's share of new loans to Latin America, 1983–86, divided by share of Latin American external debt, 1982.
Source: World Bank, *World Debt Tables, 1987–88.*

at odds with the Reagan administration's admiration for Pinochet,[4] suggests a geopolitical motive for the burst of lending from the multilateral institutions. The Reagan administration used the multilateral institutions to get around congressional prohibitions against official lending to regimes that grossly violated human rights. This conjecture is supported by the fact that the IDB, whose Latin American lending pattern had been evenhanded logrolling, focused most of all on lending to Chile during the four years. The IDB also happens to be the most firmly under United States control of the three institutions.

Currently, the multilateral institutions are lending disproportionately to Mexico, this time in consort with bilateral lending from Japan and the United States. The case for favoritism is again strongly geopolitical: Mexico's proximity to the United States, the need for another liberalization success story, etc. Mexico's actual performance record is problematic; dismal on the dimensions of Table 1.5 and weak on inflation, but outperforming most other Latin American debtors in debt servicing; Table 1.5 shows that since 1983 it has generally been able to cover its interest bill with its trade surplus. The problem is that U.S. bilateral lending is again restricted, this time not by human rights but by Gramm-Rudman constraints. Hence the emphasis of the Brady Planners on capital flight repatriation and the resumption of long-term bank lending to sustain economic growth after restructuring.

In this regard the capital flight data of Table 1.9 support both the "progress" and the "lost decade" views of restructuring.[5] The impressively large foreign asset holdings of the nationals of many of the debtor countries are indeed a large potential resource for financing recovery. Repatriating private foreign assets, or even the annual income from the assets, would solve the debt payment crisis for Argentina, Mexico and Venezuela and go a long way toward restoring their creditworthiness in international financial markets. The dark side is that the volume of capital flight is also evidence that debt burden sharing in the three countries has been even more inequitable than is indicated by the wage-consumption data of Table 1.5. The outward resource transfers shown in Table 1.4 are overstated, part of them merely reflecting portfolio shifting from domestic to foreign assets by the affluent classes of the three countries. This has enabled them to protect their net worth, but the foreign exchange losses to their economies have further depressed output, employment, and the net worth of those lacking adequate means to internationalize their portfolios.

Whether market liberalizing restructuring is likely to induce large-scale repatriation remains to be explored. We do this in the concluding part of the paper, after first offering estimates of external financing requirements for sustaining economic growth in four of the debtor countries, with and without Brady Plan debt write-offs.

II. TESTING A 15 PERCENT BRADY SOLUTION TO LATIN AMERICA'S EXTERNAL FINANCING PROBLEMS

How much additional external borrowing is needed to make debt servicing compatible with sustained economic recovery? In this section we estimate requirements for Argentina, Brazil, Chile and Mexico. We choose these four countries because they collectively account for around 70 percent of the Latin American debt and allow us to bring a fairly wide range of country differences to bear on our estimates.

Table 1.9.
Foreign Debts and Foreign Assets of Six Major Latin American Debtor Countries (in Billions US$ at End of 1977, 1981, 1985)

	Foreign Debt	Private Capital Outflow	Private Foreign Assets	Ratio of Outflow to Debt	Ratio of Assets to Debt
Argentina					
1977	11.4	2.8	3.2	0.25	0.28
1981	35.7	20.5	23.1	0.58	0.65
1985	48.3	26.1	42.4	0.54	0.88
Brazil					
1977	41.3	5.9	4.4	0.14	0.11
1981	80.0	12.2	12.8	0.15	0.16
1985	106.7	19.0	24.4	0.18	0.23
Chile					
1977	5.9	0.2	0.3	0.03	0.06
1981	15.7	1.2	0.0	0.08	0.00
1985	20.4	-1.8	0.0	-0.09	0.00
Mexico					
1977	31.2	11.9	12.0	0.38	0.39
1981	78.3	32.4	39.5	0.41	0.50
1985	97.1	59.4	88.5	0.61	0.91
Peru[a]					
1977	9.1	1.9	2.4	0.21	0.26
1981	10.3	0.7	6.6	0.06	0.64
1985	13.6	0.5	2.7	0.03	0.20
Venezuela					
1977	10.7	6.2	4.5	0.58	0.42
1981	31.9	26.2	25.7	0.82	0.80
1985	32.1	40.7	52.3	1.27	1.63

Note: (a) Peruvian private foreign assets include domestic dollar deposits.
Sources: World Bank, *World Debt Tables, 1987–88;* U.S. Federal Reserve Bulletin, Central de Reserva de Peru, *Memorias Anuales.*

These estimates are made both with and without Brady Plan debt write-offs. In the Mexican agreement, the write-off seems to be minimal, although how small will not be known precisely until all the individual creditor banks announce their choices between the three options in the agreement. For our estimates, we assumed each country gets a 15 percent write-off of its total foreign debt. In light of the Mexican agreement, this is probably an overoptimistic assessment of the impact of the Brady approach. However, for our purposes, it is better to err on the side of optimism.

Our financing projections are, alternatively, for two percent and one percent annual growth of GDP per capita over the period 1990–2000. The only explicit internal structural requirement that our model imposes for such growth is that the investment/GDP ratio of each country rebound gradually to its 1970–1980 average (somewhat less for the one percent growth target). Import elasticities, derived from regressing imports on investment for the period 1970–1986, determine import requirements. Export elasticities, obtained by regressing export growth on OECD real GNP growth (U.S. GDP growth in the case of Mexico), plus projected changes in the terms of trade, determine foreign exchange earnings net of borrowing. Since the two elasticities from the regressions are above unity, we have applied a slight dampening to give more sensible long-run properties to the model. The gap between export receipts and import requirements plus interest on the outstanding debt determines annual external borrowing requirements. We have simplified the exercise further by assuming the same initial fixed real interest rate on loans prevails throughout.

The economic model underlying this exercise is the two-gap model prominent in the economic development literature in which the foreign exchange gap is the dominant constraint on growth. In the concluding section we point to the presence of serious internal financial impediments to growth that have developed in the Latin American countries during their "lost decade." For now they are put aside pursuant to that widely used analytic strategy, *divide et impera*.

Changes in the external state of the world that can affect the foreign exchange gap are handled by making the projections under three alternative sets of assumptions about OECD and/or U.S. GDP growth and about the terms of trade.[6]

The "Base" case assumes an annual OECD income growth rate of 2.25 percent and an annual terms of trade improvement of 0.50 percent. In the "Pessimistic" case these parameters are 1.75 percent and − 1.00 percent respectively. The "Optimistic" case projections assume a 2.75 percent annual income growth rate and a 2.00 percent terms of trade improvement.

The simulation model, it should be noted, has properties characteristic of continuous full capacity planning models. Since we have tied investment to the targeted growth rate, imports to investment, and exports to OECD (U.S.) growth, consumption is necessarily a residual. Booming export growth, as in the Optimistic scenario, requires, therefore, more inputs, which can only be made available by squeezing consumption. Conversely, slumping export growth, as in the Pessimistic scenario, requires a compensating shift of resources from exports to consumption in order to keep GDP growth on target. Implicitly, the model assumes that the authorities restrict their borrowing to

Table 1.10.
Projected Percentage Change in Per Capita Consumption Between 1990 and 2000

	Base Case	Pessimistic Case	Optimistic Case
Assuming two percent annual per capita real GDP growth:			
Argentina	17.4	24.9	7.6
Brazil	22.9	27.9	16.4
Chile	26.9	44.6	4.2
Mexico	22.0	31.0	10.2
Assuming one percent annual per capita real GDP growth:			
Argentina	1.9	9.6	-8.0
Brazil	7.7	12.9	1.1
Chile	-0.6	18.0	-24.1
Mexico	4.5	13.7	-7.6

Source: See discussion in text.

the minimum essential, exploiting favorable external conditions by directing resources from consumption to exports and reducing external borrowing, reversing the procedure when export conditions worsen. This is, of course, the exact opposite of the actual behavior of the debtor governments during the 1970s, when favorable terms of trade, which made them appear creditworthy to the bankers, were the occasion for increasing the rate of borrowing to finance debt service and a domestic consumption boom. In our model we assume *nunca mas*, not from conviction but in order to present best behavior estimates.

We have, however, imposed a lower limit to the movement of consumption. Given the drastic drop of consumption per capita during the "lost decade," we discard as politically untenable all growth scenarios in which consumption per capita fails to rise by year 2000 to at least 5 percent above the 1988 level.

We turn now to the results. Table 1.10 reports the percent change in the level in consumption per capita as of year 2000 under the two alternative growth rates and the three alternative external conditions. Note that in the model the 15 percent write-off reduces required external borrowing but has no effect on consumption. Applying our 5 percent minimum consumption improvement requires excluding as politically untenable the Optimistic scenario for all the countries when the growth target is one percent GDP per capita growth, and for Chile the Optimistic scenario with a 2 percent growth target as well. In the Pessimistic scenario, on the other hand, all countries pass the consumption test with both GDP growth rates. In the Base scenario they all do so under 2 percent GDP growth, but only Brazil makes it with one percent GDP growth.

Table 1.11.
Projected Annual Net New Lending Requirements (Billions US$)

	Argentina		Brazil		Chile		Mexico	
Scenario	1990	2000	1990	2000	1990	2000	1990	2000
No debt write-off and 2 percent per capita growth rate:								
Base	4.5	6.0	1.7	12.4	(.4)	.3	3.7	21.8
Pessimistic	4.7	12.1	2.6	33.2	(.2)	4.9	4.5	42.5
Optimistic	4.2	(1.7)	.7	(13.7)	NR	NR	2.8	(4.6)
Write-off of 15 percent of foreign debt and 2 percent per capita growth rate:								
Base	3.7	5.0	.3	10.2	(.6)	0.0	2.5	19.9
Pessimistic	4.0	11.0	1.3	31.0	(.4)	4.6	3.3	40.5
Optimistic	3.5	(2.8)	.7	(16.0)	NR	NR	1.6	(6.5)
No debt write-off and 1 percent per capita growth rate:								
Base	NR	NR	(1.6)	(9.4)	NR	NR	NR	NR
Pessimistic	3.7	7.0	(.6)	12.0	(.5)	(.1)	.3	17.2
Optimistic	NR	NR	NR	NR	NR	NR	NR	NR
Write-off of 15 percent of foreign debt and 1 percent per capita growth rate:								
Base	NR	NR	(2.9)	(11.6)	NR	NR	NR	NR
Pessimistic	3.0	5.9	(2.0)	9.8	(.7)	(.4)	(.9)	15.2
Optimistic	NR	NR	NR	NR	NR	NR	NR	NR

Note: "NR" indicates not relevant, a case with insufficient consumption growth.
Source: See discussion in text.

Annual net borrowing requirements are reported in Table 1.11 for the politically tenable cases. The main results are:

1. With 2 percent GDP growth, under the Optimistic scenario all countries pass the consumption growth requirement except Chile and all move from borrower to debt repayer by year 2000.

2. With 1 percent GDP growth, under the Base scenario Brazil passes the consumption test and can immediately begin to repay its external debt.

3. Almost all the other politically tenable cases require what appear to be improbably high net new borrowing by year 2000.

4. A onetime write-off of 15 percent of the total foreign debt initially reduces the annual borrowing need between 15 and 80 percent, but, with the partial exception of

Chile, the borrowing requirements for financing the growth targets and debt servicing rebounds strongly.

The viability of these projected borrowing requirements is assessed in Tables 1.12 and 1.13 on the basis of trends in the Debt/GDP, Debt Service/export ratios, and dependence on new lending to cover interest payments. The findings are:

1. Under the Optimistic scenario, Argentina, Brazil and Mexico show improvement by all three debt servicing indicators, while also meeting the minimum consumption requirement when the growth target is 2 percent, but fail to meet the consumption improvement requirement when the target is 1 percent growth.
2. In the Base scenario, Brazil under the 2 percent growth target improves by two of the three debt servicing indicators and meets the consumption requirement. Chile does the same. In both countries, however, the dependence on new lending to cover interest obligations rises. Argentina and Mexico improve only their interest/export ratios, their Debt/GDP ratios worsen and their dependence on new loans to cover interest payments becomes total or nearly so by year 2000. With the 1 percent growth target, Brazil improves by all three debt service indicators and meets the consumption requirement. Chile, Argentina and Mexico do not meet the consumption requirement.
3. All the debt service indicators deteriorate for all four countries in the Pessimistic scenario with the 2 percent growth target. With one percent growth, two of the three ratios improve for Brazil and Chile while almost all the ratios deteriorate for Argentina and Mexico.

For prospective lenders, the panorama is not very appealing. They would not only have to bet that the conditions of the Optimistic scenario will prevail during the next decade, but also that the debtor governments will impose fiscal-monetary austerity to control consumption spending so as to keep external borrowing at the minimum necessary to meet the growth target. Lending to Chile, which is viable under the Base scenario, looks less foreboding but is far from a sure bet. Thus, for at least three of the four countries, it is questionable whether banks would voluntarily provide the financing to meet the growth targets.

The import and export elasticities used in the exercise are derived from past behavior. How would they be altered by market liberalization? Probably very little for Chile: its trade regime was already liberalized during most of 1970–1986. Imports per unit of GDP would rise in the other three countries as a result of liberalization. Whether it will raise exporting enough to compensate for the higher import intensity is debatable.

The general inference is that liberalization does not warrant lowering projected borrowing needs or the risks of supplying them. Bankers burnt in the recent past and contemplating Latin America's prospects are likely to stick cautiously to well collateralized and creditor club guaranteed loans and to say

Table 1.12.
Projected Debt Burden Ratios (Percentages)

	Argentina		Brazil		Chile		Mexico	
	1990	2000	1990	2000	1990	2000	1990	2000
Base Scenario, 2 percent per capita growth, no write-off:								
Debt/GDP	75.2	77.3	34.1	25.6	82.8	48.9	65.0	72.7
Interest/exports goods & services	38.0	32.8	22.2	14.7	12.6	6.5	21.0	19.6
New lending/ interest	6.0	8.8	65.7	-41.1	105.5	20.9	36.4	-75.5
Pessimistic Scenario, 2 percent per capita growth, no write-off:								
Debt/GDP	75.7	100.9	34.3	42.6	84.0	123.5	65.6	107.2
Interest/exports goods & services	38.9	53.6	22.7	29.8	13.0	18.5	21.6	36.3
New lending/ interest	0.0	-45.9	54.8	-116.4	86.5	-134.8	25.2	-129.6
Optimistic Scenario, 2 percent per capita growth, no write-off:								
Debt/GDP	74.9	49.2	33.8	5.3	NR	NR	64.4	31.1
Interest/exports goods & services	37.1	17.8	21.6	3.8	NR	NR	20.5	7.6
New lending/ interest	12.1	135.2	76.6	429.7	NR	NR	47.7	130.8
Base Scenario, 2 percent per capita growth, 15 percent write-off in 1990:								
Debt/GDP	63.9	65.2	28.6	20.2	69.1	34.3	54.8	62.8
Interest/exports goods & services	32.3	27.7	18.8	11.5	10.7	4.6	17.9	16.8
New lending/ interest	7.1	10.5	77.2	-52.2	124.1	29.2	42.8	-88.1

Table 1.12.
(continued)

	Argentina		Brazil		Chile		Mexico	
	1990	2000	1990	2000	1990	2000	1990	2000
Pessimistic Scenario, 2 percent per capita growth, 15 percent write-off in 1990:								
Debt/GDP	64.2	88.7	28.9	37.3	70.3	108.9	55.4	97.3
Interest/exports goods & services	33.1	46.9	19.3	25.7	11.0	16.1	18.3	32.6
New lending/ interest	0.0	-52.4	64.5	-134.5	101.8	-154.5	29.7	-144.1
Optimistic Scenario, 2 percent per capita growth, 15 percent write-off in 1990:								
Debt/GDP	63.5	37.0	28.3	-0.1	NR	NR	54.3	21.2
Interest/exports goods & services	31.5	13.8	18.4	1.3	NR	NR	17.4	5.5
New lending/ interest	14.3	173.9	90.2	1200.8	NR	NR	56.1	181.7

Note: "New lending/interest" is the current account balance excluding debt interest payments as a percentage of foreign debt interest obligations. "NR" indicates not relevant, a case with insufficient consumption growth.
Source: See discussion in text.

nunca mas to the expansive general obligation bank lending of the pre-crisis years, at least until memories dim.

III. INTERNAL FINANCIAL OBSTACLES TO ECONOMIC RECOVERY

Our simulation exercise assumed that the financial barrier to sustained recovery is merely a shortage of foreign exchange. Were that really so, a lack of success with the Brady Plan would reflect merely coordination failure. Were the Plan able to evoke stronger instruments of coercion and seduction of the banks, the U.S. Congress, and the other major industrial powers to augment debt write-offs, new lending and loan guarantees sufficiently to meet foreign exchange needs, the restructuring would succeed and growth revival would ensue. We contend, however, that the flaw in the Brady Plan is also conceptual. Like past creditor rescue programs, its financial liberalization policies are strengthening internal financial obstacles to the recovery of investment and GDP growth.

Table 1.13.
Projected Debt Burden Ratios (Percentages)

	Argentina		Brazil		Chile		Mexico	
	1990	2000	1990	2000	1990	2000	1990	2000
Base Scenario, 1 percent per capita growth, no write-off:								
Debt/GDP	NR	NR	33.4	6.6	NR	NR	NR	NR
Interest/exports goods & services	NR	NR	22.2	4.8	NR	NR	NR	NR
New lending/ interest	NR	NR	102.1	314.3	NR	NR	NR	NR
Pessimistic Scenario, 1 percent per capita growth, no write-off:								
Debt/GDP	75.0	85.8	33.7	25.9	83.6	36.5	63.5	64.3
Interest/exports goods & services	38.9	42.1	22.7	17.2	12.9	5.7	21.6	20.4
New lending/ interest	22.7	-7.1	91.0	-48.8	108.4	51.1	78.2	-75.9
Optimistic Scenario, 1 percent per capita growth, no write-off:								
Debt/GDP	NR	NR	NR	NR	NR	NR	NR	NR
Interest/exports goods & services	NR	NR	NR	NR	NR	NR	NR	NR
New lending/ interest	NR	NR	NR	NR	NR	NR	NR	NR
Base Scenario, 1 percent per capita growth, 15 percent write-off in 1990:								
Debt/GDP	NR	NR	27.9	0.6	NR	NR	NR	NR
Interest/exports goods & services	NR	NR	18.8	1.6	NR	NR	NR	NR
New lending/ interest	NR	NR	120.1	909.5	NR	NR	NR	NR
Pessimistic Scenario, 1 percent per capita growth, 15 percent write-off in 1990:								
Debt/GDP	63.6	72.3	28.2	20.0	69.8	20.2	53.3	53.3
Interest/exports goods & services	33.1	35.4	19.3	13.2	10.9	3.4	18.3	16.8
New lending/ interest	26.8	-8.4	107.1	-63.7	127.6	86.8	92.0	-92.4

Table 1.13.
(continued)

	Argentina		Brazil		Chile		Mexico	
	1990	2000	1990	2000	1990	2000	1990	2000
Optimistic Scenario, 1 percent per capita growth, 15 percent write-off in 1990:								
Debt/GDP	NR	NR	NR	NR	NR	NR	NR	NR
Interest/exports goods & services	NR	NR	NR	NR	NR	NR	NR	NR
New lending/ interest	NR	NR	NR	NR	NR	NR	NR	NR

Note: "New lending/interest" is the current account balance excluding debt interest payments as a percentage of foreign debt interest obligations. "NR" indicates not relevant, a case with insufficient consumption growth.
Source: See discussion in text.

These obstacles emerged because the cutoff of voluntary lending in 1982 not only ended an external borrowing boom, but also collapsed domestic financial bubbles and the liquidity and solvency of many overleveraged firms and banks in the debtor countries. Foreign loans had facilitated the leveraging, but stimulus came also from the deregulated financial environment put in place in many Latin American countries during the 1970s. The high real interest rates and large spreads that followed the lifting of "financial repression" augmented opportunities and pressures for speculative gaming with borrowed funds. As is typical of financial bubbles, domestic lenders bemused by booming asset values eagerly collaborated, leaving many of them with unmanageably large accumulations of bad loans when the bubble burst.

The comparative data on leveraging in Table 1.14 indicates that the fastest run-up of private domestic debt occurred in Argentina and Chile, the two countries that had most liberalized their financial sectors. The link between rising external debt and rising domestic lending was especially close in these two countries, domestic banks fueling much of their expanding domestic loans with borrowed foreign funds. Causality was, however, reciprocal. In Chile, for example, the massive increase of foreign debt during 1977–1981 was primarily, to quote from a recent statistical autopsy, "a reaction of private financial speculators to the opening up of the economy" (Scheetz, 1987, p. 1068).

The stable Peruvian and declining Brazilian ratios at the lower end of Table 1.14's spectrum are deceptive indicators of financial sobriety. Peru had authorized its banks in 1978 to take dollar deposits and make dollar loans, which led to rapid dollarizing of private domestic financing and to a major insolvency

Table 1.14.
Internal Debt of Private Sector as Percent of GDP, 1975–85

	Argentina	Brazil	Chile	Mexico	Peru	Venezuela
1975	8	25	5	5	10	19
1976	6	25	5	5	9	24
1981	26	14	39	14	9	26
1982	22	14	60	13	11	28
1983	18	12	57	10	10	30
1984	--	10	53	8	9	28
1985	--	--	52	9	8	30

Note: Entries show credit of the financial system to the private sector at the end of first half of
each year.
Source: Carlos Massad y Roberto Zahler, "Otro Angulo de la Crisis Latinoamericana: La
Deuda Interna." *Revista de la CEPAL* no. 32 (Santiago do Chile, Agosto, 1987), Cuadro 1.

crisis in 1982–83. The crisis followed an accelerated rise of the dollar/sol exchange rate that overwhelmed dollar-indebted firms whose defaults threatened to topple the private banks. Emergency central bank credit lines to the
distressed firms inflated out the bankruptcy threat, at considerable cost to less
favored sectors of the economy (Beckerman, 1987; Webb, 1987).

Brazil's declining ratio juxtaposes with the rising fiscal outlays required to
adjust the nominal value of indexed government debt to inflation. "Monetary
correction" rose from 5.1 percent of GDP in 1979 to 20.7 percent in 1984.
Indexing gave the Brazilian middle and upper classes a domestic alternative to
capital flight, but the outlays on monetary correction were financed primarily
through central bank emissions, as were a rising volume of unindexed lending
by government banks to the private sector (Baer, 1987). The Brazilian foreign
debt crisis was thus associated with a faster acceleration of inflation but less
capital flight and a milder domestic financial crisis than in the other debtors,
thanks to monetary correction and the inflating out of unindexed private debt.

The ubiquity of domestic financial crises during the early 1980s thus reflected varying combinations of excessive private domestic and foreign borrowing.[7] Left to the market and bankruptcy law, "the magnitude and perva-
siveness of private internal indebtedness and its close linkages to the national
financial systems would have required a massive transfer of property rights.
Such a transfer was impossible to carry out due to the important political and
social costs it would have involved" (Massad and Zahler, 1987, p. 19). In any
event, none of the governments were willing to try it. Resource mobilization
for foreign debt servicing and investment has thus been constrained by the
competing goal of restoring solvency and capital value to overindebted firms
and banks, at least to the larger ones.

The instruments included government takeovers of bad loans and excessive liabilities of private banks and firms at subsidized interest and/or exchange rates and with generous grace periods, tax relief, wage controls and the "inflation tax." These were used in differing proportions. The decline after 1981 of the Argentine leveraging ratio shown in Table 1.14 was engineered mainly through the "inflation tax." The high point was July 1982, when the central bank rediscounted at 5 percent and for five years assets of Argentine banking institutions equal to their deposits and concurrently froze the deposit interest rate at 5 percent in the midst of three-digit inflation (Piekarz, 1987, p. 30). The transfer from depositors to debtors was around 8 percent of GDP (Massad and Zahler, 1987). The further rise of the Chilean debt ratio after 1981 reflects, on the other hand, official takeovers of bad loans and excessive domestic and foreign liabilities from the private sector in exchange for negotiable government bonds, with indexing of both sides of the exchange. This minimized monetary expansion and the acceleration of inflation, while putting the private sector's debt overhang in storage and easing its debt service. The bad loans of the Chilean banks in 1982 alone were three times their capital and reserves (Zahler, 1984, p. 326), while total government transfers to private banks and firms that year are estimated at (US)$7 billion, or over 27 percent of the 1982 GDP and over twenty times the outlay on unemployment relief.[8]

A direct consequence of the expansive rescue efforts was fiscal "overstretching," to use the terminology of a recent OECD study (Reisen and Van Trotsenburg, 1988, p. 64). Contributing also to the rising fiscal deficits shown in Table 1.15 were reductions in the effective tax base due to capital flight originating largely in the business classes that were being rescued. Due mainly to capital flight and rising inflation, income and property taxes fell during the 1980s as a percent of GDP, as is shown in Table 1.15. Concurrently, the added burden of servicing private foreign liabilities raised the interest share of fiscal expenditures, as shown in Table 1.16. The most precipitous rise occurred in countries like Mexico and Brazil that had rapidly widening deficits and were financing them mainly through the sale of securities in unrepressed domestic markets.

Pressured by foreign creditors to be fiscally responsible, the debtor governments responded by drastically reducing public investment, as shown in Table 1.16, as well as real outlays on public services, infrastructure maintenance, and public sector salaries and employment. As a result, the primary budget—the overall fiscal budget less interest payments and transfers—moved into surplus in many of the debtor countries. Mexico's primary budget, for example, has been in the black since 1983, the surplus averaging 3.6 percent of GDP, whereas the overall fiscal deficit averaged 14 percent of GDP in 1986–87 (Reyes Heroles, 1987, Cuadro 2). In varying degrees, however, financing the rescue operations and widening budget deficits also created accounting losses for the central bank that are outside the fiscal budgeting—losses from negative real interest rate credits to the public and private sectors and from overpriced

Table 1.15.
Fiscal Deficits and Tax Revenues as Percent of GDP

	1980–81	1982–83	1984–85	1986–87	1988
Argentina:					
Fiscal deficit	-4.0	-8.9	-5.9	-5.7	n.a.
All Taxes	9.2	7.2	7.3	10.7	3.8
Direct Taxes	1.9	0.9	0.8	2.6	0.8
Brazil:					
Fiscal deficit	-2.2	-4.0	-8.8	n.a	n.a.
All Taxes	17.9	19.1	15.8	n.a.	n.a.
Direct Taxes	8.0	8.7	7.0	n.a.	n.a.
Chile:					
Fiscal deficit	3.3	-3.1	-2.4	-1.5	n.a.
All Taxes	21.7	19.1	20.2	20.1	19.8
Direct Taxes	3.7	3.1	2.2	3.0	3.4
Mexico:					
Fiscal deficit	-4.5	-9.8	-7.6	-14.0	n.a.
All Taxes	14.4	15.6	15.9	13.2	n.a.
Direct Taxes	5.3	4.2	3.9	3.3	n.a.
Peru:					
Fiscal deficit	-3.1	-5.2	-3.1	-4.7	n.a.
All Taxes	14.4	11.4	11.7	9.7	8.6
Direct Taxes	4.5	2.9	2.4	2.7	2.6
Venezuela:					
Fiscal deficit	-1.1	-3.6	2.5	-1.0	n.a.
All Taxes	20.9	18.2	20.2	17.4	14.6
Direct Taxes	15.8	11.8	12.5	8.2	10.3

Note: "Direct taxes" are income and property taxes.
Source: Inter-American Development Bank, *Economic and Social Progress Reports,* 1988 and
   1989, Appendix Tables C-1, C-4, C-7, C-8.

purchases of dubious bank assets. Central bank and IMF economists are now
trying to estimate these off-budget losses, which they dub "quasi-fiscal deficits." The estimate for Argentina is 2.0 percent of GDP during 1984–87 compared to 4.4 percent for the fiscal deficit proper (Piekarz, 1987, Appendix table). In Uruguay they averaged 4.7 percent of GDP during 1982–86, compared
to 4.9 percent for the fiscal deficit (Onandi and Viana, 1987, Cuadro 10), and
have probably been quite high in Chile. The estimates are, however, tentative,
since measurement conventions are still under discussion.

Table 1.16.
Interest and Public Investment Shares of Fiscal Expenditure, 1970–88

	1970	1980	1982	1984	1986	1988
Interest Payments as Percent of Fiscal Expenditure:						
Argentina[a]	3.2	0.3	1.2	5.9	12.8	4.2
Brazil[b]	4.5	7.2	13.0	24.0	n.a.	n.a.
Chile[c]	2.5	2.7	1.4	3.9	4.9	7.9
Mexico[b]	9.4	9.8	33.4	35.8	46.7	n.a.
Peru[b]	5.2	18.4	18.3	23.5	15.0	17.1
Venezuela[b]	1.6	5.9	7.3	11.7	11.4	12.6
Government Investment as Percent of Total Fiscal Expenditures:						
Argentina[a]	6.7	15.9	16.1	10.6	7.4	15.3
Brazil[b]	9.9	5.9	6.0	3.3	n.a.	n.a.
Chile[c]	17.5	8.4	5.6	7.4	9.6	10.1
Mexico[b]	12.2	12.1	8.4	5.5	3.4	2.4
Peru[b]	13.2	15.3	17.7	16.5	8.8	8.9
Venezuela[b]	12.9	6.1	7.5	4.6	9.2	n.a.

Note: (a), (b), and (c) are respectively national administration, central government and general
   government.
Source: Inter-American Development Bank, *Economic and Social Progress Reports*, 1988 and
   1989, Appendix Tables C-17, C-20.

One unsettled matter is whether to record income from nonperforming
loans on a cash or accrual basis. The matter is important, as private debtors
have been treating emergency payment extensions and interest subsidies as
permanent entitlements. "Perhaps the principal negative aspect of these type
measures is that they did not provide incentives for the domestic debtors to
carry out their financial commitments: they expected instead to obtain re-
newal of these facilities" (Massad and Zahler, 1987, p. 23). This may explain
why the quasi-fiscal deficits of Argentina and Uruguay have declined less than
the fiscal deficits from the early crisis years.

The rescue efforts and capital flight have made most of the larger stricken
firms and banks of 1982–83 solvent again. With debts substantially written
down and portfolios, including liquid assets, "internationalized"—see Table
1.17—they are fairly well insulated against the roaring inflation and collapsing
exchange rates. Output may be down, but profits from financial operations are
up, notably from playing the treasury bill market. That market has grown
enormously as fiscal deficits expand and funding is shifted from central bank
to open market deficit financing in response to creditor restructuring demands. The maturities and yields are market determined, which means in the
liberalized financial environment that they compete against the real return on
dollar securities. Since that environment is also in inflationary disorder, the

Table 1.17.
Private Foreign and Domestic Deposits, 1980–85
(in billion US$)

	1980–81	1982	1983	1984	1985
Argentina					
In Domestic Banks	27.4	7.9	8.2	7.6	7.0
In Foreign Banks	6.6	5.7	8.6	8.4	9.0
Foreign/Domestic (percent)	24.0	72.4	105.3	110.7	128.1
Brazil					
In Domestic Banks	41.0	45.5	33.0	36.0	23.5
In Foreign Banks	4.8	4.3	11.4	17.3	16.6
Foreign/Domestic (percent)	14.6	9.4	34.4	48.1	70.6
Mexico					
In Domestic Banks	59.6	30.9	34.8	42.9	34.6
In Foreign Banks	10.8	10.9	18.0	21.8	21.5
Foreign/Domestic (percent)	18.2	35.1	51.9	50.8	62.2
Venezuela					
In Domestic Banks	28.0	34.6	42.6	26.8	--
In Foreign Banks	17.2	12.9	17.1	19.1	22.2
Foreign/Domestic (percent)	61.2	37.4	40.1	71.2	--

Note: Domestic deposits include demand, time and savings deposits in domestic currency converted to dollars at yearly exchange rate. Foreign deposits are the gross liabilities of banks in the reporting system of the Bank for International Settlements to each of the above countries.

Source: Helmut Reisen and Axel Van Trotsenburg, *Developing Country Debt: The Budgetary and Transfer Problem* (Paris, OECD Development Centre, 1988), Table 1.19.

maturity on the treasury bills are extremely short—"Overnights" in Brazil, 2–4 week CETES in Mexico—with annualized real interest rates of 30 to 50 percent. In Argentina in the first half of 1989, the real interest rate on treasury bills reportedly reached 15 percent per *month*.

Here then is one obvious domestic financial obstacle to economic recovery. In these depressed economies with widespread excess capacity, there are not many physical investment projects that can compete with 30 to 50% real interest on safe liquid assets. Trying to reduce the rate in order to stimulate investment encourages shifting to foreign assets, namely, capital flight. Raising the real rate to induce capital repatriation further deters real investment. With public investment depressed by the need to curb fiscal deficits and private investment held down by safe high returns to firms from deficit financing and capital flight, economic recovery in the debtor countries appears blocked by financial barriers that transcend the foreign debt overhang and inadequate foreign lending.

How long this gridlock prevails depends on the interplay of two sets of opposing forces, each political as well as economic. Pushing toward hyper-inflation, popular explosions and debt moratoria is the further erosion of the tax base and monetary control as the informal sector spreads and with it the increased tax evasion and "currency substitution," that is, dollarization, on which it thrives. Pressure to cut further public investment, social outlays and maintenance augment, and the cumulative effect is infrastructure and human capital deterioration. The latter, accelerated by emigration of the skilled and unskilled in response to the prolonged slide of real wages and salaries, undercuts X-efficiency benefits from market liberalizing restructuring. As the 1980s depression persists in the debtor countries such trends gain momentum.

Working to break the gridlock from the opposite direction are pressures from the business elite to accelerate privatization, shrink the public sector, and erode what remains of the "conquistas sociales" that had benefited large segments of the urban wage-salary classes in happier times. Made solvent again by the debt write-downs that overstretched the fiscal budgets, kept profitable by financial operations in treasury bills and dollar assets, the business elite now denounces fiscal irresponsibility in order to build public backing for its objectives. It can also wait in comfort for deficits and economic deterioration to force the sale of public assets at distress prices. Repatriated capital may be needed to help purchase the privatized assets, but not much will probably be required, given distress prices and the penchant of Latin American businessmen for leveraging with domestic credits.

The debt crisis did not create the antipodal political forces; it merely reinforced them. Their origin is in Latin America's unusually concentrated distribution of income and wealth. In the past, concentration intensified during periods of fast growth and tended to fall back during slack periods (Felix, 1983). Thanks in part to the uniquely high incidence of capital flight, the 1980s is the first prolonged depression in which concentration has risen rather than slackened. Capital flight has been made easier by exogenous innovations: the electronic transfer of funds, and a widening array of flexible, liquid international financial instruments. It has also been made easier by the relaxing of controls on international capital movements in the debtor countries.

Financial liberalization extended to international capital movements has, therefore, negative long-term implications for the viability of fiscally responsible reforms to improve distributional equity, because even under more orderly fiscal-financial circumstances it reinforces the effectiveness of capital flight as a protective barrier against such reforms. There is no way that financial liberalization can create in small, technologically dependent economies thick, flexible, and highly liquid financial markets that provide value protection comparable to that offered by the major money centers of the capitalist world. Domestic real interest rates, even under financially orderly circumstances will have to incorporate a large risk premium to check portfolio "internationalizing" by the wealthy. Financial liberalization also makes it easier for the wealthy to resort to capital flight and thus create financial disorder when threatened with tax and/or expenditure reforms that are not to their liking. In Latin America, with its notoriously high inequities and class hostilities, financial liberalization reinforces the region's propensity for fiscally irresponsible but politically less confrontational reformism.

It is unlikely that the designers of market liberalizing restructuring recipes in Washington either anticipated the current internal financial gridlock or had thought through the adverse long-term implication of extending market liberalization to the financial markets of the fragile, conflictual debtor economies. In that sense, the contribution of the restructuring to the travail of the debtor economies is the unintended result of conceptual flaws. Nevertheless, the economists who rationalized the case for financial liberalization should have at least have been more aware of the tenuousness of its grounding in economic theory. Recently, however, Latin American economists, including IMF staffers, have begun pointing out that liberalizing financial markets when the state is also compelled by formal and informal commitment, as in Latin America, to save politically powerful but insolvent enterprises and to act as lender of last resort is a destabilizing recipe (Le Fort, 1989).[9] If the state wants the benefits of allowing financial prices to be market-determined, then it cannot avoid close supervision of other dimensions of credit such as its quality and quantity in order to contain financial instability. This was already demonstrated by the financial disasters of the liberalizing Southern Cone countries, but apparently some economists need a repetition in order to recognize a trend.

In the realm of creditor movers and shakers meanwhile, the most encouraging development is the emphasis on the need to stanch capital flight and promote capital repatriation. If our gridlock analysis is valid this should lead next to the awareness that neither stanching nor desired large-scale repatriation is likely with the gridlock that financial liberalization has helped create. This could set the stage for serious consideration of proposals for compulsory repatriation.

One such proposal, inspired by British and French foreign asset mobilization during World Wars I and II, would have the debtor government require registration of foreign assets, which it would then purchase with negotiable domestic currency bonds of staggered maturity. The foreign assets thus acquired would be placed in escrow abroad to collateralize the foreign debt. Concurrently, the debtor government would limit debt servicing from export receipts to a low fraction, which would free foreign exchange for importing and serve as a bargaining chip to induce creditor governments to collaborate in fingering clandestine asset ownership so as to build the escrow account.

When the proposal was first advanced by the senior author of this paper in 1985, his main intent was to dramatize the capital flight phenomenon, which then went largely unmentioned in the official pronouncements of creditors and debtors (Felix, 1985). It also, however, appeared to be a neat neoclassical positive-sum solution to the debt crisis, technically feasible if politically improbable. It would collateralize the dubious bank loans, solve the debt crisis of many of the major debtors and restore their credit standing in international financial markets. It would also raise transactions costs of future capital flight, thus restoring fiscal and monetary autonomy to debtor governments and giving them some political space to implement fiscally responsible social reforms while adhering to moderate financial liberalization.

Critics, neoclassical and Marxist alike, quickly pointed out that while socializing the foreign liabilities of the Latin American wealthy was politically acceptable, socializing their foreign assets is political and even physical suicide. Four years later it seems even less likely that the demoralized debtor governments would be capable of initiating the scheme on their own. But creditor government encouragement of the sort used to sell market liberalizing restructuring might provide the required impetus. Four years later the creditor governments may be running out of other technically feasible solutions that are also politically acceptable to their own constituencies.

NOTES

1. Half the Argentine loans of the U.S. money-center banks were to the private sector.

2. See Caskey (1989) and Guttentag and Herring (1989) for discussions of different bank interests and the mechanisms used to coerce reluctant banks into participating in bailout loans.

3. Between 1984 and 1986, 41 percent of the increase of Brazil's foreign debt and 23 percent of the increase of Argentina's debt was due to currency redenomination (Calcagno and Martinez, 1988, p. 23).

4. Thus, Assistant-Secretary of State for Inter-American Affairs, Langhorne Motley, proclaimed on a visit to Chile in February, 1985, that "the destiny of Chile is in very good hands . . . the democracies of the Western World owe a debt of gratitude for what the people of Chile did in 1973." *El Mercurio*, (Santiago) February 24, 1985, as cited in NACLA (1988, p. 29). The Reagan Administration began distancing itself from Pinochet after 1985.

5. The value of foreign assets are estimated by assuming that each year's net capital flight less returned interest and dividends is invested in a portfolio of foreign assets whose dollar value rises at an annual rate proxied by the interest rate on ten-year U.S. Treasury bonds. The Chilean 1985 figures are probably underestimates; other evidence indicates that Chilean private foreign holdings were moderately positive. For discussion of the estimating method and its limitations, see Felix and Sanchez (1989).

6. Our base case assumption of a 0.5 percent annual improvement in Latin American terms of trade is optimistic in comparison to the IMF's projection of a modest de-

cline in commodity prices in real terms from 1990–94 (*IMF Survey,* July 24, 1989, p. 239).

7. Colombia, which had not fully liberalized controls on international capital transactions, avoided falling into a debt servicing crisis on its foreign debt, but nevertheless had a severe financial crisis in 1982 due to overleveraging and loose domestic lending that required the authorities to take over 70 percent of the loan portfolios of the private banks and financieras (Carrizosa and Urdinela, 1987).

8. J. Perez de Arce, "Diferencias entre recursos del Estado destinados a la banca y por combatir el desempleo," *Diario La Tercera: Informe Economico,* (May 2, 1983), cited in Zahler (1984).

9. The Le Fort paper contains numerous citations to other supportive IMF and World Bank working papers. See also the papers in Massad and Zahler (1988).

2

United States Policies and Latin America's Trade and Debt

Werner Baer and Donald V. Coes

In the 1980s the United States, joined by other creditor countries, insisted that it was Latin America's obligation to service its enormous debt, and to keep the servicing up to date.[1] At the same time, the U.S. government has been under pressure from U.S. import competing sectors to press a number of Latin American countries to eliminate various types of export incentive programs which allegedly violate GATT rules. It has also been under pressure by other groups to press Latin American governments to liberalize their import policies. As a result, the U.S. government has increasingly adopted a pluralistic, and often contradictory, policy posture. This chapter examines the circumstances which have produced this situation, and considers ways in which a more consistent set of policies can be developed.

I. EVOLUTION OF UNITED STATES–LATIN AMERICAN ECONOMIC RELATIONS

Over much of this century the United States has been a major trade partner and source of both direct investment and financial capital for Latin America. The counterpart of the U.S. capital outflow was a current account surplus with the region. This implied a transfer of real resources from the capital-rich region to a less developed one. Most economists would recognize this as a healthy pattern since it increases world economic efficiency and raises incomes in both areas. Domestic economic policy changes in the United States, however, have recently reversed this long-run trend. Since the mid1970s, and increasingly in the 1980s, the U.S. fiscal policy has become more expansionary without being accommodated by monetary policy. The net result has been an enormous increase in real interest rates in the United States and world capital markets and the disappearance of a U.S. capital surplus available to Latin America.

Table 2.1.
U.S. Merchandise Trade with Latin America (Millions US$)

Year	Merchandise Exports	Merchandise Imports	Merchandise Trade
1970	6,494	5,913	581
1971	6,433	6,115	318
1972	7,241	7,068	173
1973	9,950	9,645	305
1974	15,823	18,658	-2,835
1975	17,108	16,177	931
1976	16,843	17,204	-361
1977	17,921	21,162	-3,241
1978	22,034	23,041	-1,007
1979	28,555	30,535	-1,980
1980	38,811	37,521	1,290
1981	42,804	39,099	3,705
1982	33,164	38,561	-5,397
1983	25,581	41,867	-16,286
1984	29,767	48,366	-18,599
1985	30,788	46,110	-15,322
1986	30,877	41,426	-10,549
1987	35,089	47,258	-12,169

Source: U.S. Department of Commerce, *Survey of Current Business,* various issues.

Trade Relations

In the period 1970–1981 the United States trade balance with Latin America was positive in seven out of twelve years, as is shown in Table 2.1. But since 1982, when the debt crisis became acute, the United States has had very large and continuing deficits with the region. These deficits were due to a combination of decreases in exports to Latin America and substantial increases in imports from the region. It can be noted in Table 2.1 that U.S. exports to Latin America reached a maximum value of US$ 42.8 billion in 1981, declining thereafter to US$ 25.6 billion in 1983, rising in the following four years, but not again reaching the 1980–82 levels. U.S. imports from Latin America, on the other hand, rose considerably in the period; they were at a level of US$ 30.5 billion in 1979, rising to US$ 37.5 billion in 1980; and in 1987 they stood at US$ 47 billion. Although prior to 1981 the U.S. trade balance with Latin America alternated between small surpluses and deficits, since 1982 the continuing deficits were larger than at any time in the previous decade.

The United States has borne a relatively large share of the current account consequences of Latin America's adjustment after 1982. This is clear from Table 2.2, which shows Latin American trade and investment earning balances with the United States as a percentage of total Latin American trade and investment balances. Although the United States has been the recipient of only a

Table 2.2.
Latin American Trade and Investment Earning Balances with the United States
(Percentage of Global Balances)

	Investment Earning Balances	Trade Balances	Net Investment Service Payments	Net Non-Investment Service Payments
1980	25.9	*	74	**
1981	16.8	*	57	**
1982	37.6	71.0	38	4
1983	33.7	54.5	33	42
1984	27.3	48.3	27	79
1985	27.5	46.3	28	76
1986	28.5	61.4	28	102
1987	20.0	60.4	29	NA

Note: Entries are percentages of global trade and investment balances, calculated from data in *Survey of Current Business,* and in Inter-American Development Bank, *Economic and Social Progress in Latin America,* 1988. (*) Latin American trade deficit in 1980 and 1981. (**) Negligible.

third or fourth of the service payments on Latin America's external debt, more than half the current trade surpluses which Latin America has had to generate to finance these payments have been earned in trade with the United States. Although this might be explained in the mid 1980s by overvaluation of the dollar in relation to the other Latin American creditors and trade partners, the share of Latin America's trade surplus generated with the United States has actually risen since 1985. In this sense the earnings of non-U.S. creditors of Latin America are being maintained through a U.S. trade deficit with Latin America. The decline of U.S. exports to Latin America is due to a number of factors:

1. The recession in many countries of the region resulting from the adjustment programs forced upon them by the debt crisis. The real yearly GDP growth rate of Latin America in the period 1971–1980 was 5.9 percent; it fell to 1.0 percent in 1981–83; and recovered to 3.4 percent in 1984–87.[2] This explains, in part, the U.S. export decline from 1981 to 1983 and the weak recovery in the period after 1984.

2. The large real devaluations of a number of the region's key currencies, which have made foreign goods more expensive. For the region as a whole, the real effective exchange rate rose by 51 percent from 1980 to 1987.

3. The results of import-substitution investments in the 1970s. This was especially the case in Brazil, where a large proportion of international borrowing was used to build up the capital goods industry.

Table 2.3.
U.S. and Latin American Trade Shares (Percentages of Total Flow)

a) Share of U.S. in Latin American Exports and Imports

Yearly Average	Exports	Imports
1960-3	37.2	41.8
1977-9	35.0	32.9
1984-6	49.4	48.7

b) Share of Latin America in U.S. Exports and Imports

Yearly Average	Exports	Imports
1970-2	14.9	13.6
1977-9	15.3	13.8
1985-7	14.0	12.1

Sources: Calculated from data in U.S. Department of Commerce, *Survey of Current Business,* various issues; Interamerican Development Bank, *Economic and Social Progress in Latin America,* 1982 and 1987.

4. Tariff and non-tariff barriers which were used to squeeze the imports of countries in the midst of the debt crisis.

The growth of U.S. imports from Latin America can be attributed to three factors:

1. An active export diversification program carried out by a number of countries. This was highly successful in a number of countries. The growth of nontraditional exports was in part due to the use of tax and credit incentives.
2. Substantial real devaluations of the currency of a number of Latin American countries, which made exports increasingly competitive.
3. The high growth rate of the U.S. economy in the 1980s after the brief downturn in the early part of the decade.

It is noteworthy that the relative decline of the United States as a trading partner for Latin America was reversed in the 1980s. Table 2.3 shows that the U.S. market's share in Latin American exports rose from 35 percent in the latter 1970s to 49.4 percent in the mid 1980s, while imports from the U.S. rose from 32.9 percent to 48.7 percent. One explanation for the increasing share

Table 2.4.
Net U.S. Service Trade with Latin America (Millions US$)

Year	Net Direct Investment Earnings	Net Other Private Receipts	Net U.S. Government Receipts	Net Services Investment	Net Services Non-Investment	Net Total
	(a)	(b)	(c)	(d)	(e)	(f)
1970	1,380	107	150	1,637	-230	1,407
1971	1,432	274	129	1,835	-301	1,534
1972	1,258	286	132	1,676	-508	1,168
1973	1,594	377	136	2,107	-256	1,851
1974	1,934	930	220	3,084	-480	2,604
1975	1,542	1,438	188	3,168	-35	3,133
1976	1,931	2,085	223	4,239	-249	3,990
1977	3,558	2,651	211	6,420	-563	5,857
1978	4,463	3,828	210	8,501	-650	7,851
1979	5,770	4,766	243	10,779	-496	10,283
1980	5,846	7,891	157	13,894	447	14,341
1981	4,832	10,924	92	15,848	1,960	17,808
1982	2,382	12,127	258	14,767	-423	14,344
1983	405	10,835	371	11,611	-1,981	9,630
1984	516	9,570	17	10,103	-2,924	7,179
1985	2,434	7,905	-288	10,051	-2,055	7,996
1986	4,216	5,697	-620	9,293	-2,477	6,816
1987	4,179	2,449	-299	6,329	-3,257	3,072

Source: U.S. Department of Commerce, *Survey of Current Business,* various issues.

enjoyed by the United States in Latin American trade is that the United States has had a higher rate of growth than many of the other industrial countries during most of the 1980s, which resulted in a greater degree of U.S. import absorption from the region. This was apparently more important than the competitive advantage which Latin American countries gained in trade with other industrial countries as a result of the devaluation of the dollar. It is also probable that the decline of the dollar made U.S. goods more attractive to Latin Americans than those from other industrial countries, which would explain the growth of the U.S. share in Latin American imports. The share of Latin America in U.S. exports fluctuated only slightly, declining 1.3 percentage points in the 1980s, while its share in U.S. imports decreased slightly more.

The Service Balance

An examination of Table 2.4 shows that Latin America's service balance with the United States was always negative in the decades of the 1970s and

1980s, but that it worsened substantially in the late 1970s, peaking in 1981. After that year the service deficit declined, but continued at a level substantially higher than before the late 1970s.

The major explanation for the growth of the service deficit can be found in column (b) of Table 2.4, which consists of "Net Other Private Investment Receipts" and represents primarily interest payments. This item ballooned from less than one billion to over twelve billion dollars in 1982 and is responsible for most of the growth in the overall service deficit. The steep rise of this item after 1979 is in great part due to the rapid increase of U.S. interest rates. The use of very tight monetary policy in the United States in the late 1970s and early 1980s to cope with inflation, in conjunction with the continuation of expansionary fiscal policy, had a repercussion on interest rates throughout the world. The annual average prime rate, for example, rose from 6.83 percent in 1977 to 18.87 percent in 1981, while LIBOR rates rose from an annual average of 6.2 percent in 1977 to 16.5 percent in 1981. Since most of the Latin American debt was contracted on a flexible interest rate basis, these developments substantially increased the burden of the debt to the region.

Column (c) of Table 2.4 shows that net U.S. government interest receipts were positive, but became negative in 1985. This trend was partially due to negotiated reductions of official debt and debt servicing under the Paris Club arrangements. Unfortunately, this easing of official debt service was small in relation to the large private debt service payments which the region had to make to U.S.-based creditors. Tax payers of the United States and other major creditor countries, in effect, accepted a reduction in income on official debt in order to maintain and even increase Latin American payments to private creditors.

Column (a) of Table 2.4 shows earnings from direct investments. This item was always positive for the United States, since it was primarily profit remittances by U.S. companies in Latin America. The decline after 1980 reflects the economic crisis the region was undergoing in the 1980s. As the economies stagnated, profits of U.S. firms declined, as did their profit remittances. This trend was reinforced in some countries by controls on the remittance of profits as the balance of payments situation worsened.

Capital Flows

During most of the post-World War II period, Latin America has been a major recipient of capital flows through both direct investment and loans. Following its replacement of Great Britain as the dominant foreign economic power in the region after World War I, the United States became the major source of net capital inflows to Latin America. The high point of U.S. predominance was reached shortly after World War II, when more than 50 percent of direct investment and capital flows were of U.S. origin. With the recovery and more rapid growth of Western Europe and Japan, U.S. shares have declined, despite the absolute increase of investments through the 1970s. Although the United States declined in relative terms, it remained the major source of external capital.

One should also consider that in addition to its importance as the origin of a substantial share of Latin America's foreign capital, the role of the United States as the world's leading financial intermediary was particularly important in Latin America, especially after 1973, when U.S.-based multinational banks were responsible for recycling a substantial part of the OPEC surplus to Latin American borrowers. U.S. influence was also important in multilateral organizations, such as the World Bank and the Inter-American Development Bank. This historical pattern was abruptly changed in the early 1980s. With the explosion of the debt crisis, Latin America became a net exporter of capital to its creditor countries, particularly the United States.

The major trends in the U.S. capital account with Latin America are summarized in Table 2.5. The U.S. was a net lender of capital to Latin America in every year between 1970 and 1983, with the exception of 1979, as may be seen in column (a). Most of this capital was financial, particularly after 1973, as is clear from column (b) of Table 2.5. There were several reasons for the preponderance of financial capital flows rather than equity investment. First, the international financial community at the time regarded such loans as less risky than equity investments, particularly when the loans were made to sovereign governments, since they presumably rested on the taxing capacity of the borrower governments. However incorrect this assumption may appear with the advantage of hindsight and in the light of current emphasis on debt for equity swaps, financial capital flows were clearly preferred in the 1970s. A second reason was the development and perfection of variable interest rate loans, which appeared to remove interest rate uncertainty for both borrowers and lenders.

Finally, in some countries, such as Brazil, there were technical reasons for the preference for financial capital flows over equity investment, since direct investment regulations did not allow for the effects of inflation in the lending country, while such inflation was automatically incorporated in the nominal interest rate paid on the loan.

Most of this financial capital flow was net lending by U.S. banks, as is shown in column (c) of Table 2.5. The net figures, however, do not tell the whole story. Gross U.S. bank lending to Latin America, as measured by the change in U.S. claims on Latin American borrowers by U.S. banks, was always positive (a minus indicates a U.S. outflow), except for 1985. Gross U.S. lending reached a peak in 1982, sharply dropping off after that period. Much of the gross lending after 1982 was, in fact, forced lending induced by the necessity to renegotiate and roll over earlier loans.

Latin American capital outflows to U.S. banks are shown in column (e). A substantial part of this flow was private capital flight, which increased dramatically after 1977. In 1979, despite the maintenance of gross U.S. lending to

Table 2.5.
U.S. Financial Capital Flows to Latin America: Banking and Total Net Capital Flows
(Millions US$)

	U.S. Banking Claims	U.S. Banking Liabilities	Net U.S. Banking Claims	Total Nonbank Financial Flows	Total Financial Capital Flows	Total Capital Flows
	(a)	(b)	(c)	(d)	(e)	(f)
1970	-376	-815	-1,191	-244	-1,435	-1,997
1971	-589	-325	-914	-24	-938	-1,569
1972	-1,480	876	-604	-173	-777	-1,080
1973	-1,471	2,109	638	-316	322	-298
1974	-6,950	4,344	-2,606	-1,049	-3,655	-5,880
1975	-9,041	3,217	-5,824	-509	-6,333	-7,716
1976	-14,841	4,457	-10,384	-1,025	-11,409	-11,441
1977	-7,038	4,878	-2,160	-374	-2,534	-5,979
1978	-10,449	8,404	-2,045	-576	-2,621	-6,333
1979	-10,549	18,102	7,553	492	8,045	5,273
1980	-26,697	5,186	-21,511	-3,230	-24,741	-26,170
1981	-43,995	29,799	-14,196	5	-14,191	-12,826
1982	-51,471	28,092	-23,379	2,518	-20,861	-14,316
1983	-13,740	25,821	12,081	-773	11,308	14,752
1984	-1,624	15,327	13,703	9,060	22,763	24,907
1985	4,483	-1,513	2,970	2,593	5,563	2,372
1986	-8,037	26,173	18,136	4,426	22,562	12,661
1987	-6,634	8,288	1,654	3,203	4,857	-2,118

Note: A minus sign (−) implies an outflow from the United States. Column (d) consists of
changes in net holdings of securities plus net changes in U.S. nonbanking claims. Column c
= a + b; column e = c + d; column f = e + (net direct investment from Table 9).
Source: U.S. Department of Commerce, *Survey of Current Business,* various issues.

Latin America, shown in column (d), the doubling of capital outflows resulted
in a net capital inflow to the U.S. banking system of more than 7 billion dollars.

Examination of columns (c), (d) and (e) together reveals that much of the
growth of the gross Latin American debt owed to U.S. banks financed a large
capital outflow to these banks. This reflects the capital flight induced, in part,
by overvalued exchange rates, combined with domestic crises, especially in
such countries as Argentina, Chile, Mexico and Venezuela.

The dramatic reversal of net bank lending to Latin America between 1982
and 1983, when the record 1982 inflow of more than 20 billion dollars was
succeeded in 1983 by a net outflow of more than 12 billion, was due both to
the sharp drop in gross bank lending to Latin America and the maintenance
of private capital outflows to U.S. banks.

Table 2.6.
U.S Financial Capital Flows to Latin America: Securities and Non-Banking
(Millions US$)

	U.S. Holdings of Latin American Securities	Latin American Holdings of U.S. Securities	Net Securities Flows	U.S. Non-banking Claims	U.S. Non-banking Liabilities	Net U.S. Non-banking Claims
1970	-135	66	-69	-365	190	-175
1971	-33	56	23	-249	202	-47
1972	-45	-9	-54	-234	115	-119
1973	-107	43	-64	-548	296	-252
1974	-93	24	-69	-779	-201	-980
1975	-347	43	-304	-303	98	-205
1976	-219	198	-21	-1,080	76	-1,004
1977	-151	280	129	-643	140	-503
1978	181	351	532	-1,372	264	-1,108
1979	310	88	398	-377	471	94
1980	37	330	367	-2,090	-1,507	-3,597
1981	27	97	124	-241	122	-119
1982	3	449	452	2,502	-436	2,066
1983	658	674	1,332	-2,207	102	-2,105
1984	2,190	862	3,052	3,355	2,653	6,008
1985	1,957	543	2,500	781	-688	93
1986	3,309	4,360	7,669	-1,485	-1,758	-3,243
1987	913	2,290	3,203	NA	NA	NA

Source: U.S. Department of Commerce, Survey of Current Business, various issues.

Other financial capital flows from the U.S. to Latin America were relatively unimportant by comparison with bank lending, as may be seen from column (f) in Table 2.5. Most of these flows consisted of trade in U.S. and Latin American securities and nonbank financing. Much of the latter was related to multinational operations, resulting in financial flows between U.S. parent and Latin American subsidiaries. As was the case with bank lending, there was a reversal in the other net financial flows after 1982.

Table 2.6 shows the trends in these two types of nonbank lending on a gross and net basis since 1970. One of the most interesting aspects of these capital flows between these two regions is that Latin America became a net lender in securities trade as early as 1977, five years before the debt crisis. In the post 1982 period, net securities outflow from Latin America amounted to more than US$ 5 billion annually. This may be another manifestation of capital flight.

Direct foreign investment, which is shown in Table 2.7, was a less important component of the U.S. capital account with Latin America than were financial flows, in part for reasons stated earlier. Like trade in securities, the reversal in

Table 2.7.
U.S. Direct Investment Balance with Latin America (Millions US$)

Year	U.S. Direct Investment in Latin America	Latin American Direct Investment in U.S.	Net Direct Investment (- is an outflow from U.S.)
1970	-601	39	-562
1971	-691	60	-631
1972	-279	-24	-303
1973	-673	53	-620
1974	-2,270	45	-2,225
1975	-1,347	-36	-1,383
1976	-146	114	-32
1977	-3,632	187	-3,445
1978	-4,207	495	-3,712
1979	-4,043	1,271	-2,772
1980	-2,655	1,226	-1,429
1981	58	1,307	1,365
1982	5,820	725	6,545
1983	3,066	378	3,444
1984	1,625	519	2,144
1985	-3,875	684	-3,191
1986	-7,450	-2,451	-9,901
1987	-7,336	361	-6,975

Source: U.S. Department of Commerce, Survey of Current Business, various issues.

net direct investment preceded the 1982 debt crisis. Gross direct U.S. investment in Latin America peaked in 1978 and rapidly declined to a net outflow, which reached nearly US$ 6 billion in 1982.

II. CONFLICTING POLICY GOALS IN U.S. ECONOMIC RELATIONS WITH LATIN AMERICA: AN INTERPRETATION

The economic relations between any country and the rest of the world potentially flow through two major channels: the goods market and the capital (or assets) market. These correspond, respectively, in the balance of payments to the current and the capital accounts, which together in the long run must offset each other. In most of the postwar period until the 1970s both market participants and policymakers paid much more attention to trade, and the current account.

The Capital Account Reversal

With the rise of multinational banking, beginning in the 1960s and significantly expanded in the 1970s by the availability of petrodollars after the first oil shock, asset market (or capital account) transactions came to eventually upstage trade questions, presenting policymakers with a new series of constraints. In earlier, and apparently simpler days, the makers of U.S. economic policy toward Latin America were primarily concerned with trade questions, notably the maintenance of markets for U.S. exports to Latin America and the secure access to essential imports from the region. Any resulting current account deficit was assumed to be easily financed via the capital account, implying a capital inflow from the United States and other creditor countries to Latin America. This arrangement worked especially well in the mid 1970s, when the international financial community was flush with petrodollars, available to lend at nominal interest rates close to or even below inflation in the creditor countries. Past debts and their servicing requirements were financed by new net borrowing, as was shown above.

It should now be clear that the asset market disequilibrium or capital account deficit of Latin America could not continue indefinitely. Some capital market participants appeared to have perceived this point sooner than others. As we noted in the preceding section, increases of Latin American holdings of U.S. securities began to accelerate as early as 1976 (see Table 2.6), while increases of U.S. holdings of Latin American securities peaked in 1975 and actually decreased from 1978 onwards. A similar trend is evident in trade in nonbank financial assets, in which net U.S. outflows peaked in 1980. Latin American bank deposits in the United States began to accelerate sharply in 1978 (Table 2.5). Direct investment flows to Latin America began to fall off after 1978 (Table 2.7).

Although our data mask considerable variations in capital flows between the United States and individual Latin American countries, it is clear from the aggregate data that the bank debt crisis of 1982 was anticipated by a number of years in other international capital markets. In retrospect, one wonders why the U.S. banking community steadily increased its lending through 1982, when gross U.S. bank lending to Latin America reached more than US$ 51 billion.

Although the turnabout in U.S. bank lending to Latin America came later than any other reversal in capital flows, when it did occur, it was brutal. Gross lending fell by nearly US$ 40 billion between 1982 and 1983, and in 1985 there was an outflow (see Table 2.5). At international bankers' insistence prospects for any new lending became contingent on a sharp improvement in the current account which, given the insistence on the maintenance of interest payments, required an even larger improvement in the trade surplus.

Conflicting Interests of Participants in U.S.–Latin American Trade and Capital Movements

Until it belatedly recognized the long-run inviability of continued growth of Latin American indebtedness, the international banking community was a willing partner in expansionary Latin American fiscal policies. In any economy, when domestic savings are not sufficient to finance domestic investment as well as the common excess of public expenditures over tax receipts, the balance must come from abroad in the form of a current account deficit. In this sense Latin America's worsening current account imbalances in the 1970s were intimately linked to insufficient domestic savings and particularly to growing public sector deficits. In many of the countries of the region the growth of public sector expenditures outstripped both overall economic growth and the growth of tax receipts. Such public sector deficits could be financed either through money creation, or through local or foreign borrowing. The last of these three means of financing the deficit, foreign borrowing, was little used by most Latin American countries before the end of the 1960s. With the vast increase in international capital availability in the 1970s, few Latin American governments resisted the temptation to go to the international capital markets rather than to their domestic savers and taxpayers. This demand for financing by Latin American governments proved profitable for the international banking community, which was often as willing to lend to a sovereign government in Latin America as to private investors at home.

With their heightened perception of the long-run risks inherent in the process, as well as its ultimate inviability, the international banking community began to sound like the bankers they once had been. From 1982 on the bankers insisted on evidence of creditworthiness as a precondition to roll over expiring debt, which had become increasingly short term.

The bankers' central aim was the achievement of trade surpluses large enough to finance interest payments on the outstanding debt, given their new reluctance to advance new loans. The means by which this was to be accomplished were less important to them than the end. As a trade surplus can be achieved through either export expansion or import contraction, both types of policies received the bankers' support, as well as that of the IMF. In the short run, it is probably much easier to generate a trade surplus by reducing imports than by increasing exports. As Table 2.1 suggests, most of the sharp reversal of Latin America's trade balance in the early 1980s came through a reduction of imports rather than an export expansion. This decrease of imports was the result of several factors: direct import restrictions, real devaluation, and, perhaps most importantly, a decline in the GDP growth rate, which in some countries became negative for the first time since the Great Depression of the 1930s. Poor Latin American performance on the export side was due, in part, to the worldwide recession in the early 1980s, as well as to sharp declines in the price of a number of important Latin American primary exports. The aggregate export figures, however, hide the tremendous strides which were made by some Latin American countries in pushing manufactured exports, notably by Brazil and Mexico.[3] Thus, by the mid 1980s one might judge the banking communities to have attained their objective, in that the region was producing the trade surpluses necessary to service the debt.

This may have solved the immediate problem from the viewpoint of the international banking community, but the achievement of the trade surplus was not in the interest of other U.S. policy constituencies. Latin America had long been one of the major U.S. export markets, particularly for capital goods. The sharp decline of Latin America's imports fell particularly hard on U.S. manufacturers, already hard hit by the overvalued U.S. dollar, high interest rates, and the domestic recession of the early 1980s.

Although the initial burden of Latin American trade adjustment fell primarily on U.S. exporters, the subsequent success of Latin American exporters of manufactured goods affected a different group, U.S. producers of import competing goods. For the first time, Latin American manufactured goods posed a serious threat in sectors such as steel, textiles, machinery, clothing, footwear, transport equipment, and others. These new pressures led to predictable reactions by the threatened domestic producers. They were not long in filing charges against Latin American countries for using tax and credit subsidies, allegedly in violation of GATT rules. Even when these charges were rejected, they often forced potential Latin American exporters to incur substantial additional costs.

U.S.-based multinationals located in Latin America in some respects enjoyed a more favorable position in the Latin American trade balance turnaround, since they enjoyed a better access to U.S. markets. They benefited from the sharp fall in relative real wages and other domestic costs within Latin America, as well as from a variety of export incentives instituted by Latin American countries. This was partially offset, however, by increased administrative barriers to imports, which were particularly severe in industries using a large amount of imported components.

The Decapitalization of Latin America and U.S. Political Interests

The sharp reversal in net capital flows to Latin America occurred, perhaps not coincidentally, with a reversal in the political tide. Between the mid 1970s and mid 1980s authoritarian governments were replaced by democratic regimes in most Latin American countries.[4] This trend was particularly evident in several of the major countries of the region, notably Argentina and Brazil. Few would question America's long-term interest in encouraging the trend towards increasing political openness. Short-term U.S. economic policy, however, may work at cross-purposes and even undercut our long-term political goals.

Governing Latin American countries has never been easy, either for dictators or democrats, as the region's century of political instability has shown. When the burden of effecting a net resource transfer to the rest of the world is added to existing problems, the survival of fragile new democracies is even more precarious. U.S. policymakers have not been blind to this, as U.S. promptness in arranging bridge loans to major borrowers when credit markets closed in 1982 and 1983 has shown. In the longer run, U.S. support for World Bank, IDB, and other multilateral assistance is based, in part, on the belief that it may be less expensive to provide modest help to the region now than face the costs of major upheavals in the future.

The time may have come when such incremental assistance is no longer sufficient to deal with Latin American economic conditions in the last decade of the 20th century. Past U.S. pressure on Latin American debtor countries to follow IMF-endorsed austerity programs has been a short-term success in the narrow sense of avoiding default and major international financial crises, by keeping debt servicing up to date as a condition for periodic rolling over of the principal. These short-run benefits, however, have incurred enormous long-run costs. They have caused a severe decline in the standard of living of the region today, and perhaps even more ominously, tomorrow, through a decline of investment.

The available data are unmistakably discouraging. Latin America's real minimum wages decreased by over 15 percent between 1980 and 1985 (in Mexico the decline was 43 percent and in Brazil 16 percent), while the output per capita, which had increased by 33 percent between 1970 and 1981, declined by 3.3 percent in the years 1982 to 1987. Latin America's investment/GDP ratio, moreover, was 22.6 percent in the period 1970–1981, falling to 16.6 percent in 1982–87, as the net yearly transfer of capital abroad in the years 1983–87 totalled US$ 25 billion.[5] For many Latin Americans, the 1980s have been a decade of stagnation.

Not only does the decline in the region's standard of living threaten the long-term survival of democratic governments, but the decline of investment activity will make it increasingly difficult for Latin American economies to keep up with the rest of the world. Low investment activity will result in Latin America's falling increasingly behind in productivity and technology, which will make it difficult to maintain, let alone increase, its share of the world market.

The region's trade surpluses in the 1980s, especially with the United States, as noted above, resulted from efforts to compress imports and, in some countries, to promote exports through incentive programs and real depreciation. The consequent pressures from U.S. interest groups anxious to maintain their sales to Latin America and from other groups, who feel threatened by Latin America's penetration of U.S. markets have placed additional constraints on U.S. policy.

It is in the interest of both the United States and Latin America to find a more permanent solution to reduce the real burden of the debt. The markets' own mechanism of debt relief, in the form of discounts on the face value of the debt in the secondary market, is not a satisfactory solution, since it is uncertain and arbitrary, providing little incentive for long-term investment.[6]

Once the debt burden is substantially decreased, Latin American will have more foreign exchange available to allow itself to liberalize imports and thus increase economic efficiency. A substantial increase in Latin American imports would also make it possible to raise the region's investment ratio and thus expand and modernize its productive capacity. Finally, a substantial increase in Latin America imports could also disarm the opposition to the penetration of nontraditional goods from Latin America into the U.S. market.

NOTES

1. Current U.S. banking regulations force banks to insist on maintenance of interest payments. Interest payments which are in arrears beyond a grace period require the banks to recognize a loss by increasing their loan reserves.

2. The decline of growth in some of the major countries in the same period was much more pronounced: in the same periods, Argentina's growth declined from 2.6 to −2.9 percent and recovered to only 1.2 percent; Brazil's growth declined from 8.7 to −1.7 percent and recovered to 6.1 percent; and Mexico's growth declined from 6.6 to −1.2 percent and recovered to only 0.9 percent.

3. Brazil's overall manufactured exports increased from US$ 6.6 billion in 1979 to US$ 15.1 billion in 1984 and are expected to reach US$ 18 billion in 1988. Mexico's nontraditional exports rose from US$ 1.2 billion in 1981 to US$ 4.1 billion in 1985.

4. In the mid 1970s the nineteen Latin American nations (Spanish- and Portuguese-speaking) could be classified into fourteen authoritarian regimes and five democracies. By the mid 1980s the number of democratic governments had risen to thirteen.

5. These data were taken from: Inter-American Development Bank, *Economic and Social Progress in Latin America: 1988 Report;* U.N., *Economic Commission for Latin America and the Caribbean, Economic Panorama of Latin America 1988.*

6. In November 1988, for example, Brazilian debt was selling in the secondary market at about 40 percent of its face value, while Mexican debt was selling at about 45 percent and Argentine debt at less than 20 percent (*The Economist,* 26 November, 1988, p. 112).

3

Economic Growth and External Debt: Some Analytical Macroeconomic Issues for the "Baker Plan"

Paul Beckerman

Over the medium to long term, heavily indebted developing nations face a trade-off between real GDP growth and external-liability accumulation. The terms of each nation's trade-off may become more or less acute over time through changes in such variables as the national saving rate, the incremental capital-output ratio, technological improvement, and the physical-capital depreciation rate, as well as through changes in such external circumstances as world interest rates and terms of trade. Nevertheless, the broad generalization remains that, in outlining their medium-term development strategies, national economic authorities must choose between higher real GDP growth with higher external-liability growth and lower real GDP growth with lower real external-liability growth. This is the essential dilemma of what is still generally called the "debt crisis," although it is surely now more accurate to call it "the chronic debt condition."

Recent analyses by Selowsky and van der Tak (1986) and by Nogueira Batista Jr. (1986) have clarified the relationships among a developing economy's real growth rate, external-saving inflow, and net external liability stock. After developing a simplified model incorporating this theory, this essay develops a rough indicator called the "debt-stabilizing real growth rate," defined as the theoretical long-term GDP growth rate that would maintain a constant ratio of net external liabilities to GDP. The numerical value of this growth rate is a benchmark indicator of the nation's debt burden. If the nation's real GDP growth exceeds this benchmark, its net external liabilities-GDP ratio must increase, and so its net external liabilities would have to grow faster than its real GDP. Alternatively, if the net external liabilities-GDP ratio is to decline, the real growth rate must be lower than the benchmark growth rate.

Economic analysts have often used the external debt-total exports ratio (or other ratios with total exports in the denominator) to indicate whether a nation's external-debt burden is stabilizing. (See, for example, Simonsen 1984.) In the current circumstances, however, precisely because they are so high for most indebted developing nations, improvements in debt-export ratios hold out little hope of renewed access to international financial markets. The debt-export ratio measures a nation's external liquidity—its capacity to weather external fluctuations without having either to draw down reserves or to secure emergency financing. The most indebted developing nations are now so illiquid by this measure that even very significant improvements would still leave their ratios unacceptably high, even after rescheduling of amortization payments.

Since most heavily indebted developing nations are unlikely to achieve acceptable liquidity ratios in the short term, the fundamental question for nations now caught in the "debt crisis" must be: can they secure sufficient real growth without unduly worsening their external debt burden? Until their circumstances improve, indebted nations' disposition to keep cooperating with their creditors must depend in large measure on whether they can secure adequate real growth. Since the ratio of net external liabilities to GDP, when multiplied by the average interest rate on the debt, indicates the proportion of GDP taken by external factor payments on liabilities, and hence unavailable for capital formation, it is a more appropriate indicator of the real-resource burden of the external liability stock, and hence of the external liabilities' effect on the nation's real-growth prospects.

The announcement of the "Baker Plan" in September 1985 indicated that the U.S. government effectively recognized that the most heavily indebted developing nations could not improve their external-debt ratios without bearing an unacceptable medium- to long-term cost in output growth. Since the U.S. authorities still hoped to prevent the commercial banks from having to write down their loans, and since this required the developing nations to continue "to play the game," the Baker Plan amounted to the U.S. government encouraging the commercial banks to continue to provide additional credit to nations whose external debt was already excessive. In return, so to speak, the Baker Plan exhorted the indebted nations to undertake "structural reforms" consistent with improving their growth potential, including such measures as higher public-sector saving, trade liberalization, financial liberalization, "privatization," and other measures. These measures would presumably serve to increase domestic saving and capital productivity, which would make the medium-term debt-growth trade-off less acute.

It seems reasonable to say that the Baker Plan's results thus far, both for the indebted nations and for their external creditors, have been less than fully satisfactory. The indebted nations have proven unable or unwilling fully to implement the liberalizing advice; the alternative of a debt-service moratorium still receives serious consideration, and occasional implementation, in many of the fifteen "Baker Plan nations"; and the commercial banks continue to provide funds with understandable reluctance. A full review of the Baker Plan is beyond this essay's intended scope, however. Its purpose, rather, is to outline a deliberately simple macroeconomic framework within which the Baker Plan and alternative approaches to it may be understood and evaluated.

Section I outlines the basic analytical structure from which the "debt-stabilizing real growth rate" is derived. Section II outlines a simple simulation model, and discusses some simulation results. Section III offers some concluding observations.

I. AN ANALYTICAL FRAMEWORK

Following an approach suggested by Nogueira Batista Jr. (1986), an economy's real GDP growth rate may be related to the external-saving inflow and to the growth of external liabilities through an extension of the familiar Harrod-Domar growth model (See Jones, 1975). The most elementary version of the Harrod-Domar analysis assumes that the economy has no external relationships. Let Y represent real gross domestic product, K the physical capital stock, and I gross investment. Suppose each unit of capital added to K permits Y to increase by "$1/v$" times I, assuming an adequate supply of other factors of production, so that "v" is the incremental capital-output ratio ("ICOR"). Assume for the moment that "v" is approximately constant over time. If the domestic saving flow is the constant "s" times Y, the addition to the capital stock per unit time is $I = sY$. Since this addition to the capital stock permits an increment to production of $[(1/v)\ I]$, or $[(1/v)\ sY]$, it enables production to grow at a rate of

$$g = [(1/v)\ sY]/Y = s/v. \tag{1}$$

In the theory of economic growth this is known as the "warranted growth rate." As long as no factor of production besides physical capital (such as labor, natural resources, or imported inputs) is in short supply, this would be the economy's maximum feasible long-term growth rate.

The elementary Harrod-Domar analysis neglects capital depreciation for simplicity, but this may be a significant consideration. Suppose the capital stock depreciates at a periodic rate of "d" (implying that physical capital has an average lifetime of $(1/d)$ periods). Let v^* represent the capital-output ratio for the existing capital stock. The net addition to the capital stock over any time period is $I - d\,K = s\,Y - d\,K$, and the warranted growth rate with capital depreciation is then given by

$$g = \{[(1/v)\ sY] - [(1/v^*)\ d\,K]\}/Y = (s/v) - d. \tag{2}$$

To take account of external liabilities and saving inflows from abroad, the closed-economy assumption must be replaced and the external-saving inflow introduced.[1] In the national-income accounts, the inflow of external saving over any time interval is taken to be the negative of the "net resource flow," that is, the difference between imports and exports of merchandise and non-factor services (assuming for simplicity that the flow of unrequited transfer payments is negligible).[2]

Net exports, defined as exports less imports of goods and non-factor services, is therefore the negative of external saving. In what follows, let net exports be the proportion "z" of GDP.

The relationship between external-saving inflows and net external-liability accumulation is described by the balance-of-payments accounts. Define an economy's "net external liabilities" as total external liabilities less external-asset holdings (including the central bank's gross international reserves). Let $L_{(-1)}$ represent the net external-liability stock at the start of the period in question (i.e., at the end of the preceding period), and "r" represent the real rate of return due during the period on the net external liabilities outstanding at the start of the period. Approximately enough, the current account of the balance of payments equals net exports of goods and nonfactor services less net factor payments (interest, dividends and profit remittances) on net external liabilities (i.e., payments on the liabilities less receipts on the assets). Let B represent the current-account surplus; then, approximately enough, $B = (X - M) - r L_{(-1)}$.[3] Assuming that convertible-currency movements and other valuation effects on external liabilities and assets are negligible, net external liabilities increase over time by the current-account deficit—that is, $-B$ gives the increment to L over any time interval. Since

$$-B = (M - X) + r L_{(-1)}, \tag{3}$$

and $(M - X)$ is the external-saving inflow, the addition to the net external liabilities equals the external-saving inflow plus net payments on finance. The growth rate of the net external-liability stock, "h", is given by Equation (3) divided by $L_{(-1)}$, or

$$h = -B/L_{(-1)} = (M - X)/L_{(-1)} + r [L_{(-1)}/L_{(-1)}] = -z/d + r. \tag{4}$$

This essay has referred thus far to "external liabilities," which include accumulated foreign-investment stocks as well as external debt. In the present analytical structure, foreign-investment inflows are as good as debt inflows—arguably better, in the sense that the pressure to repatriate profits on foreign investment is far less than the pressure to make interest payments. This is of course one of the arguments in favor of debt-equity swapping: conversion of external debt (following a valuation reduction in the external debt) into foreign investment replaces some of the interest-payments obligation with a profit flow that may be lower but is, in any case, subject to obligatory retention within the nation for several years.[4] Although debt conversion is significant or potentially significant in all the Baker Plan nations, for simplicity, the present analysis continues to treat all external liabilities the same.

Suppose now that national saving is a proportion "s" of GDP less net external interest payments, that is, a proportion "s" of gross national product.[5] Gross national product is given by $Y - rL_{(-1)}$. Total saving available to the economy then equals the sum of national saving and the current-account deficit, $s [Y - rL_{(-1)}] - [zY - rL_{(-1)}]$. Net capital formation is then given by $I - dK = s [Y - r L_{(-1)}] - [zY - rL_{(-1)}] - d K$. The Harrod-Domar warranted growth rate for an open economy with capital depreciation then becomes

$$g = \{[(s - z) + (1 - s) r d]/v\} - d, \tag{5}$$

or, for easy comparison with Equation (2), $g = \{[(s - z)/v]\} - d + \{[(1 - s) r D]/v\}$, where $D = L_{(-1)}/Y$, the ratio of net external liabilities at the start of the period in question to GDP during the period. This extended Harrod-Domar equation shows that, all other things being equal, the warranted growth rate should be higher, the lower is the value of "z," which is the net non-factor goods-and-services export surplus as a proportion of GDP.

This last observation does not imply that a nation can increase its long-term growth rate by reducing exports and increasing imports. The relevant magnitude for the present analysis is the difference between exports and imports. The present argument in no way contradicts well-known arguments that higher export-GDP and import-GDP ratios may improve overall economic efficiency and long-term growth rates.

As they now stand, Equations (4) and (5) are different equations in L, since the value of $D = L_{(-1)}/Y$ varies as L grows at the rate "h." The two equations are mutually valid for brief time intervals over which "D" remains at its initial value. For appropriately brief time intervals, Equations (4) and (5) may be combined in simple equations giving "g" and "h" in terms of one another:

$$g = \{[s (1 - rD) + rD]/v\} - d + (h - r) (D/v) \tag{6-a}$$

and

$$h = [(g + d) v - s (1 - rD)]/D. \tag{6-b}$$

For given values of "s," "z," "v," "d," and "r," and a given net-external-liability growth rate "h," Equation (6-a) gives the warranted real growth rate; Equation (6-b) indicates the net-external-liability growth rate required to attain a given real growth rate "g." These equations express the trade-off between "g" and "h": as long as "v" exceeds "D," higher values of "g" are associated with higher values of "h."

As a simple numerical example, consider a nation in which (i) the capital-output ratio "v" is 3.5; (ii) the capital stock lasts an average of 25 years (so that "d" is 4 percent); (iii) the saving rate is 20 percent of GNP; (iv) the real rate of return on net external liabilities is 3.5 percent per year; and the initial net external liability-GDP ratio is 50 percent. Equation (6-a) implies that if net external liabilities grow at a real rate equal to their real rate of return (so that the external-saving rate "z" equals zero and external liabilities grow at a rate of h = r = 3.5 percent per year. With "z" equal to zero, net external liabilities grow at a real rate of 3 percent, (by the real interest rate). If real external liabilities were to grow at 4 percent per year, the external-saving rate would be 0.5 percent, and the warranted real growth rate would rise to about 2.1 percent per year. Equation (6-b) implies that in order for this economy to grow at a real annual rate of 2.5 percent, net external liabilities would have to grow at a real rate of 6.2 percent. Latin American population growth rates are typically between 2 and 3 percent per year, and labor-force growth rates slightly higher. These GDP growth rates, accordingly, would imply non-positive per-capita income and productivity growth rates for the country in question.

With some further development of the relevant equations, this analysis can be adapted to determine the possibilities for "stabilizing" a nation's external-liability growth without unduly constraining real growth. In the simple, analytical structure outlined thus far, a nation's net external liabilities may be said to be "stabilized" if the net external liability-GDP ratio "D" can be maintained constant. Since "D" grows at a rate precisely equal to $[(1+h)/(1+g)]$ − 1, (approximately, h − g) it will remain constant if g = h. By setting Equation (4) equal to Equation (5), a simple equation for the "debt-stabilizing" values g^* and h^* may be determined, given "s," "v," "d," and "r":

$$g^* = h^* = [s (1 - rD) - v^*]/(v - D), \qquad (7\text{-a})$$

and

$$z^* = [s + (1 - s) rD] - v (g^* + d). \qquad (7\text{-b})$$

For the numbers given in the example above, the "debt-stabilizing" real growth rate g^* would be 1.9 percent per year—that is, when real net external liabilities grow at 1.9 percent, real GDP grows at 1.9 percent per year. Note that since "D" becomes a constant in Equations (7-a) and (7-b), it gives a long-term growth rate for "h", unlike Equations (5) and (6-b); since $L_{(-1)}/Y$ is constant by assumption, Equation (7) is no longer a difference equation in L.

If "g" exceeds g^*, then "h" must exceed g^*, and "D" must increase. This can be seen as follows. Rearranging Equation (5) slightly, g = [s (1 − rD) − dv]/(v − D) + h D/v; therefore g = [(v − D)/v] g^* + h D/v. Further rearrangement leads to $h - g = (h - g^*) [1 - (D/v)]$. As long as "v" exceeds "D", $[1 - (D/v)]$ exceeds zero. It follows that, if "h" exceeds $g^* = h^*$, "h" must be greater than the corresponding value of "g". This value of "g" must exceed g^*, since higher values of "g" are associated with higher values of "h". That is, if "h" exceeds $g^* = h^*$, even though "g" will exceed g^*, "D" will tend to increase. Conversely, if "h" is less than $g^* = h^*$, "D" will tend to diminish.

The accompanying Table 3.1A and Table 3.1B indicate some of the possibilities. Consider an economy whose annual capital-depreciation rate is 4 percent. For possible values of "v" ranging from 2.75 to 3.5 and 4.25, and possible annual real interest rates ranging from zero to 1.5, 3, and 4.5 percent, the table gives values of g^* for values of "s" ranging from 17.5 to 20, 22.5, 25, and 27.5 percent, and for values of "D" ranging from zero to 15, 30, 45, 60, and 75 percent. By reading down the columns of Tables 3.1A and B, the reader can observe the consequences for g^* of increases in the value of "D". On the whole, increases in the value of "D" to be preserved by the growth rate g^* do not imply substantial increases in the value of g^*, given the values of "s", "v", "d", and "r". Increases in the value of "s", on the other hand—reading across the table—appear to have substantial effects on the value of g^*. Comparing the changes in "s" with changes in "D" is rather like comparing apples and oranges. Nevertheless, it seems noteworthy that a nation that increases its saving rate by 2.5 percentage points—all other things being equal—can, in general, achieve an increase in g^* equal to or greater than it could attain by reducing the value of "D" from 75 percent to zero, even when the interest rate is relatively low.

By examining the table values for different parameters, the reader may observe the consequences for g^* of increases in the real rate of return on external liabilities. Roughly speaking, an increase in the real rate from zero to 4.5 percent per year reduces the value of g^* by, at most, about two percentage points when "D" is equal to 75 percent—again, all other things being equal.

By comparing the entries in Tables 3.1A and B, one can observe the consequences for g^* of different values of "v". The value of the ICOR inevitably has a powerful effect on the debt-stabilizing real growth rate, as these tables make clear. Unfortunately, the value of any economy's ICOR is a rather elusive number. So, for that matter, is the value of any economy's capital-depreciation rate, which also has a significant effect on the real growth rate. The problem of pinning down believable values for the ICOR and for the capital-depreciation rate is one of the most troublesome aspects of the present analysis. Since the analysis is intended as a planning exercise for the future, it is important to consider different plausible values for "v" and for "d".[6] The model described below permits some variation in the values of "v" and "d" over time, which is a somewhat different matter from their appropriate initial values.

To place this discussion in some perspective, Table 3.2 presents recent data from nine Latin American nations regarding their capital formation, external saving, domestic saving, and net factor-service payments as proportions of

Table 3.1A.
Debt Stabilizing Real Growth Rates

D	s: 17.5	20.0	22.5	25.0	27.5
$r = 0.0$					
0.0	2.4	3.3	4.2	5.1	6.0
15.0	2.5	3.5	4.4	5.4	6.3
30.0	2.7	3.7	4.7	5.7	6.7
45.0	2.8	3.9	5.0	6.1	7.2
60.0	3.0	4.2	5.3	6.5	7.7
75.0	3.3	4.5	5.8	7.0	8.3
$r = 1.5$					
0.0	2.4	3.3	4.2	5.1	6.0
15.0	2.5	3.4	4.4	5.4	6.3
30.0	2.6	3.6	4.6	5.7	6.7
45.0	2.7	3.8	4.9	6.0	7.1
60.0	2.9	4.0	5.2	6.3	7.5
75.0	3.0	4.3	5.5	6.7	8.0
$r = 3.0$					
0.0	2.4	3.3	4.2	5.1	6.0
15.0	2.5	3.4	4.4	5.3	6.3
30.0	2.6	3.6	4.6	5.6	6.6
45.0	2.6	3.7	4.8	5.9	6.9
60.0	2.7	3.9	5.0	6.2	7.3
75.0	2.8	4.0	5.3	6.5	7.7
$r = 4.5$					
0.0	2.4	3.3	4.2	5.1	6.0
15.0	2.4	3.4	4.4	5.3	6.3
30.0	2.5	3.5	4.5	5.5	6.5
45.0	2.6	3.6	4.7	5.8	6.8
60.0	2.6	3.7	4.9	6.0	7.1
75.0	2.6	3.8	5.0	6.2	7.5

Source: See discussion in text.

GDP. These are rough calculations based on data drawn from the International Monetary Fund's *International Financial Statistics*. Nonetheless, despite their "back-of-the-envelope" character, these calculations clearly indicate some of the most important trends that accompanied the debt crisis, including (i) a marked decline in capital formation rates in the early 1980s, particularly after 1982, notably in the cases of Argentina, Bolivia, Brazil, Chile, Ecuador, Mexico, Peru, and Venezuela; (ii) a substantial decline at

Table 3.1B.
Debt Stabilizing Real Growth Rates

D	s: 17.5	20.0	22.5	25.0	27.5
$r = 0.0$					
0.0	1.0	1.7	2.4	3.1	3.9
15.0	1.0	1.8	2.5	3.3	4.0
30.0	1.1	1.9	2.7	3.4	4.2
45.0	1.1	2.0	2.8	3.6	4.4
60.0	1.2	2.1	2.9	3.8	4.7
75.0	1.3	2.2	3.1	4.0	4.9
$r = 1.5$					
0.0	1.0	1.7	2.4	3.1	3.9
15.0	1.0	1.8	2.5	3.3	4.0
30.0	1.1	1.8	2.6	3.4	4.2
45.0	1.1	1.9	2.7	3.5	4.3
60.0	1.1	2.0	2.8	3.7	4.5
75.0	1.1	2.0	2.9	3.8	4.7
$r = 3.0$					
0.0	1.0	1.7	2.4	3.1	3.9
15.0	1.0	1.8	2.5	3.2	4.0
30.0	1.0	1.8	2.6	3.3	4.1
45.0	1.0	1.8	2.6	3.5	4.3
60.0	1.0	1.9	2.7	3.6	4.4
75.0	1.0	1.9	2.8	3.7	4.6
$r = 4.5$					
0.0	1.0	1.7	2.4	3.1	3.9
15.0	1.0	1.7	2.5	3.2	4.0
30.0	1.0	1.8	2.5	3.3	4.1
45.0	1.0	1.8	2.6	3.4	4.2
60.0	0.9	1.8	2.6	3.4	4.3
75.0	0.8	1.7	2.6	3.5	4.4

Source: See discussion in text.

roughly the same time in external-saving flows as a proportion of GDP, notably in the cases of Argentina, Bolivia, Brazil, Chile, Ecuador, Mexico, Peru, and Venezuela; and (iii) a sharp increase in net factor-service payments as a proportion of GDP (i.e., factor-service payments less receipts, which for Latin American economies largely represent financial-service payments), notably in the cases of Argentina, Brazil, Chile, Colombia, Ecuador, and Mexico.

Table 3.2.
Domestic Saving in Latin America, 1976–86

	Gross Capital Formation		External Saving		Domestic Saving		Net Factor Service Payments /GDP
	percent current GDP	percent 1980 GDP	percent current GDP	percent 1980 GDP	percent current GDP	percent 1980 GDP	
Argentina:							
1976	25.5	22.8	-4.1	-3.7	29.9	26.7	3.3
1977	27.1	25.7	-3.1	-2.9	30.2	28.6	1.0
1978	25.2	23.2	-3.9	-3.6	28.7	26.4	1.2
1979	23.4	23.0	-0.2	-0.2	23.7	23.2	0.8
1980	22.2	22.2	2.2	2.2	20.6	20.6	0.9
1981	18.7	17.4	0.4	0.4	17.8	16.5	3.0
1982	16.5	14.8	-3.2	-2.9	21.3	19.0	7.4
1983	17.8	16.3	-4.9	-4.4	22.8	20.8	8.7
1984-86	NA	NA	NA	NA	NA	NA	NA
Bolivia:							
1976	18.3	16.8	1.7	1.5	18.3	16.8	-1.7
1977	17.1	16.4	1.4	1.4	17.1	16.4	-1.4
1978	20.0	20.3	7.5	7.6	15.0	15.2	-7.5
1979	18.9	19.2	3.3	3.4	16.7	16.9	-3.3
1980	16.7	16.7	-8.3	-8.3	25.0	25.0	8.3
1981	13.3	13.4	-6.7	-6.7	20.0	20.1	6.7
1982	14.3	13.9	-9.5	-9.3	23.8	23.2	9.5
1983	13.3	12.2	-6.0	-5.5	16.0	14.6	6.0
1984	13.1	11.8	-4.9	-4.5	15.9	14.4	4.9
1985	12.4	11.0	-1.4	-1.3	10.7	9.5	1.4
1986	NA	NA	NA	NA	NA	NA	NA
Brazil:							
1976	22.5	17.5	2.4	1.9	20.7	16.2	2.0
1977	21.3	17.4	0.7	0.6	21.3	17.4	2.2
1978	21.8	18.6	1.2	1.0	21.4	18.3	2.4
1979	22.8	20.9	2.1	1.9	20.5	18.8	2.2
1980	22.0	22.0	2.1	2.1	20.3	20.3	3.3
1981	21.4	21.7	0.3	0.3	21.3	21.5	4.1
1982	20.3	20.7	0.7	0.7	19.3	19.7	5.3
1983	16.1	15.9	-2.4	-2.4	17.1	16.9	5.8
1984	15.5	16.1	-5.6	-5.9	21.1	22.0	5.7
1985	16.7	18.9	-5.1	-5.8	21.8	24.6	5.3
1986	18.5	22.7	-2.6	-3.1	21.1	25.9	4.2

Table 3.2.
(continued)

	Gross Capital Formation		External Saving		Domestic Saving		Net Factor Service Payments /GDP
	percent current GDP	percent 1980 GDP	percent current GDP	percent 1980 GDP	percent current GDP	percent 1980 GDP	

Chile:

1976	13.3	9.6	-4.8	-3.5	17.6	12.7	3.8
1977	13.3	10.6	1.1	0.9	13.3	10.6	-3.7
1978	14.7	12.6	2.7	2.3	15.1	12.9	5.0
1979	14.9	13.8	2.3	2.2	15.5	14.3	3.9
1980	16.6	16.6	3.7	3.7	17.2	17.2	3.8
1981	18.6	19.6	10.0	10.6	12.7	13.4	4.8
1982	14.6	13.3	1.4	1.3	9.8	8.9	8.5
1983	12.0	10.8	-3.2	-2.9	13.0	11.7	9.4
1984	12.3	11.8	0.5	0.5	13.1	12.5	10.7
1985	14.2	13.9	-3.1	-3.1	16.8	16.5	11.8
1986	14.5	15.0	-4.3	-4.5	19.2	19.9	11.3

Colombia:

1976	15.9	12.8	-3.5	-2.8	21.0	17.0	2.8
1977	14.5	12.2	-3.9	-3.3	22.7	19.0	2.2
1978	15.4	14.0	-3.1	-2.9	21.4	19.5	2.3
1979	15.4	14.8	-2.1	-2.1	20.3	19.5	0.9
1980	16.8	16.8	-1.1	-1.1	20.2	20.2	2.2
1981	17.7	18.1	2.9	3.0	17.7	18.1	3.2
1982	17.5	18.0	3.8	4.0	16.6	17.2	4.4
1983	17.2	18.0	2.4	2.5	17.5	18.4	5.8
1984	17.0	18.4	-0.2	-0.2	19.2	20.8	4.6
1985	19.0	21.3	-2.6	-2.9	23.2	25.9	9.1
1986	18.0	21.1	-9.0	-10.6	27.2	32.0	10.0

Ecuador:

1976	22.2	17.7	0.8	0.6	23.0	18.3	-0.1
1977	23.6	20.0	2.5	2.1	24.1	20.4	2.8
1978	26.2	23.7	5.1	4.6	23.3	21.1	5.1
1979	23.7	22.6	-0.9	-0.8	26.2	25.0	7.9
1980	23.6	23.6	0.0	0.0	26.1	26.1	6.0
1981	22.3	23.1	-1.2	-1.2	24.3	25.3	8.6
1982	22.7	23.8	2.1	2.2	23.1	24.3	6.9
1983	16.6	17.0	-4.2	-4.3	21.8	22.2	4.4
1984	15.4	16.4	-6.6	-7.0	23.8	25.4	7.9
1985	16.1	17.8	-6.4	-7.1	24.6	27.3	6.0
1986	18.4	21.1	-0.8	-0.9	21.2	24.4	6.6

Table 3.2.
(continued)

	Gross Capital Formation		External Saving		Domestic Saving		Net Factor Service Payments /GDP
	percent current GDP	percent 1980 GDP	percent current GDP	percent 1980 GDP	percent current GDP	percent 1980 GDP	
Mexico:							
1976	21.0	15.9	1.2	0.9	21.1	15.9	2.8
1977	19.6	15.3	-0.3	-0.2	23.1	18.1	2.8
1978	21.1	17.8	0.4	0.3	23.2	19.6	2.9
1979	23.4	21.6	1.1	1.0	24.9	22.9	3.1
1980	24.2	24.2	0.8	0.8	27.3	27.3	3.7
1981	25.7	27.7	1.5	1.6	27.5	29.6	4.4
1982	22.3	23.9	-6.4	-6.8	27.6	29.6	10.3
1983	17.3	17.6	-10.3	-10.4	30.5	31.0	6.7
1984	18.0	18.9	-8.3	-8.8	30.0	31.6	6.1
1985-86	NA	NA	NA	NA	NA	NA	NA
Peru:							
1976	16.7	15.9	5.3	5.0	12.7	12.0	3.9
1977	14.5	13.8	3.1	2.9	11.9	11.3	4.7
1978	14.0	13.0	-3.8	-3.5	18.3	17.0	6.1
1979	14.1	13.7	-13.3	-13.0	27.7	26.9	9.0
1980	17.0	17.0	-4.7	-4.7	22.4	22.4	5.1
1981	20.4	21.0	3.7	3.8	18.5	19.0	5.7
1982	21.7	22.6	2.9	3.0	19.7	20.5	5.9
1983	18.2	16.6	-1.6	-1.4	18.6	17.0	8.3
1984	16.4	15.7	-5.5	-5.3	21.6	20.7	7.8
1985	14.3	14.0	-7.8	-7.6	21.9	21.3	7.8
1986	13.3	14.0	1.0	1.0	13.2	14.0	4.8
Venezuela:							
1976	31.7	29.2	-0.7	-0.6	35.1	32.4	NA
1977	38.8	38.3	8.5	8.4	33.0	32.6	NA
1978	42.5	42.8	14.1	14.2	28.7	28.9	NA
1979	31.6	32.2	-1.1	-1.1	32.7	33.4	NA
1980	25.2	25.2	-7.5	-7.5	32.2	32.2	NA
1981	24.5	24.4	-5.2	-5.2	28.1	28.1	NA
1982	24.1	24.2	4.0	4.0	21.9	21.9	NA
1983	19.1	18.1	-10.6	-10.0	22.3	21.1	NA
1984	13.7	12.8	-11.0	-10.3	27.0	25.2	NA
1985	15.4	14.5	-9.6	-9.0	24.2	22.7	NA
1986	19.2	18.9	1.1	1.1	19.2	18.9	NA

Source: See discussion in text.

The following section presents the analysis discussed thus far in a formal structure, which can be used more flexibly to plan or project a developing nation's strategy for managing the trade-off between its economic growth and its external liability accumulation.

II. A SIMULATION MODEL

The model listed here formally presents the analytical structure that lies behind the external debt-GDP growth trade-off. It begins with a "potential" production relation,

$$
\begin{aligned}
Y' &= [1 - d_{(-1)}] \, K(-2)/v'_{(-1)} + I_{(-1)}/v, \\
&= [1 - d_{(-1)}] \, Y'_{(-1)} + I_{(-1)}/v,
\end{aligned} \tag{8}
$$

where Y' represents the real GDP that could be produced as long as there is no shortage of any factor of production other than capital, K the real period-end capital stock; I gross domestic capital formation, and v' and "v" are exogenous constants (the capital-output and incremental capital-output ratios respectively); d represents the physical capital-depreciation rate. The second element is a production function,

$$
Y = \min \, [Y', N_{(-1)}/q], \tag{9}
$$

where Y represents real GDP, N the labor force, and "q" is an exogenous constant;

$$
S = s \, [Y - r \, L_{(-1)}], \tag{10}
$$

where S represents the national saving flow, "r" the real world interest rate, "s" is an exogenous constant, and L the period-end stock of net external liabilities;

$$
Z = z \, Y, \tag{11}
$$

where Z represents the external-saving flow (imports less exports of goods and non-factor services), and "z" is an exogenous constant;

$$
H = Z - r \, L_{(-1)}, \tag{12}
$$

where H represents the real current account;

$$
I = S - H, \tag{13}
$$

where I represents gross domestic capital formation;

$$N = N_{(-1)} (1 + n), \tag{14}$$

where "n" is an exogenous constant labor-force growth rate;

$$K = K_{(-1)} + I - d K_{(-1)}, \tag{15}$$

where "d" is an exogenous constant, the rate at which physical capital depreciates; and

$$L = L_{(-1)} - H. \tag{16}$$

Some simple and obvious extensions of the model enable it to take account of unemployment, consumption, real export and import flows, and external assets. The fixed-proportions production function implies that the unemployment rate "u" is given by

$$u = 1 - q Y/N_{(-1)}. \tag{17}$$

Next,

$$C = Y - I - Z, \tag{18}$$

where C represents real consumption;

$$Q = c C + y Y + k I, \tag{19}$$

where Q represents real imports of goods and non-factor services, taken to be a simple function of consumption, production, and investment through the exogenous constants "c", "y", and "i";

$$X = Z + Q, \tag{20}$$

where X represents real exports of goods and non-factor services;

$$A = (m/12) [Q + r L_{(-1)}], \tag{21}$$

where A represents real external assets, taken to be targeted by the authorities to be "m" months' worth of imports and net interest payments; and, finally,

$$D = L + A, \tag{22}$$

where D represents gross external liabilities.

This model may be used to simulate an indebted developing economy's future real growth and external-debt accumulation. While it can reproduce the results outlined in the preceding section—that is, while it can confirm that an appropriate external-saving rate will ensure that the ratio of external liabilities to GDP remains unchanged—a more helpful application of the model would be to help plan a medium-term policy strategy. For example, suppose a nation has reason to believe that it could resume voluntary borrowing from external sources if it first worked its external liabilities-GDP ratio down to some value D^* that is significantly lower than its current value. The model could be used to determine how fast the economy could grow during the work-down period, according to whether the work-down period were longer or shorter. Presumably the nation would thereafter borrow only what it required to hold the ratio fixed at D^*, so it would also be important to determine whether the g^* consistent with this D^* would be satisfactory. The model could be used to evaluate simultaneous improvements in other variables over the work-down period, including higher values of "s" or lower values of "v" and "d". The consequences of improving or worsening values of "r" may be analyzed as well.

Table 3.3 presents a stylized simulation based on the imaginary economy described in the preceding section. For purposes of this simulation, real GDP is taken to be 80 [billion U.S. dollars] and the labor force is taken to total 15 [million people] in the base year [1989]. Taking "n" = 2.8 percent, "d" = 4 percent, "s" = 20 percent, "v" = 3.5, "D" = 50 percent, and "r" = 3.5 percent, if "z" = 0, real GDP growth "g" will be 2.1 percent and real external-liability growth "h" will be 3.5 percent. In this simulation, unemployment is assumed to equal 3 percent of the labor force in the initial year 1989. This is done by calculating an appropriate assumed value for the parameter "q" in the production function.[7] The unemployment rate rises to 7.3 percent in 1996. The value of Y/N (productivity) declines by 0.7 percent per year, and the value of C/N (consumption per worker) declines at the same rate.

A similar simulation carried out with "z" = −1.3 percent—that is, with positive external saving flows—shows that "g" would increase to 2.5 percent, but "h" would increase to 6.2 percent. Unemployment rises only to 5 percent by 1996, rather than to 7.3 percent, but "D" rises to 62 percent rather than to 55 percent. Productivity and consumption per worker diminish in this simulation by 0.3 percent per year.

In yet another simulation, "z" is set equal to z^*, the value that leads to equal growth rates for "g" and "h" and hence to an unchanging value of "D". The value of "z" turns out to be about 0.8 percent per year, and the values of g^* and h^* turn out to be 1.9 percent per year. Unemployment reaches 8.9 percent by 1996, and productivity and consumption per worker decline at an annual average rate of 0.9 percent.

As an illustration of a policy "strategy" simulation, suppose that a nation's authorities decide to work their real external liabilities down by 5 percent in real terms from 1989 through 1991, then slowly increase their growth rate to 1.5 percent per year through 1993, and finally maintain a constant debt-GDP

Table 3.3.
Simulation of Economic Growth and External Debt
(in Billions US$ Except as Noted)

	1989	1990	1991	1993	1995	1996
Potential GDP	80.0	81.7	83.4	87.0	90.8	92.7
Real GDP	80.0	81.7	83.4	87.0	90.8	92.7
Domestic savings	15.7	16.0	16.4	17.1	17.8	18.2
External savings	0.0	0.0	0.0	0.0	0.0	0.0
Factor service payments	1.4	1.4	1.5	1.6	1.7	1.8
Real current account	-1.4	-1.4	-1.5	-1.6	-1.7	-1.8
Gross domestic capital formation	17.1	17.5	17.9	18.7	19.5	20.0
Labor force	15.4	15.9	16.3	17.2	18.2	18.7
Capital stock	285.9	292.0	298.2	311.0	324.5	331.5
Net external liabilities	41.4	42.8	44.3	47.5	50.9	52.7
Growth rate of net external liabilities	3.5%	3.5%	3.5%	3.5%	3.5%	3.5%
Unemployment rate	3.0%	3.6%	4.3%	5.5%	6.7%	7.3%
Real consumption	62.9	64.2	65.5	68.3	71.2	72.8
Real imports of goods and non-factor services	4.4	4.5	4.6	4.8	5.0	5.1
Real exports of goods and non-factor services	4.4	4.5	4.6	4.8	5.0	5.1
Real external assets	1.5	1.5	1.5	1.6	1.7	1.7
Gross external liabilities	42.9	44.4	45.9	49.1	52.6	54.4
Real GDP growth	2.1%	2.1%	2.1%	2.1%	2.1%	2.1%
Real external liability growth	3.5%	3.5%	3.5%	3.5%	3.5%	3.5%
Debt/GDP	50.0%	50.7%	51.4%	52.8%	54.2%	54.9%
Change in Debt/GDP		0.7%	0.7%	0.7%	0.7%	0.7%
Capital/person	100.0	99.3	98.7	97.4	96.1	95.5
Income per capita	100.0	99.3	98.7	97.4	96.1	95.5
Growth rate of income per capita	--	-0.7%	-0.7%	-0.7%	-0.6%	-0.6%
Consumption per capita	100.0	99.3	98.6	97.3	96.0	95.4
Growth rate of consumption per capita	--	-0.7%	-0.7%	-0.7%	-0.7%	-0.7%

Source: See discussion in text.

ratio thereafter. The simulation analysis indicates that this would require setting values of "z" equal to about 4 percent during the first three years, then
about 2 percent during 1992 and 1993, and finally about 0.7 percent in 1994,
1995 and 1996 to maintain a debt-GDP ratio of 39.5 percent (compared with
the initial 50 percent) with equal real GDP and real debt growth rates of 1.8
percent. Unemployment would rise to 12.1 percent by 1996, and productivity

and per-capita consumption would diminish to just under 91 percent of their initial values.

These would be disappointing and probably unacceptable outcomes. Accordingly, policymakers might try to improve the outcome by taking steps to increase domestic saving. For example, maintaining the preceding strategy in all respects, but increasing the domestic-saving rate in one-percentage-point steps from 20 to 25 percent between 1989 and 1994 and maintaining it thereafter, would permit the economy to reach a higher final "debt-stabilized" growth rate by 1995 and 1996—3.4 percent compared with 1.8 percent. The improvement in the domestic saving rate would come about, presumably, through better control of public-sector finances and measures to encourage private saving, including establishment of increased confidence. The debt-GDP ratio would be stabilized at 32.4 percent. Unemployment in the final year would be lower—8.7 percent compared with 12.1 percent, and moreover would be on a declining path, since the 3.4 percent real growth rate would exceed the population growth rate. The 1996 productivity level would be only 94 percent of its 1989 value, but higher than it would have been had the saving rate remained unchanged. On the other hand per-capita consumption would be 89 percent of its 1989 value, lower than it would have been had the saving rate remained unchanged.

Finally, suppose that the scenario just now described were accompanied by an increase in the productivity of new capital—that is, suppose that the value of the reciprocal of the ICOR $[(1/v)]$ rises by 1 percent per year. This would permit an additional improvement in the outcome. The debt-stabilizing real growth rate would be 3.9 percent rather than 3.4 percent. The debt-GDP ratio would be stabilized at 30.9 percent compared with 32.4 percent. Unemployment in the final year would be lower—7.9 percent compared with 8.7 percent. The 1996 productivity level would be only 95.5 percent of its 1989 value, and per-capita consumption would be 90.1 percent of its 1989 value.

III. CONCLUDING REMARKS

In addition to being a chronic cause of external liquidity crises, the developing nations' heavy external debt burden has significantly affected these nations' real-growth capacity. Now that the "debt crisis" has clearly become a medium- to long-term condition, it is essential that the issue of external-debt "stabilization" be understood and addressed in terms of nations' medium- and long-term growth capacity, rather than in terms of their capacity to withstand liquidity crises. The Baker Plan did at least do this, whatever its shortcomings.

Over the 1990s, the indebted developing nations and their external creditors will continue to deal with each other within the macroeconomic framework sketched in this essay. After a decade of generally disappointing growth, the developing nations' growth requirements are likely to become a higher priority; nevertheless, it is unlikely that their creditors will be any more forthcoming than they have been thus far. Since 1982, external creditors have sought to persuade nations that by cooperating and accepting lower growth rates in the near term, they would enjoy access to more credit and grow faster over the medium term. This approach, which has come to be regarded as the Baker Plan's premise, appears to have become, perhaps inevitably, less credible for many of the indebted nations since 1985. In part, the problem is that, as time passes, the commercial banks are gradually shoring up their capital positions. At some point the commercial banks will be in a strong enough position to be able to decide not to provide new funds to their developing-nation clients, not even to finance interest due, let alone to finance trade deficits. That is, it is at least possible, if not likely, that commercial banks are planning never again to carry out significant lending operations with developing nations. To the extent developing nations perceive that this is likely, their incentive to continue "playing the game" is diminished. To the extent this is true, the Baker Plan's fundamental premise would be invalidated.

In effect, each nation must now decide whether its highest medium-term growth rates are more likely to be achieved with (i) continued low or negative external saving for several years to come, accompanied by the kinds of "structural reform" and debt-negotiation positions that external creditors presumably regard favorably, with some possibility that this will then induce external creditors to provide positive external saving thereafter; or (ii) a debt-service moratorium, which would permit external saving to rise toward zero in the near term but, presumably, no further thereafter.[8] (The moratorium need not be declared.) The second alternative, it must be noted, requires genuine structural reform, no less—indeed, even more—than the first alternative. Since the second alternative assumes, probably realistically, that external saving will not be forthcoming, improved saving rates and more efficient resource allocation are even more essential than they would be under the premises of the Baker Plan.[9]

NOTES

An earlier version of this chapter was written while the writer was associated as Visiting Professor with the Faculdade de Ciências Econômicas da Universidade Federal da Bahia, under a grant from the Commission for Educational Exchange between the United States and Brazil. The views expressed in this chapter are those of the writer and do not necessarily represent those of any institution with which he is now or has recently been associated. Comments by José Affonso Ferreira Maia and José Sergio Gabrielli are gratefully acknowledged. Special assistance by Dionísio Carmo-Neto is also gratefully acknowledged. The writer alone is responsible, however, for any errors of fact or judgment.

1. Intuitively, an economy receives external saving to the extent the value of the goods it receives from abroad exceeds the value of the goods it sends out. In the national-

income accounts identity, if C represents private consumption, I total (public and private) gross capital formation, S gross private saving, T public-sector revenues (net of transfers), G public-sector consumption expenditure, J public-sector capital formation, M imports and X exports of goods and non-factor services, and R net unrequited transfer payments to foreigners, $C + I - J + (G + J) + (X - M) = C + S + T + R$; subtracting C from both sides and transposing, $I = S + (T - G) + (M - X + R)$, that is, total investment identically equals the sum of private, public and external saving, the three components of the right-hand side of this last equation. Since the current-account deficit equals $M - X + R$ plus net external factor payments, while national saving is equal to domestic saving $[S + (T - G)]$ minus net external factor payments, capital formation is therefore equal to national saving plus the current-account deficit. Some analysts define "external saving" as the current-account deficit rather than the net resource inflow.

2. Net unrequited transfer payments are negligible (less than errors and omissions in the balance of payments) for most Latin-American nations, and are therefore disregarded in our analysis.

3. The assumption that interest is paid on $L_{(-1)}$, rather than on the average of $L_{(-1)}$ and L, and working with $d = L_{(-1)}/Y$ rather than with $d = \{[L_{(-1)} + L]/2\}/Y$, permits Equations (4) and (5) to be written in relatively simple ways without sacrificing essential points. Most analysts use $d' = L/Y$ in their work—that is, they take a nation's 1987 debt-GDP ratio to be the year-end debt stock over 1987 GDP. Moreover, for relatively longer time intervals the interest bill may more accurately be calculated as $r [L + L_{(-1)}]/2$, based on the average net liability stocks at the beginning and the end of the year. With these changes, Equation (4) becomes $h = [-z/d' + r]/[1 + zd' - (r/2)]$, (4') since $B = Z + r\{[L + L_{(-1)}]/2\}$, $B/L_{(-1)} = -Z/L_{(-1)} + r\{[L/L_{(-1)}] + 1\}/2 = h = \{[-Z/L_{(-1)}] [L/L] [Y/Y]\} + \{r [1 + (h/2)]\} = \{[-Z/Y] [L/L_{(-1)}] / [L/Y]\} + \{r [1 + (h/2)]\}$, so $h = [z (1 + h)/d'] + r [1 + (h/2)]$. For simplicity, however, the remainder of the analysis is carried on using Equation (4).

4. The pressure to repatriate profit flows arising from converted debt may become a problem in future years.

5. National saving is defined as gross national product less the current account deficit; domestic saving is defined as gross domestic product less external saving as defined above, that is, less the difference between national-accounts imports less exports.

6. Taking historical values of the ratio of the change in real gross investment to the change in real GDP (adjusted for depreciation) is a problematic approach to evaluating the likely ICOR, first, because the past is an unreliable guide to the future; second, because GDP is influenced by factors of production other than capital; third, because terms of trade and other price movements influence GDP growth. As many researchers can attest, historical ICOR series tend to "run uselessly all over the place."

7. Since employment is given by qY, the unemployment rate is given by $u = 1 - (qY/N)$, which can easily be solved for q given initial values for "u", Y, and N.

8. Unfortunately, developing nations can no longer assume, if they ever could, that the "structural reforms" recommended by external creditors are necessarily in the nation's best interests. External creditors' recommendations for structural reforms in such areas as fiscal deficits, financial reform, trade liberalization, and privatization are likely to be affected by the creditors' interest in being repaid in the short term. If policymakers are advised to carry out some policy that will (a) probably cause net economic damage but (b) probably make external creditors more inclined to provide ex-

ternal credit, then policymakers must evaluate whether the probable benefit of (b) is likely to exceed the probable cost of (a).

9. There is a well-known argument that nations that have foreign debts must service them because they are legally, if not morally, obligated. Again, this argument merits careful examination, which is beyond the scope of the present essay. On the question of moral obligation, it is important to remember that a large part of what may be called the "original" external debt (as opposed to the debt undertaken to finance debt service) was undertaken by de facto governments and by private borrowers. De facto governments assumed substantial amounts of debt owed by private borrowers in the early 1980s, notably in Argentina and Chile. Legitimate questions may be raised on moral grounds about whether entire societies ought to be burdened with the continuing debt service on such debt. It is true that there is a simple principle in international law that any government inherits its predecessor's external obligations. Nevertheless, it is questionable whether it is wise for external creditors to insist on this legal principle in the face of the economic reality that the debt may be too excessive to service.

4

Privatization and the State Sector

William Glade

Now and then an issue comes along that is singularly useful, because of the policy discussion it generates, for illuminating the institutional field in which economic processes play themselves out. Privatization is this kind of issue. The light thrown on the larger scheme of social organization by the controversy privatization provokes is of particular value for framing U.S. policies and expectations regarding Latin America, for it clarifies the structure of interests that undergirds the state and so provides us a good sense of the architecture of the region's economic systems. If one can assume that current policy aims in the hemisphere include such objectives as restructuring national economies, depoliticizing decisionmaking in favor of market-constrained allocations, and paring back the unproductive absorption of resources in the public sector, then the quiet but determined tug-of-war that has been going on over privatization policies will most likely set, for a good many years to come, the alignment of business and government through which these objectives shall be sought.

To be sure, the situation is not everywhere the same. At one extreme, the odd repudiation of perestroika in Cuba reverses what, fleetingly (in the early 1980s), looked to be a glimmer of liberalization. This setback has already begun to return that country to an economic anorexia that is only partly concealed by heavy Soviet subsidies. Most probably, too, the ostensible willingness of the Nicaraguan regime to tolerate a mixed economy is a tactical maneuver, designed as much to provide a marketable decor for its foreign sympathizers as to rectify the grosser economic miscalculations associated with Sandinista engineering—a tropical NEP therapy, as it were. Once external political factors are under control, the country is likely to resume a "politica de estatización" to assist in the consolidation of domestic political hegemony, preparatory to eventually extending a command style of economic organization to neighboring Honduras and El Salvador, if not Guatemala. On the other hand, the re-engagement of the private sector in Jamaican development that the Seaga administration brought about will no doubt continue, albeit in possibly modified form, under the second Manley government, whose erstwhile socialist vision has come to resemble somewhat palely that of the Gonzalez government in Spain.

Most of the countries seem to be sorting themselves out along such a spectrum, closer to the Jamaican than to the Cuban end. Such is the case in Uruguay, Costa Rica, the Dominican Republic, and Bolivia. Colombia, never as interventionist as the rest of the region to begin with, has also initiated a number of privatizations. Even in Venezuela, whose huge public and parastatal sectors dominate the economic landscape even more than in Brazil or Mexico, the second Carlos Andres Perez administration has announced its intention to decontrol some parts of the economy, to lift the prices of public enterprise output to more realistic levels, and to sell some of the smaller public enterprises. A major exception to the liberalizing trend is Peru, where an *Izquierda Unida* victory would position that country, in economic policy terms, somewhere nearer the Nicaraguan pole. Under the current Garcia presidency, the problem posed by a large resource-consuming state that is ineffective in actually administering government have come to the fore again, as it did under Velasco two decades earlier. The difficulties so cogently examined several years ago in the Saulniers study of Peruvian parastatals have yet to be taken into account in the formulation of development policy.[1] There, as in El Salvador, political decomposition appears to be a factor in shaping relations between the public and private sectors. It remains to be seen whether the opposition forces captained, at present, by Peru's leading literary light can master enough of a constituency to halt the drift to a regimented economy.

A general observation is in order before we review the privatization issue in four country cases. This concerns the "retreat of the state" that privatization is often thought to imply. What seems to be in store bears little or no resemblance to the "withering away" on which Marxian and neoclassical liberal eschatologies curiously seem to converge. Although contemporary institutional reform generally envisages the removal of significant productive assets from direct management by the state, whether through outright divestiture of ownership or through replacing the political guidance of state-owned enterprises with a professionalized management responsive to market signals, this is certainly not the end of the matter. In virtually every country, a prime, though usually unstated, objective in privatization is to relinquish resources for alternative public uses once the fiscal deficit has been brought down to tolerable levels. The vast need everywhere to strengthen economic infrastructure and social overhead capital ensures a continuing prominence for public investment within a reconfigured government sector, to say nothing of the immense backlog of welfare outlays that are required in nearly all the countries to alleviate the most acute destitution. For that matter, when deregulation is called for to enhance allocational efficiency there is a strong case for extending the geographical compass of the rest of the administrative apparatus. Only by broadening the delivery of myriad public services is there hope of lowering entry barriers and transactions costs for the tens of thousands of firms, small ones in particular, that have been historically handicapped by severe problems of access.

In the short and intermediate term, programs of privatization are part of a general process of structural adjustment. They aim at putting the structure of production on an internationally competitive footing, thereby establishing a sounder basis for the eventual resumption of employment expansion and enabling countries to grow out of the debt problem. The role of privatization is to increase the efficiency of resource use, heighten management flexibility, and promote technological advance. Gains in allocational efficiency through the substitution of competition for rent-seeking behavior are presumed to be substantial, though in cases like some of the successful Asian economies, where rents are customarily ploughed back into investment, it is conceivable that there could be some offsetting reduction in capital formation rates. Of the four cases to be reviewed here, however, such an offset would most likely be a factor only in Brazil and, more arguably, Mexico.

A further offset, in the short to intermediate run, concerns the drop in living standards that has accompanied austerity and restructuring programs and reduced the profits of the majority of firms which cater to the home market. Aside from directly depressing investment capability and incentive, the austerity-bred transition from the accumulation of capital to the accumulation of discontent has produced an environment that bodes ill for the future security of capital and creates considerable uncertainty in the process. Either outcome encourages capital flight and ups the risk premium that must be added to the marginal efficiency of capital so far as the exceptional requirements of new investments are concerned.

CHILE

It has been conventional wisdom to ascribe the Chilean preference for privatization to the ideology espoused by the post-Allende government and its foreign advisors, the "Chicago Boys."[2] This, however, misses the special political and economic circumstances that have driven Chilean economic policy from the beginning. Privatization antedated the debt crisis and was a response to other considerations. The conventional wisdom also misses the point that, whatever the initial impetus for privatization, a process of policy refinement, based on learning-by-doing, has clearly taken place along the way. The systemic privatization that Chile, alone in Latin America, has attempted did not, in other words, spring full-blown from the brow of some neoclassical (and ideological) Zeus. Rather, it has emerged, over time, from a whole set of circumstantial exigencies that have given the policy its particular shape. In fact, a major midcourse correction had to be instituted in order to rectify an institutional blindness that had marred the program from the outset. Even though it was appreciated fairly early that deregulation and trade liberalization were necessary to help ensure that the privatization of enterprises did not merely redistribute economic rents, it was only after a major financial collapse occurred that the government took full cognizance of the counterproductive distortions that had been introduced into the program by the concentration of private financial power.

The political trigger for privatization appears to have been an acute problem of administrative/managerial overload. This resulted from the Allende government's haste in bringing the bulk of economic organization under the direction of the state by whatever means. Although Mexico also experienced a bad case of organizational indigestion when its public sector grew so luxuriantly during the administrations of Echeverria and Lopez Portillo, Chilean state expansion had been even more abrupt and, on the whole, more disorderly. Indeed, because the displacement of private management was so sweeping and, in many instances, procedurally irregular, and because an intense amount of partisan infighting seems to have characterized relations among the bureaucratic cadres of the ruling coalition, the effects of rapid state expansion were far more disruptive in Chile than either Mexico or Peru, the latter having also greatly enlarged its public sector in the course of the state-led economic transformation that began in 1968.

Confidence in the state was undermined from another quarter as well, albeit much more gradually. By 1970, the country had experienced some four decades of interventionist policies that were almost archetypal for Latin America. Like the other major countries, Chile had centered its development policy on import-substituting industrialization, notwithstanding the fact that its internal market was much smaller than those of Brazil, Mexico, and Argentina, or even Venezuela. In the mid-1960s, in fact, the Chilean economy was just slightly larger than Colombia's (though today the latter is three quarters larger). The prevailing perception was that the national economy had turned in a rather lackluster performance for much of the postwar period, thanks in part to policies that, as Mamalakis has shown, discriminated against a potentially productive agriculture, neglected mining and forestry, and favored an industrial plant whose size was increasingly constricted as the limits of the domestic market were approached. There was concern, too, that investment levels were low, with scant likelihood of significant improvement. With a 4.5 percent average annual growth in GDP during the 1960s, a figure that was certainly respectable by world historical standards, Chile would not seem to have merited quite such dissatisfaction. Nonetheless, among its reference group, the major Latin American economies, only troubled Argentina turned in a worse (4.2 percent) performance. To be sure, on a hemispheric level, Cuba, with 1.1 percent growth, and Uruguay, with 1.2 percent growth, set the bottom of the scale for Latin America, but this was small consolation considering how well the larger countries were doing. To make matters worse, distributional struggles were heating up to the extent that it became quite impossible for Chile to adopt the production-enhancing policy sequence argued by, for example, the German Social Democrats in the postwar period: profits today, investment tomorrow, jobs the day after. The "social question" in Chile proved too longstanding for this, as a mobilized population jockeyed for control of the levers of state policy.

Given the failure of the Frei government to improve matters substantially through state guidance of a conventional Latin American variety, though with a stronger redistributive hue, the country next lurched into an extreme interventionism that only made matters worse—significantly so. By the time Allende was overthrown, no mean amount of zealotry was required to adhere to the old Cepaline faith. Circumstances had, in effect, paved the way for the market option the country was to eventually embrace under military rule.

Against this background, three other factors must be appreciated in order to understand the relative success of Chilean privatization. First of all, the slow, gradualistic growth of the parastatal sector up to 1970 and the quality of human resources Chile had developed (and was able to enlist in public sector employment) gave the country a tradition of management in its state-owned enterprises, including the Chileanized copper companies, that was respectably conservative and professional. Only during the 1970–73 interval were parastatal firms and newly expropriated enterprises wildly mismanaged. Second, save for the same aberrant interval, the Corporación de Fomento, or CORFO, seems to have been quite competently run as the spearhead of state entrepreneurship, and for years has played a key, oversight role in the parastatal sector. As things worked out, the organizational capabilities of CORFO were to be a special asset in implementing the privatization program when it got underway. CORFO's experience in making diagnostic microeconomic studies, in carrying out managerial rectification, in evaluating investment options, and its connections into the developing Chilean financial markets were to stand it in very good stead.

The third factor was that the program was able to gain considerable momentum early on, owing to a peculiar combination of circumstances. The pell-mell expropriations of the Allende period endowed the government with a large inventory of financially troubled firms that had no extensive roots in the public sector, nor a long tradition of respected public management. Devolution of these firms to the private sector was, therefore, fairly simple and straightforward, especially since the means by which most had been inducted into the public sector were of questionable legality anyhow—this in a country that took pride, historically, in its observance of the rule of law. It was, moreover, plain to all but the most fanatic that something had to be done straightaway if these firms were to recover their capacity to produce. The reprivatization of these assets thus helped to chart a course for subsequent transfers and established a relatively noncontroversial precedent for moving the responsibility for supplying goods and services from the public back to the private sector.

Besides the foregoing, there were at the time severe impediments to organized criticism and to any concerted political action that might have sought to block or undo these reprivatizations. The outlines of what would eventually need to be accomplished, moreover, were not yet clear. For its part, the government came only later to a fuller appreciation of the problem of linkage, a recognition that the reduction of intervention in product markets, especially in the traded goods sector, implied a lessening of intervention in factor markets, so as to avoid jeopardizing the firms' chances for success in increasingly competitive product markets. On the other side of the picture, it is doubtful that private investors would have been so eager to regain control of their properties had they realized at the time the scale deregulation would eventually assume, particularly in respect of interest rates and commercial policy. In addition, it was not evident until later that local producers would have to confront particularly sharp competition from imports due to the government's dogged adherence, despite a general preference for free-market policies, to a fixed exchange rate as a means of braking inflation and inflationary expectations.

In the event, once the approximately 250 firms seized from the private sector by Allende were disposed of, the government embarked on a program to shape up its inventory of parastatals, applying market criteria to public enterprise management (simulated privatization) and, in other instances, bringing private, usually foreign, capital and management into the equity structure of state-owned enterprises (semiprivatization) to make them more dynamic in their operations. In still other cases, CORFO began to prepare a number of public enterprises for outright privatization (the sale of all a firm's shares to private investors) by changing the capital structure, shedding noncommercial operations, and, in the case of public utilities, introducing appropriate regulatory modifications to conform the behavior of "natural monopolies" to something approximating a market constrained firm.

The basic continuity of macro policy over more than a decade enabled improvements to be made as time went by. To avert a repetition of the financial catastrophe that ensued when pecuniary speculation, centered on the banks, enabled large corporate empires to be amassed on a flimsy financial base, regulations were introduced to limit stock acquisitions by single interests and other precautionary measures were decreed. Public disclosure requirements increased the supply of authenticated information available on concerns whose shares were moved through the stock exchange. Investment bankers, both domestic and foreign, were brought into the process and debt-equity swaps were employed as well. Pension funds were authorized, within limits, to invest in the newly issued shares, a major step forward in developing the capital market, given that social security reform had already privatized the management of pension funds. As part of a concerted effort to broaden the capital market, employee stock ownership programs were introduced, based, on occasion, on the investment of corporate funds theretofore reserved for severance pay and unemployment compensation liabilities. Small investors, including employees, were also favored by the sale of shares on credit. In one notable case, a decision to close down the informatics services of a government agency in favor of procuring such services in the open market led to the establishment, in response to a proposal from the soon-to-be-dismissed government workers, of a new worker-owned informatics company. This, in turn, emerged as an outstanding player in the local software market.

The dominant impression from the period as a whole is one of pragmatic adaptation to changing circumstances. Doctrinaire positions were surprisingly infrequent. During the 1982–83 recession, for example, the largest commercial banks, and a host of important nonfinancial corporations associated with them, were taken over by the government, notwithstanding its commitment to capitalism, in order to stave off their collapse. Further, the largest corporation in the country, CODELCO, has remained firmly ensconced and well-managed in the public sector throughout.

The foregoing should not be interpreted to mean that all has gone smoothly, apart from the financial debacle mentioned above. There have been complaints from time to time about a lack of transparency, although in fairness it must be said the point is arguable for recent years.[3] The first reprivatizations returned most firms to their former owners at no cost, but the practice seems not unreasonable in view of the fact that they had been seized illegally to begin with, and run down though poor management to boot. Thus the charges of underpricing in divestitures applies mainly to the firms hived off subsequently. During the divestitures of the mid 1970s, it is true, a relatively small group of investors with preferred access to credit were the major beneficiaries, building unstable conglomerate empires and concentrating ownership to a high degree. By the end of the 1970s there were also charges that public assets were being sold at below value, and similar charges have been raised since.[4] A careful study of the 1974–1982 and subsequent transactions by Hachette and Luders, however, raises questions about how extensive this was after the round of highly-leveraged purchases that ended around 1980.[5] In any case, for the last several years, the transfer process would appear to have been reasonably clear and open. Auctions, the issuance of stock through the exchange, and flotations underwritten by investment bankers have all been employed. Chief among the recent divestitures alleged to have been mismanaged is the steel company, but on this the evidence is contradictory.[6] The deep discount at which utility companies have been sold in recent years undoubtedly reflects uncertainty over how regulated rates will fare.

A striking feature of the Chilean experience is the degree to which a technocratic elite was given free rein to frame and implement policies in a context in which popular groups had been demobilized, the state bourgeoisie neutralized, and many questions ostensibly depoliticized. With the customary political forum suspended for the time being, it was possible for the new technocratic policymaking machinery to act on its belief that Chile, on account of its size, was inherently a structurally open economy—one that had for years, however, pursued policies inconsistent with this fundamental character. The new reformist policy was not always entirely coherent, especially with respect to exchange rates, but the remarkably long interval in which it could evolve allowed, as noted earlier, for correction and evolution. Thus, the Chilean record is of unique value for showing what a more fully evolved privatization program might look like and what are some of the more troublesome risks along the way. Of the risks, the worst by far was the increased concentration of ownership to which the early phase led during the period of debt-financed building of oligopolistic conglomerates. The negative allocational effects of the anticompetitive industrial structure this produced may have been offset, in whole or in part, by the opening of the economy to external competition. But the same cannot be said of the unstable organizational structure, which eventually collapsed amidst crisis. Distributional patterns also suffered, before the "popular capitalism" objective was introduced in the 1980s. Perhaps one of the most promising aspects of the program was the de facto fiscal forgiveness it incorporated as, in effect, foreign deposits could be repatriated on a no-questions-asked basis to purchase the firms put up for privatization; an official laundering, as it were. The pragmatic way Chile has, in fact, handled its privatization program belies the charges of ideological rigidity. Some industrial companies, such as SOQUIMCH, have been sold to foreign investors through debt-equity swaps, American Express having been the purchaser in that case. The same approach has been used in the financial sector, as in the Credit Lyonnais acquisition of an interest in the Banco Continental. When the regional electric power companies were privatized, however, the measure was seen as primarily an opportunity to expand the range of portfolio options for domestic investors. Meanwhile, CORFO, which has presided over much of the program, has used some of its new resources to set up a venture capital fund for small- and medium-sized businesses. What is more, important state-owned companies remain in operation and, as if to refute the notion that they are stepchildren of the new economic order, twenty-three of them have recently launched ambitious investment programs for the 1988–92 period.

BRAZIL[7]

Had Brazilian privatization been started well before the return to civilian rule, there is a chance that it, too, might have gained the momentum and refinement that policy continuity would provide. Even as it is, there are points in which it is surprisingly similar to the Chilean approach, though in other respects it follows a distinctly Brazilian path. At the same time it reflects, in the modest way it has developed, the policy indecision and inaction that has characterized the unfortunate Sarney government generally. Although the military governments had evinced considerable ability to stick with and refine their policy course, which was different from that taken by the Pinochet regime in Chile, the discord attendant to Brazil's return to electoral politics has at times paralyzed the government and at other times resulted in a series of policy flip-flops. No discernable lines of movement can be readily projected into the years ahead.

Some interests resist privatization, which they take as tantamount to dismantling the state sector, while others have argued on its behalf since at least the mid 1970s. In between, however, there seems to be no groundswell of opinion for anything other than tinkering with the parastatal sector's structure. Doubtless, too, Brazil's particular economic circumstances have fostered the country's tempered approach to privatization. Unlike Chile, the Brazilian home market has been so large and expansive that, despite the anxieties that were expressed in the early 1960s about approaching market constrictions, the growth rate has held up quite well on the whole. So well has the economy performed up to recent times, that privatization as a means of rejuvenation has not been perceived as an especially urgent issue, even as part of a large reform issue. That the country's economic performance has been so satisfactory, in turn, has been partly attributable to yet another feature of the Brazilian situation: namely, the success the country has enjoyed, from around the mid 1960s onwards, in penetrating export markets in nontraditional exports. The Japanese-style policies employed to engineer this success in export diversification paid off handsomely. As parastatals have figured among the new exporters, on this account, too, the perceived urgency of privatization has been lessened.

The result is that privatization has, in effect, turned out to be pragmatically targeted on rather limited objectives and in this sense very much like the character of Brazilian industrial policy all along. So entwined have been the public and private sectors historically (in a manner not dissimilar to the Japanese case, where industrial targeting has also been the dominant strategy) and so effective and dynamic have been major state-owned enterprises that a Chilean-style systemic privatization has found practically no support from any quarter. It is, in fact, in Brazil that some have ironically suggested that privatization of the public sector ought properly to take a back seat to privatization of the private sector, such is the extent to which Brazilian private enterprise has depended on "the rich widow"—the state.

Different though they have been, however, there are some points in common to Brazilian and Chilean experience. In the first place, a number of the companies initially transferred to the private sector were cases of reprivatization. Unlike Chile, where these were firms that had been expropriated for ideological reasons, the Brazilian companies had fallen into the hands of the state through receivership operations, having leaned too heavily on state-provided credits in the 1970s and early 1980s. To get the privatization program underway, then, from 1980 through 1987, some seventeen firms were sold to private investors; at least ten of these were reprivatizations. Among them were textile companies, a hotel, a publishing company, two paper companies, another in vegetable oils, one in cement, two in chemicals, one in synthetic rubber and so on—a fairly motley assortment selected mainly on the grounds that they could be readily sold. As in Chile, some were sold by competitive tenders and others were put on auction; four were sold through direct negotiation with the buyers. However, the companies sold, to put the matter in perspective, contributed only a very small part of the central government's portfolio of industrial, commercial, and financial holdings. The cumulative value of the companies divested through 1987 amounted to only US$ 220 million, which was under 0.7 percent of the overall net worth of federal public enterprises as of December 1988. Besides the seventeen firms noted, around a half-dozen others were simply shut down, the most important being the National Housing Bank, and some eighteen wholesale food marketing companies were slated for transfer from federal operation back to state or municipal control, whence they had originated. The latter step was more a matter of decentralization than privatization as such (though some sources include these in description of privatization), but it fits the "reprivatization" pattern in that these locally established organizations had been originally acquired by the federal government when local financing played out.[8] The point is relevant to the overall perspective, however, for it reminds one that in Brazil, more than in most of Latin America, the total parastatal sector includes, besides the federal government's entities, a considerable number of enterprises owned and operated by state governments and municipalities.

Since 1987, the formal privatization program has continued, picking up a bit of speed in the process. Early in 1988, the Banco de Nacional de Desenvolvimento Econômico e Social (BNDES) disposed of its controlling interest in SIBRA, a manganese alloy producer. Caraiba Metais, the only copper smelting plant in the country was also put on the block and sold to a group of copper fabricating companies. The CELPAG paper and pulp company was likewise sold, as was Aracruz Celulose, the country's largest paper and pulp operation. COSINOR, a steel mill in the northeast, along with MAFERSA, a railway car manufacturer, and CCB, a paper company in Bahia, was privatized too. Of particular interest is the decision, taken the same year, to privatize COBRA, the government's pioneering computer software company. Much of the impetus for this somewhat unexpected development came from the company itself, which felt that restraints on public-sector salaries were seriously hampering its ability to retain and attract the highly qualified professionals who are, in turn, its basic capital.

Far overshadowing the cases of outright privatization have been two other policy changes both of which enjoy a better "fit" with the Brazilian policy style. The first consists of the semiprivatization operations through which shareholding in parastatals has been opened up to private investors. Major companies like TELEBRAS, PETROQUISA, USIMINAS, and Petrobras Distribuidora have been set on this path. Again to give an idea of scale, it is worth noting that just the PETROBRAS shares sold in 1986 through the capital market amounted to US$ 450 million. It seems likely that this approach will be applied to other large parastatals in the future, including, for example, other petrochemical fertilizer enterprises, the electric power companies, and the CVRD mining conglomerate. The huge size of the main state-owned enterprises however, vastly exceeds the capacity of the Brazilian capital market to absorb them in toto, without either driving the offer price down to giveaway levels or diverting excessive amounts of capital from private-sector seekers of capital (i.e., crowding out) or both. Yet, if size precludes the outright sale of these largest parastatals, it could be argued that, from the standpoint of allocational efficiency, all that is needed is that a portion of the shares of these enterprises be listed and traded in order to get a market reading on the efficiency of their operations.

The second option that has been taken is that of simulated privatization, to which semiprivatization has often been added for additional productive benefit. This strategy, in fact, long antedates official efforts in formal privatization, but since the late 1970s the program has been more concerted than it was previously. It was in 1979, for example, that the government established the Secretariat for Public Enterprise Control (SEST), the initial emphasis of the agency being that of monitoring enterprise accounts and parastatal borrowing, especially foreign borrowing. The measure was prompted by the need to cope with the deleterious effects of the second oil shock. After a few years, however, it was evident that SEST might usefully play a role broader than that of financial budgeting, so to improve its supervisory and managerial capabilities an elaborate system of performance evaluation was developed, based on the experience of the Telebras company. Priority was given to bringing the operations of the ELETROBRAS and SIDERBRAS complexes under the scope of the new evaluation system, but in due course it was also applied to the parastatals operating under the oversight of the Ministry of Mines and Energy and those connected with BNDES. Thanks to these, and to more conventional management assessment systems, a number of projects were launched by the various ministries to improve the operating efficiency of the parastatals in their respective jurisdictions. The Minister of Industry and Commerce, for example, in 1987, went so far as to replace the whole board of directors of the money-losing COSIPA steel mill, Brazil's third largest steel maker, and to push for permission to relax the price controls imposed by the Finance Ministry on all steel manufacturers, ceilings that held prices as much as 35 percent below costs in some cases (price controls have also handicapped the operating efficiency of ELETROBRAS companies).

One of the reasons that the pressure to privatize has been less than one might expect lies in the commercial agility of the major state-owned enterprises. Few have been such a financial and technical failure as NUCLEBRAS, though in major cases price controls have concealed the level of managerial efficiency achieved. PETROBRAS has, for example, gained considerable respect for its managerial and technical competence, has succeeded in increasing domestic production considerably, and has more than held its own in winning competitive contracts abroad through one or another of its subsidiaries. It has also been regarded highly enough by foreign private-sector peers to be included in various joint ventures, as in the arrangement with Texaco for exploratory drilling in the Gulf of Mexico. TELEBRAS enjoys a generally good standing among its customers, including major industrial users of telecommunications services, while EMBRAER, the aircraft producer, has experienced spectacular success in penetrating export markets for commuter planes and military training aircraft, selling the latter, for example, to the RAF over stiff competition from European rivals. No less successful, on the whole, has been the CVRD mining combine, the fourth largest of the Brazilian public enterprises. Given the fact that seventeen of the twenty largest Brazilian nonfinancial firms (as ranked by sales) are in the public sector, it is unlikely that outright privatization will be attempted for a significant portion of these, and there is scant private-sector interest in acquiring them in their entirety in any case.

As for the formal or outright privatization process itself, a few observations are in order. When in mid 1987 the Planning Minister, Anibal Teixeira, urged an accelerated program of divestiture and proposed selling 65 of the 415 companies then under state control to the private sector, the total assets involved would have come to only about 5 percent of the assets of the 180 state firms classified as directly productive. Further, a number of companies put up for sale at one time or another had to be withdrawn, for want of interest by purchasers in some instances or because of objections from government agencies in others. For instance, the national medical service successfully protested the proposed sale of several hospitals. It may even be questioned how committed the government has ever been to privatization in the full sense. The Special Commission for Privatization ("Destatization"), ostensibly the key actor in such a program, was not created until late 1981 and, to judge from its annual reports, some years elapsed before it was even able to come up with a firm census of the public enterprises supposedly in its purview. Operations were hampered by the lack of cooperation from other government agencies, particularly those with line authority over the various clusters of public enterprise, and in principle it was up to the latter to initiate privatization procedures in any case. By November of 1985, the Special Commission was replaced by an Inter-Ministerial Council on Privatization, which, in turn, was, with its secretariat, reorganized further in 1988. Significantly, until this last revamping the agency had only a very modest number of top level technicians on its staff for most of the time, though it was allowed to contract with the private sector for the provision of a number of specialized services.

As one might expect, what could be accomplished by the official privatization agency was minimal. Thus, the chief implementation responsibility has de facto fallen on another entity, the highly respected and professional BNDES, which is in its organizational attributes, a rough equivalent to the Chilean CORFO. Although BNDES financing (loans and investments) went 100 percent to the public sector in 1952, by 1987 just under 67 percent of its financing operations were channelled toward private enterprises. As early as 1979, when serious discussion of privatization began, BNDES had large equity holding in some 185 industrial firms in fields ranging from petrochemicals to textiles to semiconductors, and had made a substantial volume of loans to other firms. As might be inferred, the Bank has accumulated a substantial organizational experience on the operating side of business, including the managerial revitalization of run down companies. Further, with impressive in-house capabilities in a wide range of business and financial services and analysis associated with investment banking, BNDES has long had extensive intimate ties with the major players in the Brazilian industrial and financial community, from which it secures supplementary services as needed for the privatization of firms. The head of BNDES today is, in fact, an engineer from one of the wealthiest Rio families in the construction industry.

What all this has meant is that BNDES, like CORFO, is organizationally well-prepared to ready enterprises for privatization through public offerings or private sales of shares, with such company reorganization and fiscal restructuring as may be warranted, with rehabilitation of plant and equipment and/or recourse to management contracts if necessary, and with an established capacity to prequalify bidders and evaluate alternative offers—all backed up by the wherewithal to finance the sale where this is essential to completing deals. From an organizational point of view, therefore, the transaction costs for BNDES of carrying out a privatization program are as low as would be possible in Brazil, and most of the outright privatization that is likely to occur over the years ahead will in all probability come from its portfolio. Moreover, as in the past, its services are sure to be contracted for handling other privatizations as well. As in the Chilean case where a similar repertoire of organizational capacities is available, the crucial importance of the policy instrument selected for privatization stands out in bold relief.

Like Chile, Brazil provides an example of the importance of the political climate for privatization, as more, surely, would have been accomplished had either the military or civilian government been more committed to the process. Yet, if privatization has not exactly been pushed by political forces external to or in charge of the state, it has emerged, determined by factors internal to the public sector's decision processes, as an adaptive response by the state technocracy to radically altered economic circumstances, which, in turn, have only sporadically been conducive to the actual implementation of the program.

ARGENTINA[9]

In Brazil, the procedural aspects of privatization are, in part, set forth in legislation (for companies supervised by the ministries) and, in part, an evolved product of BNDES practices. In Chile, CORFO-developed procedures predominate, there being no specifically prescribed procedure in legislation. In either case, however, the process appears to have worked fairly smoothly in the cases put through it. An immediate contrast is provided by the Argentine experience. Although the law that set up the privatization program (Law 22.174 of March 4, 1980) stipulates the methods and procedures to be used, these have not necessarily been followed in all cases and the whole context of privatization has been strikingly different from either Brazil or Chile. They have also been much more troubled by instability in the political and economic environments.

Part of the problem can be chalked up to political circumstances. In Chile the state has been firmly behind the process while in Brazil the presidency has been distracted by other matters since the restoration of civilian rule, apparently content to let the process run itself. In Argentina, in contrast, the privatization program has, for a variety of reasons, come to be complicated by political considerations emanating from an interplay of intensely partisan forces that seem much more strongly organized than in either of the other two countries. The party now in power, the Radicals, has no doctrinal commitment to privatization and most probably even contains a significant segment opposed to it, for ideological reasons as well as because a goodly number of the party faithful labor in the state bureaucracy. Alfonsin came to office, after all, with an economic program of the more traditional type, one that conserved a strong role for the state and that did not anticipate the fiscal pressures that eventually would build the case for privatization. The platform on which he ran made no mention of privatization, which might, in any event, have seemed at odds with the populist tone of the first two years of his administration. Thus the divided views within the government have meant that even today the government has put forward no compelling and coherent overall rationale for such measures.

Two other features of the political scene have conspired against development of a privatization priority. First, the Alfonsin government had, from the outset, to assign the top spot on its policy agenda to the ticklish matter of "domesticating" the military and bringing to justice those accused of gross human rights violation. So all absorbing—to the polity and the government—did this task become that there was little disposition to take on another controversial policy that, moreover, carried the political liability of appearing part of the policy preference of the authoritarian predecessor government. The Martinez de Hoz government, which has often been derided for its policies during the late 1970s, did more than merely flirt with privatization. Through 1980 it had, in fact, succeeded in reprivatizing a considerable number of firms that had become part of the portfolios of the Banco Nacional de Desarrollo and the Caja Nacional de Ahorro y Seguros. All of their holdings in 207 firms were sold, along with part of their holdings in twenty-nine others, and forty-six companies were shut down as unsalvageable. Some peripheral privatization was begun as well. An Interministerial Commission for Privatization presided over the process.

Beyond this, Argentina has for years exemplified the concept of the state as a self-interested maximizing agent rather than the instrumental view of state as umpire and guardian of the public interest. The peculiarity of the recent political history has accentuated this. With the military already resentful because of its defeat in the Malvinas war and aroused by Radical prosecution of human rights cases, the government thought it imprudent to add to the antag-onism by addressing the problems of the several public enterprises operated as sinecures of the military. Although one opposition party on the right has fa-vored privatization, the strength of this party has been problematic. The much larger opposition party, the Peronists, has been opposed, moreover, as have the allied militants in the labor movement, Latin America's strongest and the one with the longest tradition of sustained labor activism.

There is evidence as well that at least a part of the business sector, having been nourished for years on the favors of the state, looks askance at privati-zation. Business reservations are also colored these days by anxiety over what the embryonic integration program with Brazil is likely to do to Argentine producers. Fear that Argentine industry will prove to be no match for the more powerful Brazilian industrial sector has, in other words, bred a certain leeri-ness about too hastily abandoning state regulation and cutting back on other state-related privileges such as a national preference in state purchasing. So attached are some to the concessionary role of the state that when in 1988 the military finally proposed divesting itself of some of its business holdings in joint ventures, the private partners involved threatened to block the movement on grounds that the enterprises, once privatized, would no longer qualify for an assortment of special privileges.

Privatization is also a tall order for economic reasons, although here mat-ters are more complicated. The average annual growth rate of the economy has been -0.8 percent in the 1980–86 period, indicative of a need to restruc-ture but also of a level of performance calculated neither to brighten the ex-pectations of the investors who might be purchasers of state firms nor to pro-vide the buoyant capital markets needed for a successful underwriting of new issues—least of all in companies with the dismal track record of most of the Argentine public enterprises. So notorious have been their problems that even in good times other investment options would look more attractive, and, for the past several years the Argentine capital market has suffered by comparison with those of Brazil, Chile, and Mexico.

Economic conditions have, however, favored the privatization program in other ways. Consumers, whatever the fervor of their nationalism in other re-spects, have grown so exasperated with deterioration of public services that, to many, privatization would be acceptable if it offered a plausible remedy for these shortcomings. The state oil company, the YPF is, for example, one of the world's biggest money losers among firms in that industry, while the deficien-cies of telephone service are so great as to make it virtually impossible to access computers by telephone modem. Unlike the situation in either Brazil or Chile, the management of public companies has been so conspicuous for its ineffi-ciency, with overstaffing rampant and no track record of innovation, that even the reluctant Radicals and Peronists have been hard put to find convincing ar-guments to retain state control over so much of the economy. The deficits of these concerns have simply grown far too large—US$ 28 billion by 1988 from

117 federal and 188 provincial and municipal parastatals—for the public treasury to continue to absorb. The threat of hyperinflation has, in fact, underscored the urgency of deficit reduction.

Against this backdrop, the government has moved, albeit somewhat irresolutely, to try to impose greater accountability on the parastatals by means of the Sindicatura General de Empresas Publicas and an Interministerial Committee on Public Enterprises, the latter being replaced at the end of 1987 by a Directorate of Public Enterprises. The Directorate, in turn, was charged with modernizing the operations of thirteen major parastatals: the General Port Administration, Argentine Airlines (AA), the water and electric energy company, Argentine Maritime Lines (ELMA), the postal and telecommunications company, the national telephone company (ENTEL), Argentine Railways, the state gas company, Hidronor, the national sanitary works, Greater Buenos Aires Electricity Company, the national coal company, and the national oil company, all of which were running operating deficits. Three of these—AA, ENTEL, and ELMA—were judged prospects for privatization in one form or another. Besides the firms connected with the Directorate, however, the parastatal sector includes, as noted earlier, a great many other firms belonging to the federal government, to provincial and municipal governments, several intergovernmental corporations, and a host of mixed enterprises. There is no central oversight and coordinating agency above these, and even in the case of the Directorate, its work is hampered by having to share supervisory authority with several ministries.

A decree of November 1987 opened up broad areas of public services to private competition. Somewhat surprisingly, the Ministry of Defense has in the past couple of years taken steps to start the privatization of a number of the enterprises in which the Argentine military has held an interest, in part to cut the erosion of the military budget occasioned by the deficits of these firms. Notably absent in the overall situation, however, is any organization playing the pivotal role of CORFO in Chile or BNDES in Brazil. Neither the Banco de la Nación, which handled many of the reprivatizations of the 1970s, nor the privatization secretariat that was later set up in the Office of the Presidency has been able to assume the institutional leadership of the process.

When the privatization effort of the 1980s finally got under way it started with the reprivatization of four companies during the 1985–87 period, one of them, the SIAM S.A. complex of companies, was being parcelled out in four subdivisions, based on product lines, to as many corporate buyers. In addition, Fabricaciones Militares, the industrial holding company of the Argentine Ministry of Defense, disposed in 1988 of its 21 percent interest in the Atanor Chemical Company and sold several other mixed-enterprise holdings in the petrochemical field. FAMA, the military's aircraft manufacturing company, and Foja Argentina, a steel company, were also put into the privatization process. Meanwhile, the government reprivatized a travel company and the SIAT gas pipe factory and sent to Congress a bill to allow two of the three state-controlled TV channels to be put into private hands. Several of the service activities of the YPF were also put up for sale. Even at this modest pace, privatization did not go smoothly. Although the demonopolization law of November 1987 was followed by almost 70 proposals from private companies, a year later a dozen of these proposals had been rejected and none of the others had actually been accepted or even renegotiated despite a statutory 30-day limit for making a decision on them. Further, two of the government's privatization initiatives—to sell private capital to a large minority interest in the Argentine Airlines company and ENTEL—had run afoul of criticism based ostensibly on the government's failure to follow its own established procedures for divestiture. In neither case was competitive bidding or a public solicitation of offers made, as prescribed by law. And while one, the effort to bring SAS in as a managing partner in the airlines concern promised a probable increase in efficiency, the other, the proposed politically inspired sale of 40 percent of the telephone company to *Telefonica de España*, the Spanish state enterprise, did not look likely to bring in cutting-edge technology. In any event, the latter deal retained the telephone company's monopoly position despite an earlier exploration of the possibility of allowing privately operated local exchanges, such as one serving the financial district of Buenos Aires, to set up. The airlines case may also have had a political dimension, as Sweden, like Spain, had been particularly supportive of the Alfonsin government. It is interesting to note that in both cases the foreign investor whose participation was being sought was a parastatal rather than a private-sector company.

Obstacles of a more general nature have hampered real progress toward privatization in Argentina. Macroeconomic policy has been erratic, confounding both enterprise performance and investor expectations. There has been no comprehensive liberalization of trade with the rest of the world to pressure both state and private companies toward greater efficiency. Some state companies have a history of corruption, and the traditional way of doing business is based on high-level personal contacts, a mixture of regulations, and the dexterous use of veiled subsidies. In all of them there is a high degree of interpenetration between the public and private sectors. Sundering this established interdependence has not come easy for either side. The difficulty, on the business side, derives from the fact that the macroeconomic reforms still pending leave such broadly distributed opportunities for rent-seeking still in place, especially among suppliers of the public and parastatal sector, that it is hard to build up much impetus for change. In addition, the future is fraught with a high level of uncertainty on the political as well as the economic front. For the government's part, the same political uncertainty has colored much of the administration's actions and increased the reluctance to install policies that, however beneficial in long-run economic terms, carry the distinct short-run disadvantage of galvanizing injured parties into political opposition. Preoccupied with reforming civilian-military relations for the first part of its term of office, the administration has approached the end of its term engulfed in the failure of the *Plan Austral* and, more recently, the *Plan Primavera*. In fact, the policy of holding down parastatal prices, in a misguided effort to contain inflation, has increased the decapitalization of the public enterprises and left them in worse shape than before. Through inertia as much as anything else, therefore, the large, sprawling Argentine state—neither as strong as the state in Mexico or Chile nor as dynamic as the state in Brazil—has simply continued to limp along, despite the objective need for privatization and greater cohesion in policy and organization.

MEXICO[10]

Mexican privatization, largely a creature of the de la Madrid government, has been less halting than that of Argentina. Even so, it has been slowed by factors that are not altogether dissimilar, though to an extraordinary degree details of the program have been shrouded in aggregates and conceptual or categorical obscurity. The opaqueness of the process is probably not accidental, for as Melvin Tumin observed years ago in writing on the social functions of ignorance, obfuscation yields a number of advantages. In the main the ambiguity derives from two sources: the accuracy of the parastatal census and from the definition of privatization used in the Mexican context.

The customary total figure used nowadays is 1,155 parastatals, as of the beginning of the de la Madrid term, but the number is questionable, and not only because it differs considerably from some of the (lower) figures released by the government in the preceding two administrations. It is, in fact, probably more accurate than the earlier official tallies. Nevertheless it is lower, by a couple of hundred or so, than a painstaking count completed by the University of Texas' Institute of Latin American Studies before the Lopez Portillo administration left office. The ILAD census was also made prior to the nationalization of the commercial banks, as a result of which the government acquired the shareholdings these institutions had in over 400 industrial, commercial, and other enterprises. The 1,155 total, therefore, may reflect a substantial amount of undercounting—either that or a substantial reclassification of entities as nonparastatals. On the other hand, all of the reckonings include a very large number of small to middling operations like trust funds set up in the 1970s to finance various public sector operations on an off-budget basis, entities that might be considered regulatory or promotional agencies in other administrative contacts, and so on. These are, of course, in no sense comparable in either size or nature to the more important economic holdings of the government.

On the definitional side, the official figures on privatization generally cover outright or formal privatizations, reprivatizations of the 369 companies that came in as shareholdings of the banks, semiprivatizations, mergers of firms and agencies, liquidation of unsalvageable firms and superfluous agencies, and formal deactivation of some entities that were never operating to begin with. It also includes, apparently, the sale of some companies in which the government stock interest was slight and the transfer of parastatals held by the federal government to state and local governments. Some progress has been made on simulated privatization, as prices of a number of publicly produced goods and services have been raised to reduce the element of subsidy. No comprehensive identification and sorting out of all these transactions, however, has ever been released, and unlike the situation in Chile and Brazil, no agency has operated in a key facilitating role or as a clearing house. Indeed, Mexico does not even have anything like the Subsecretariat of Privatizations that operates as a kind of gatekeeper in the Office of the Argentine Presidency.

Beyond the foregoing, no small part of the implementation problem in Mexico has come from the country's protracted economic crisis. This has hampered the Mexican program in more or less the same way that it has stalled the Argentine program. Indeed the Mexicans entered their current economic difficulties far less accustomed than their Argentine counterparts to the experience of high inflation, the repeated collapse of the growth rate, management of the huge external debt, and general expectational uncertainty. They were also unaccustomed to political instability though this factor too, common for years in Buenos Aires, began to make a startling appearance in the run up to the elections of 1987. Inasmuch as the left opposition has excoriated the government on privatization and its other measures of economic liberalization, it is not too surprising that the government has been disinclined to present the opposition with clearer targets. The caution is understandable in that the modest restraints placed on expansion of the public bureaucracy and draconian cuts in bureaucratic real wages cost the ruling party the electoral support of one critical constituency in the 1988 elections. Privatization has thus been submerged into institutional politics. The political elite have long been past masters at managing this baroque process. From the other side of the political arena, some of the business sector have spoken out in favor of privatization, but others, historically dependent on rent-seeking, have at best been lukewarm in support. In any case, most businesses have been absorbed in a scramble for survival amidst unfamiliar economic circumstances while simultaneously preoccupied with readying themselves for the contest with the external competitors, thanks to Mexico's belated but sweeping trade liberalization. Furthermore, not until the early Salinas administration did the government feel safe in moving against the powerful labor fiefdoms that have sought to preserve lax management and worker redundancy in the parastatal sector.

It is interesting to reflect on why the economic crisis, through the dislocation and trauma it inflicted on the polity, permitted the government to move so boldly on some fronts and so hesitantly on others. By allowing the de la Madrid administration to take such a radical measure as bringing Mexico into the GATT, a move rejected under the preceding presidency, and by providing sufficient political space to accelerate the opening of the economy, the crisis seems to reflect an extreme context in which business opposition had been immobilized and opposition from the politically active intelligentsia dulled. At the same time, curiously, policy restructuring through privatization and relaxation of the restrictive treatment of foreign investment appear to have run up against more resistance, and as the government seeks to regain a political equilibrium it is far from certain how these programs will fare.

As for what has been actually accomplished, by the beginning of 1988, 657 parastatals had been officially placed in the privatization hopper, in one sense or another. Unambiguous instances have included a) divestiture of the shareholdings the nationalized commercial banks held in other businesses, b) the closing of the obsolete Fundidora Monterrey steel mill which had been acquired when it could no longer repay loans received from the government, c) sale of the luxury Presidente hotel chain, d) sale of the Mexicana de Cobre copper mining company and a major sulphuric acid producer, and e) sale of the government's interest in Diesel Nacional, Renault de Mexico, and the VAM automotive company. Semiprivatization has been employed to provide private stockholders, including employee ownership groups, with an interest in the BANAMEX, BANCOMER, and Banca SERFIN commercial banking systems. Additionally, besides a miscellaneous assortment of industrial holdings sold by BANAMEX, BANCOMER, and Banca SERFIN (e.g., bottling companies, paper products companies, automotive parts manufacturers), Nacional Financiera, the government's industrial development bank, sold several of its shareholdings, as did the Mining Development Commission and the Ministry of Tourism. Among these divestitures were manufacturers of household appliances, porcelain products, polyethylene containers, water pumps, and hotels, a mining company, and a well-known restaurant in Mexico City's Zona Rosa. Some bank-held shares in the national telephone company were also sold.

The state-owned airline company, Aeromexico, was ostensibly liquidated as bankrupt and widely touted as a case of privatization, but in fact the company was reincarnated as a firm, owned 35 percent by the former company's union and 65 percent by the Banco de Mexico. Offers to purchase the Companía Nacional de Aviación had been rejected by the end of 1988, as had tenders to purchase the large, and historic, Cananea copper mining concern. Reportedly, some 389 entities had been shut down by the middle of 1988, while some 76 had been merged and some 27 transferred to state and local governments. The overall impact, however, may be judged by the fact that public and parastatal employment in early 1988 stood 80 percent above what it was in 1977, with a total of 3.29 million employees on the Mexican federal payroll. Whatever headway was made in rationalizing employment in the smaller operations must be set against the fact that in the plummeting oil market of 1982–1987, the largest industrial employer in the country, *Pemex*, expanded its work force by 35 percent (with 220,000 on its payroll, *Pemex* has twice the workers of Exxon, which has double the assets of *Pemex*).

In short, for much of the period 1970–1988, when the interest in privatization was growing world wide, Mexico, like France in the first part of the Mitterand administration, ran counter to the trend. Nonetheless, adverse circumstances finally overtook traditional policy preferences and destatization policies were finally promulgated. Even so, the decentralized structure of the parastatal sector, reformed (in part) in the 1970s to permit ministerial oversight, was such that, in combination with political and economic factors, privatization has been exceptionally awkward. Tellingly, the institution that would seem to be best equipped to play a leading role, Nacional Financiera, has been marginal to the process.

The reluctance of the Mexican state to press forward vigorously with privatization seems as much evidence of the customary role of interventionary concessions in shoring up political equilibrium as it is of the unpropitious economic climate. From this point of view, it could be argued that the extraordinary headway made in trade liberalization has been all that the system of political economy could handle in one *sexenio*, particularly as there has also been some tension-producing rectification of the price structure. Doubtless, the next wave of reform will focus on a liberalized treatment of foreign capital, and expanding the area of freer trade with the United States along with bringing down the rate of inflation. If this comes about, it may well be that Mexico will finally be constrained to accelerate its privatization, in order to align factor and product markets in a more consistent way.

GENERAL OBSERVATIONS

The four sets of experiences reviewed demonstrate that intercountry variations in environmental variable have had a decisive effect on the scope and progress of privatization, such that no generally valid expectations can be predicated on a public announcement of the program's initiation. What might be accomplished by privatization as part of a larger program of structural adjustment is, therefore, highly indeterminate. Nonetheless, as the four countries in question do suggest that some privatization strategies are likely to have a higher payoff than others, the next research problems in this area lie in determining what amount of cross-country policy transfer and learning is possible in order to refine the policy package and enhance its contributions to improved performance. It is significant, and somewhat paradoxical, that Chile, the country which has pushed privatization the most aggressively, is the only one of the four in which the major parastatals have been able to launch, thanks to the country's macroeconomic policies as well as to the microeconomic success in simulated privatization, an ambitious investment program to expand and improve their operations.

NOTES

1. Alfred H. Saulniers, *Public Enterprises in Peru: Public Sector Growth and Reform*, Boulder, Colorado: Westview Press, 1988. See also Armando Gallegos et al.,

Mapa Económico Financiero de la Actividad Empresarial del Estado Peruano, Lima: ESAN, 1985.

2. Besides field notes taken during research in July, 1988, the following information comes from Jorge Marshall and Felipe Montt, "Privatization in Chile," mimeo., Santiago: March 1987; José Piñera Echenique, "Privatization in Chile," La Jolla: University of California at San Diego, Institute of the Americas, May 1988; Dominique Hachette, *Aspects of Privatization: The Case of Chile 1974–85,* Washington, D.C.: the World Bank, April 1988; Joseph Ramos, *Neoconservative Economics in the Southern Cone of Latin America, 1973–1983,* Baltimore: Johns Hopkins University Press, 1986.

3. Mario Marcel, *La Privatización de Empresas Públicas en Chile 1985–88,* Santiago: CIEPLAN, Notas Técnicas 125, January 1989.

4. One of the more careful critiques in this respect was made by Alejandro Foxley, "Towards a Free Market Economy; Chile 1974–1979," *Journal of Development Economics,* vol. 10 (1982): 3–29. See also Enrique Errazuriz, "Capitalización de la Deuda Externa y Desnacionalización de la Economía Chilena," Santiago: Academia de Humanismo Cristiano Programa de Economía del Trabajo, Documento de Trabajo # 57, August 1987.

5. Dominique Hachette and Rolf Luders, *Aspects of the Privatization Process: The Case of Chile, 1974–82,* Washington: the World Bank, 1987.

6. Raul Saez, "La Privatización de la Compañía de Aceros del Pacífico (CAP)," Materiales para Discusion # 180, Santiago: Centro de Estudios del Desarrollo, 1987.

7. The Brazilian information is based on field interviewing carried out in the summer of 1988, and the following sources: Rogerio L.F. Werneck, "The Uneasy Steps of Privatization in Brazil," mimeo., La Jolla: University of California at San Diego, Institute of the Americas, May 1988; *Estatização e Privatização, Os Limites da Intervenção do Estado,* São Paulo: FUNCEP, 1987; Enrique Saravia, "The Brazilian Privatization Program," *mimeo.,* Rio de Janeiro: Fundação Getúlio Vargas, Inter-American School of Public Administration, 1988; Ethan Kapstein, "Privatization in Brazil," *mimeo.,* La Jolla: University of California at San Diego, Institute of the Americas, May 1988.

8. As of this writing, it is not clear that all, or any, of these can be financed by local or state governments, so negotiations have been started to explore the feasibility of their being acquired by associations of food processors.

9. Besides field research in the summer of 1988, the following have been sources of information for this section: Javier Gonzalez Fraga, "Privatization in Argentina," *mimeo.,* La Jolla: University of California at San Diego, Institute of the Americas, May 1988; Fundación de Investigaciones Económicas Latinoamericanos, *El Fracao del Estatismo,* Buenos Aires: Sudamericana/Planeta, 1987; Horacio A. Losoviz, "Empresas Publicas en Argentina, Realidad y Nuevas Políticas," *mimeo.,* Buenos Aires: Ministerio de Obras y Servicios Públicos, 1988.

10. The discussion is based on a considerable number of printed sources, including Oscar Vera, "The Political Economy of Privatization in Mexico," mimeo., La Jolla: University of California at San Diego, Institute of the Americas, May 1988; María Amparo Casar and Wilson Peres, *El estado empresario en Mexico: Agotamiento o Renovación?* Mexico: Siglo Ventiuno Editores, 1988; Juan Perez Escamilla, *La Venta de Empresas del Sector Público, 1983–1988,* Mexico: Secretaria de Hacienda, 1988.

5

Economic Performance of Public Enterprises in Latin America: Lessons from Argentina and Brazil

Melissa H. Birch

Analysis of Latin American economies in the 1980s has frequently focused on the public sector. The dominant economic theory of the 1980s, embodied in the International Monetary Fund stabilization plans imposed on in so many Latin American countries, emphasized the role of domestic credit in stabilizing both internal and external macroeconomic variables. Such a focus necessarily curtailed public-sector activities and, by default, favored private-sector, privately financed initiatives. The presence of a large number of state-owned enterprises (SOEs) and the key role they play in both public finances and the provision of basic economic services thus came under scrutiny. Policymakers, especially in the developed countries, focused on the large deficits accumulated by some public enterprises and concluded that the firms should be privatized. Although the basis for this conclusion is unclear, one deduces from the privatization prescription that the ownership of an enterprise's assets is believed to largely determine its performance.

Using several different performance measures, the analysis in this paper examines the performance of public enterprises in Argentina and Brazil and suggests, however, that performance varies substantially across industries, between countries in the same industry, and over time. In such a case, it seems apparent that a richer policy approach may be required.

Section I this chapter reviews the origins of state intervention in the Latin American economies and the current extent of state participation. Section II describes the patterns of production, investment, and employment in a sample of Argentine and Brazilian SOEs, and Section III analyzes the performance of these firms. The final section draws some conclusions from the observed performance that may provide guidance as to the appropriate role for public enterprise in the developing countries of Latin America.

I. EVOLUTION OF STATE PARTICIPATION IN THE LATIN AMERICAN ECONOMIES

SOEs are a common feature of the economic landscape in Latin America and come from a long tradition of government intervention in economic affairs. Beginning in colonial times, the European states took responsibility for economic affairs by commissioning the exploration of Latin America and the exploitation of its resources. After colonization, the European colonial powers continued to control local economies through the granting of special concessions and monopoly rights for certain activities. This relationship between government and the private sector, combined with the small size of the market in many Latin American countries, created a collaborative attitude toward economic activity. Economic agents in Latin America tend to see themselves as working in cooperation with the government and, therefore, entitled to protection.

Many of the existing SOEs in Latin America were created in the late 1940s. In general, Latin American economies had prospered during the Second World War, as they exported raw materials and foodstuffs to North American and European countries whose resources were diverted to wartime production. Some companies, owned by citizens of Axis countries, were nationalized as "enemy property," and their operations were taken over by the state. After the war, Latin American countries began to look inward for ways to use the accumulated international reserves to develop their national economies. The establishment of domestic industries became an important objective of economic policy, and a key role for state enterprises was found in preventing bottlenecks in economically "strategic" sectors. The nationalistic political climate that existed in many Latin American countries during this period also favored the creation of state enterprises.

While many SOEs were created in the 1940s, they proliferated in the 1960s and 1970s. In Brazil, for example, 128 out of 251 SOEs existing in 1980 were created between 1960 and 1975. The activities of international development institutions, able to lend only with a government guarantee, favored the development of SOEs, especially in infrastructure creation and heavy industry. In the private sector, international capital flows from private sources increased. In some Latin American countries, although the entrance of multinationals was permitted, it was regulated, sometimes with the requirement that the government be included as a financial partner to mitigate the unpleasant political connotations of "foreign capital."

As economic growth and social development became an explicit objective of many governments in the 1960s and early 1970s, distribution of income and wealth became an issue. Further concentration of ownership of state-granted monopolies in the hands of a few local or foreign interests came under attack. In response, many countries adopted programs providing for state ownership of productive capacity in industries thought to be critical for future develop-

Table 5.1.
Distribution of Nonfinancial State Enterprises by Major Sector and Sphere of
Government in Brazil and Argentina

	Agriculture, Mining and Forestry	Manufacturing	Services	Total
Argentina				
Federal	7	20	116	143
State or Provincial	12	13	58	83
Municipal	0	0	6	6
Inter-governmental	1	0	2	3
TOTAL	20	33	182	235
Brazil				
Federal	20	56	115	191
State or Provincial	11	33	223	267
Municipal	1	3	96	100
Inter-governmental	0	0	0	0
TOTAL	32	92	434	558

Sources: Trebat (1983), p. 38; Ugalde (1984), pp. 28–38.

ment. During this period, SOEs were also used in an effort to create new development "poles" and increase regional integration. In other cases, failing firms were taken over by the state to protect or maintain employment. By the mid1980s, there were 235 SOEs in Argentina and 558 in Brazil. They are represented in almost every sector of the economy but, as can be seen in Table 5.1, are heavily concentrated in basic services and are less commonly found in manufacturing. In both countries, they play only a minor role in the agricultural sector.

To understand the behavior of these Argentine and Brazilian SOEs, the political and economic environment in which the firms operate needs to be considered. The two countries offer quite different macroeconomic and political settings for their respective SOE sectors. In Argentina, sustained economic growth has eluded the authoritarian, populist, and democratic regimes that have alternated in power over the last 20 years. In Brazil, neither the rapid growth during the Brazilian "Miracle," nor the shock of the oil crisis, nor the onset of the debt crisis brought to an end the long period of military rule (1964–1984). The rest of this section summarizes the contrasting political and economic developments in the two countries between 1965 and 1983, focusing on the impact of changing policy environments on the public-enterprise sector.

Argentina

The last thirty years of Argentine economic and political history have been extremely turbulent. Between 1955 and 1982, Argentina experienced 16 changes of government and twice as many changes of finance minister. In terms of the environment created for public enterprise, the different administrations can be divided into four distinct policy periods.

The data used in this chapter begin in 1965, very nearly the end of the Illia government, which had followed expansionary monetary and fiscal policies to revive an ailing economy. Those policies, combined with good harvests in 1964 and 1965, led to rapid economic expansion. As inflation erupted, however, economic growth began to stagnate in 1966.

The orientation of the government of General Ongania that replaced Illia in 1966 was politically authoritarian and economically laissez faire. With regard to public-sector activities, the economic plan that came into effect called for increasing utility prices (mostly state owned), decreasing employment in the public sector, and reducing the financial losses of SOEs. Contractionary economic policy combined with political repression to create popular unrest, and the Ongania government was overthrown in 1970.

During the next three years, Argentina was governed by a succession of military presidents (Generals Roberto Livingston and Alejandro Lanusse) who relaxed economic and political controls somewhat and tried to win labor support by increasing wages. In free elections held in 1973, however, Lanusse lost to Hector Campora, a stand-in for Juan D. Peron, the extremely popular former president of Argentina, who then returned from exile.

Peronist policy was populist in style and gave the state a significant role in economic affairs, especially in employment creation and wage policy. During this period, SOEs expanded, but prices for their output were kept low to reduce the cost of living for the working class. Deteriorating economic conditions and increasing civil disorder led to a coup in March 1976 and a return to the policy combination of political authoritarianism and laissez-faire economics experienced some ten years earlier under the Ongania rule.

Under the very powerful finance minister José Martinez de Hoz, prices were freed from controls, employment and investment were cut, and an attempt to sell SOEs to private interests was made. By 1982, however, the military government was beginning to crumble. The defeat by the British in the war for the Malvinas (Falkland) Islands, rising inflation, and a deteriorating financial and industrial system brought on the collapse of this model of government. During its last years, some loosening of economic policies occurred as the government prepared for upcoming elections to be held in 1984.

In summary, the 1965–1985 period may be divided into four distinct policy periods for Argentine SOEs. Expansionary economic policy prior to 1965 should have provided a favorable environment for SOE expansion, but the authoritarian period that followed (roughly 1966–1973), stressed financial performance over the expansion of SOE services. In contrast, the Peronist period (1973–76) emphasized the role of the SOEs as providers of essential services to working-class families and critical inputs in industrial production. Financial performance thus may have been sacrificed for national policy objectives. The military period that followed (1976–1982), represented a return to a more orthodox economic policy and an economic climate similar to the 1966–1973 period. Unfortunately, data for the democratic period beginning with the Alfonsin government in 1984 are not yet available.

Brazil

The Brazilian economic and political experience over the period under consideration here was quite different. The military government that came to power in 1964 inherited economic stagnation coupled with high inflation and was swift to adopt policies to stabilize the economy and promote growth. The full effect of these policies was not seen, however, until 1968, when the country began eight years of consistently high rates of real growth. During what has become known as the "Brazilian Miracle," for the period 1968–1974, real growth averaged 11.3 percent per year. Although the onset of the oil crisis in 1973 spurred inflation, persistent trade deficits, and increased foreign debt, the effect on growth was not immediately felt. The Second National Development Plan announced in 1974 delineated a key role for SOEs in maintaining high rates of economic expansion through continued public investment in infrastructure and heavy industry.

In the late 1970s, as the military began to contemplate a return to civilian government at some future date, it adopted policies aimed at increasing real wages and improving living standards. By 1979, the emphasis of economic policy had shifted toward the curbing of rising inflation, and the early 1980s saw a move to increase the prices of SOE output to dampen the inflationary spiral. To supplement the lower level of public investment required as government spending was reduced, foreign borrowing and investment were encouraged.

Economic policy under the Brazilian military government promoted rapid growth through substantial investment in productive capacity. Foreign, private domestic, and state capital were all part of a package of policy tools to be used to catapult the country into the category of world power. The new government aimed to stabilize the economy and promote economic growth through the creation of a system of incentives to direct investments into areas and sectors deemed essential by the government, the attraction of foreign capital (both private and official) to finance the expansion of the country's productive capacity, and the use of public investments in infrastructural projects and in certain government-owned heavy industries.

The results of this relatively comprehensive, long-run approach to economic policy, as compared with the stop-and-go policies in Argentina, can be seen in Table 5.2. Rapid economic expansion provided a growing market for the output of Brazilian SOEs, and as growth slowed in the 1970s, the multiplier effects of continued SOE investment prolonged growth and postponed recession and adjustment. Argentine economic policy, in contrast, changed almost constantly, and the Argentine economy stagnated throughout most of the period. Economic growth, when it occurred, was much more modest and less enduring than in Brazil. At the same time, inflation was higher in Argentina, and markets for output much less stable.

II. PRODUCTION, INVESTMENT, AND EMPLOYMENT IN THE SOEs

In the following sections we examine the behavior of SOEs in these two very different environments. The varying levels of output, investment, and employment are discussed, basic measures of efficiency and productivity are calculated, and explanations for the observed patterns of performance are explored.

The Sample

Public utilities and state firms considered to be occupying critical or strategic sectors of the economy are heavily represented in the samples considered in this paper. The two sets of data, one from Argentina and another from Brazil, cover the mining, petroleum, electric power, railroad transportation, and telecommunications industries. The Argentine data were collected by the author in Argentina and are based primarily on data from the Sindicatura General de Empresas Publicas (SIGEP), an oversight agency charged with "collecting information on compliance with financial, legal, and fiscal directives." While SIGEP oversees some seventeen firms, to maintain comparability with the Brazilian data, only five are included in this sample. The Brazilian data are taken from work by Thomas Trebat. The firms included and the period covered are found in Table 5.3.

The two data sets are not entirely comparable. The methodology used in the calculations is the same unless otherwise noted, but coverage varies. For Brazil, "mining" refers to the iron mining operations of the CVRD, a company internationally known for its performance standards. In Argentina, the mining industry is represented by YCF, a small coal mining operation. Oil industry coverage also varies somewhat. Although the Brazilian oil company PETRO-BRAS clearly dominates the measures, the Brazilian data also include some petrochemical firms. In Argentina, only YPF, the petroleum drilling and refining company, is included.

Table 5.2.
Indicators of Economic Performance, 1965–83 (Percent Change Except as Noted)

	1965	1970	1975	1980	1983
Argentina					
Real GDP	11.6	2.6	0.0	0.9	3.0
Industrial Output	17.9	6.4	-2.7	4.0	--
Gross Fixed Investment	--	7.7	0.1	3.6	-1.8
Consumer Prices	28.5	13.6	182.3	100.8	343.8
Current Account (billions US$)	--	.2	-1.3	-4.8	-2.4
Total External Debt (billions US$)	--	--	7.9	27.2	45.1
Brazil					
Real GDP	3.5	2.6	5.6	8.5	--
Industrial Output	9.8	6.2	3.9	--	--
Gross Fixed Investment	--	--	-2.2	--	--
Consumer Prices	65.9	22.3	31.2	86.3	--
Balance of Trade (billions US$)	.7	.2	-3.5	-2.8	--
Current Account (billions US$)	-.3	.8	-6.7	-12.1	--
Total External Debt (billions US$)	--	5.3	21.1	54.4	--

Sources: IMF, *International Financial Statistics*; Trebat (1983), p. 134.

Table 5.3.
Enterprises Included and Years Covered

Argentina	Brazil
Mining:	
Yacimientos Carboníferos Fiscales (YCF) (1965-83)	Companhia Vale do Rio Doce (CVRD) (1965-79)
Steel:	
SOMISA (1965-83)	Companhia Siderúrgica Nacional (1965-79)
	Companhia Siderúrgica Paulista (1966-79)
	Usinas Siderúrgicas de Minas Gerais (1965-75)
	Companhia Ferro e Aço de Vitória (1968-72)
	SIDERBRAS (1975-79)
Petroleum:	
Yacimientos Petrolíferos Fiscales (YPF) (1965-83)	PETROBRAS (1965-79)
	PETROBRAS Química (1968-79)
Telecommunications:	
ENTEL (1965-83)	Companhia Telefônica Brasileira (1966-72)
	Telecomunicações do Rio de Janeiro (TELERJ) (1973-79)
	Telecomunicações de São Paulo (TELESP) (1973-79)
	EMBRATEL (1967-79)
	Eight state telephone companies

Table 5.3.
(continued)

ARGENTINA	BRAZIL

Electricity:

Servicios Eléctricos del Gran Buenos Aires (SEGBA) (1965-83)	ELETROBRAS (1970-80)
Agua y Energia Eléctrica (A y EE) (1965-83)	Cia. Brasileira de Energia Elétrica (1970-75)
	Cia. Eletricidade de Manaus (1970-75)
	Cia. Hidroelétrica de São Francisco (1965-75)
	Other regional firms

Railways:

Ferrocarriles Argentinos (FF AA) (1965-83)	Rede Ferroviária Federal (1966-79)
	Ferrovia Paulista (FEPASA) (1965-79)

The samples also differ in terms of time period under consideration. The Trebat data start in the mid 1960s and end in the late 1970s. The Argentine data begin in the mid 1960s and end in the early 1980s, but for some variables, many observations are missing between 1965 and 1970. The problem of different chronological periods may be mitigated somewhat when one considers that, in analyzing the behavior of a firm, the political regime under which the SOE exists may be a more important environmental factor than the calendar year.

Production

The behavior of Argentine and Brazilian SOEs with respect to levels of production has been quite different (see Table 5.4). In Argentina, production peaked in most industries in 1975 or 1976 and declined thereafter. In Brazil, physical output continued to increase through the 1965–1979 period in all but the petroleum industry. In Argentina, steel and electricity output showed the largest gains, while in Brazil electricity, mining, and rail transportation showed the most substantial increases. Railroads, a declining industry internationally, showed an early and steep decline in Argentina but a steady gain in Brazil.

Investment

Public-enterprise investment represents a significant share of public-sector investment in both countries, but only a modest share of total investment. In

Table 5.4.
Indices of Output of State-Owned Enterprise (1966 = 100)

	Argentina	Brazil	Argentina	Brazil	Argentina	Brazil
	Mining[a]		*Steel*[b]		*Petroleum*[c]	
1965	87	98	98	74	93	81
1970	186	241	118	132	138	141
1975	151	523	174	813	139	148
1976	186	527	169	203	140	143
1977	161	477	152	281	151	138
1978	131	536	199	310	159	133
1979	219	655	200	361	165	138
1980	117	--	194	--	172	--
1983	147	--	185	--	170	--
	Telecommunications[d]		*Electricity*[e]		*Railroads*[f]	
1965	100	--	101	92	102	96
1970	103	--	141	145	96	155
1975	107	100	223	288	75	303
1976	100	--	234	328	78	361
1977	104	--	261	368	82	388
1978	100	--	268	411	70	439
1979	--	247	324	464	77	544
1980	--	--	330	--	66	--
1983	--	--	296	--	94	--

Note: (a) For Brazil, iron ore production in tons; for Argentina, coal production in tons; (b) Index based on equivalent ingot tons of flat steel products; (c) Index of domestic crude oil production in cubic meters; (d) Local calls completed; (e) Gigawatt Hours (GWh, equal to a billion kilowatts); (f) Rail freight in billions of ton-kilometers.
Sources: Trebat, p. 135; SIGEP.

1965, SOE investment accounted for 14.5 percent of total investment in Argentina, and by 1981, it accounted for almost 17 percent. Brazilian SOEs accounted for 13.6 percent of total investment in 1965 and 22 percent in 1979. During the same period, Brazilian SOE investment increased from about one-third of all public-sector investment to two-thirds (by 1979), while in Argentina, the share declined from 45 percent in 1970 to 35 percent in 1977 before increasing again to almost 40 percent in 1981.

In Argentina, despite policy changes toward the role of the state, SOE investment increased nearly 60 percent in real terms between 1965 and 1983—out-pacing private domestic investment by a large margin. The pattern of SOE investment over the period was quite irregular, but the rate of its increase tended to decline in the second half of the period (see Table 5.5). In Brazil, public-enterprise investment increased continuously between 1966 and 1976 and declined only slightly thereafter. Also out-pacing private-sector invest-

Table 5.5.
Real Rates of Growth of Public Enterprise Investment and Output (Percent Change)

	Public Enterprise Investment		Public Enterprise Output[a]		Total Industrial Output	
1966	--	11.9	--		-1.5	9.8
1967	46.0	24.4	1.0		1.5	3.0
1968	9.1	3.4	2.6		9.2	13.3
1969	2.4	12.4	8.9		9.8	12.1
1970	22.2	24.4	7.0		6.4	10.4
1971	7.4	27.1	15.3		9.6	14.3
1972	-7.5	19.1	5.0		6.6	13.4
1973	5.7	27.5	5.2		6.2	15.8
1974	20.1	29.2	2.7		5.8	9.8
1975	11.0	21.5	-0.6		-2.7	6.2
1976	0.6	32.9	2.2		-4.7	10.7
1977	-6.8	-0.01	2.9		3.9	3.9
1978	-0.9	-0.01	0.6		-10.5	8.1
1979	-12.4	-0.04	13.2		10.6	6.9
1980	14.7	-1.5	4.7		4.0	8.3
1981	-18.9	--	-2.1		-16.0	--
1982	-10.4	--	--		--	--
1983	-7.9	--	--		--	--

Note: (a) Output data not available for Brazil.
Soruces: World Bank (1985); Trebat (1984), p. 131.

ment, the total increase in Brazilian SOE investment between 1966 and 1980 amounted to more than 232 percent. This kind of consistent trend is far more typical of the Brazilian data than of the Argentine.

One indication of the relative importance given to the various industries in the SOE sector is their relative share of total SOE investment. The allocation by industry of public-enterprise investment in Brazil and Argentina is found in Table 5.6. Not surprisingly, both countries have devoted a significant share of SOE investment to the energy sector—petroleum and electric. Argentina, a country rich in petroleum, natural gas, and coal, spent an average of 40 percent of SOE investment between 1965 and 1983 developing such resources. Another 22 percent, approximately, was spent to develop electric (primarily hydroelectric) energy potential. In Brazil, the emphasis was the reverse. On average, slightly more than one third of all investment was directed toward electric energy, but in the 1966–69 period, more than half of all investment funds went to this industry. Petroleum and petrochemicals received an average of 21 percent of public-enterprise investment in Brazil.

Brazil appears to have invested relatively more in steel (an average of 18 percent) than did Argentina, where steel has accounted for only about 8 percent of Argentine SOE investment. Both countries have devoted an average of about

Table 5.6.
Sectoral Allocation of Public Enterprise Investment (Percent of Total)

	1965	1966-69	1970-75	1976-79
Argentina				
Steel	4	4	10	6
Fuels	47	42	34	45
Communications	6	9	11	9
Electric Energy	24	23	22	21
Transport (Railroads)	15	16	13	13
Water	4	4	10	6
Not Classified	--	43	--	--
TOTAL:	100	100	100	100
Brazil				
Mining	6	4	6	4
Steel	46	4	9	13
Petroleum and Petrochemicals	20	19	21	23
Telecommunications	--	6	9	10
Electrical Energy	13	55	43	40
Railroads[a]	10	12	12	10
Not Classified	5	--	--	--
TOTAL:	100	100	100	100

Note: (a) Also includes other transportation enterprises.
Sources: SIGEP; Trebat (1983), p. 120.

12 percent of all SOE investment to telecommunications. Investment in transportation as a share of total SOE investment seems to have declined in both countries over the period under consideration.

Employment

Employment in the SOE sector accounts for some 16 percent of public-sector employment in Argentina. Total SOE employment increased between 1966 and 1976 but decreased in the following ten years. Workers in SOEs accounted for 4.1 percent of the Argentine labor force in 1975 but only 2.4 percent in 1980. In Brazil, SOE employment represented some 14 percent of employment in manufacturing in 1968 but less than 9 percent of the total by 1979.

Trebat notes that Brazilian public enterprises have not pursued aggressively the social objective of employment creation nor would they appear to fit comfortably within the common stereotype of the public enterprise as being an overstaffed bureaucracy.

Table 5.7.
State-Owned Enterprise Employment (1966 = 100)

	Argentina	Brazil	Argentina	Brazil	Argentina	Brazil
	Mining		Steel		Petroleum	
1966	100	100	100	100	100	100
1970	75	110	95	102	82	100
1975	144	213	151	147	124	116
1976	153	215	145	174	120	129
1977	157	228	139	181	107	133
1978	116	178	137	187	92	137
1979	112	194	135	192	87	143
1980	108	--	140	--	82	--
1983	102	--	129	--	80	--
	Telecommunications		Electricity		Railroads	
1966	100	100	100	100	100	100
1970	106	177	93	327	85	93
1975	121	198	176	595	89	83
1976	116	190	173	622	90	87
1977	109	197	157	667	73	73
1978	111	210	145	693	64	71
1979	106	213	137	997	62	71
1980	108	--	131	--	56	--
1983	114	--	71	--	60	--

Sources: Trebat (1983), p. 157; SIGEP data.

In Argentina, however, employment creation seems to have been an important objective for the SOEs under some governments, although it was decidedly not a priority under the 1976–1983 military government. Despite the observed decline in SOE employment in Argentina, the SOEs are still widely perceived to be "overstaffed bureaucracies."

Although Trebat termed employment growth in the Brazilian SOEs "very slow," employment in the SOE sector has generally grown more rapidly in Brazil than in Argentina (see Table 5.7). Mirroring the emphasis seen previously on investment in the Brazilian electric energy sector, employment in this sector in Brazil increased almost tenfold in the years between 1966 and 1979. The greatest increase in employment in Argentine SOEs was also in the electric energy sector. Employment in this industry in Argentina increased 76 percent to reach its peak in 1975, but has declined steadily since then. By 1981, this sector employed fewer people than in 1966. Employment in rail transportation declined substantially and quite consistently in both countries. In Argentina, the only exceptions to this steady decline occurred during the Peronist period of the mid 1970s and again ten years later as the military government ended.

The patterns of production, investment, and employment observed here follow quite closely the changing political and economic climates in the two countries. In Argentina, political support for the SOEs started with Peron in the 1940s and peaked with his return to power in the early 1970s. The military government that came to power in 1976 adopted a strictly free-market ideology. Although unable to realize its objectives fully, it was able to reduce the resources allocated to SOEs. In Brazil, a military government of a different type was in power throughout the period under consideration here. Although the president changed, the political rhetoric and economic objectives experienced only minor variation. The ideology of the Brazilian government during this period acknowledged an important role for the state in the production of goods and services, especially in key sectors of the economy. The industries included in this sample, with the exception of the railroads, fall squarely within the group over which the state wished to maintain control.

III. PRODUCTIVITY AND PERFORMANCE IN THE SOE SECTOR

The Brazilian SOE sector shows a dramatic increase during the period in its use of capital relative to labor (see Table 5.8). By 1979, the average worker in the sector was employed in conjunction with from two to twelve times more capital than in the mid 1960s. This finding is consistent with the high levels of investment undertaken by the SOEs during the late 1960s and early 1970s and the moderate increase in employment noted previously. This pattern is typical of the development strategy adopted by the government that came to power in 1964: to emphasize infrastructure creation and eschew social objectives of employment creation, at least within the SOE sector. The rising capital/labor ratios thus reflect modernization and the adoption of new technology, favorable relative prices created by the investment incentives and import-duty exemptions for capital goods, and managers' and politicians' preference for expanding plant capacity to enhance political visibility and the perception of achievement.

Whatever the reason for the increase in the capital intensity of the SOE sector, the question of the productivity of such investments naturally arises. The capital/output ratios found in Table 5.9 reveal that the amount of capital used to produce a unit of output rose from about 2.7 units in the mid 1960s to about 4.1 units in 1975 and 6.7 units by 1979. These figures must be interpreted with great care, however, because they are sensitive not only to the rather notorious difficulty of measuring capital, but also to capacity-utilization rates and the effect of price controls on the measure of output. With this caveat in mind, one is reluctant to state that capital use has doubled in ten years, but clearly it has increased substantially.

In Argentina, over a much shorter period, there has also been an increase in the use of capital relative to labor for some industries. In petroleum and elec-

Table 5.8.
Capital/Labor Ratios, Selected Years

Argentina (1977 = 100)	1977	1979	1980	1982
Mining	100	142	149	164
Steel	100	100	133	66
Petroleum	100	165	190	214
Communications	100	96	96	94
Electricity[a]	100	130	144	294
Railroads	100	205	284	368

Brazil (1970 = 100)	1966-68	1970	1975	1979
Mining	52	100	155	260
Steel	122	100	227	297
Petroleum	36	100	296	471
Communications	97	100	282	473
Electricity[a]	99	100	139	201
Railroads[b]	--	100	838	1850

Note: (a) Excludes predominantly distribution firms; (b) Trebat suggests estimates for railroads are less reliable than those for other sectors.
Sources: (Argentina) Author's calculations on the basis of data from SIGEP; (Brazil) Trebat (1983), p. 155.

tricity generation, capital per worker appears to have doubled, and in rail transport, it has more than tripled. Bearing in mind the investment and employment data presented previously, this increase in the capital/labor ratio in Argentina appears to be less the result of consistent investment over time than of declining employment in these industries. In the period 1976–1982, employment in railroads, electricity generation, petroleum, and mining fell markedly, while employment in steel and communications was roughly constant. At the same time, investment increased dramatically in the railroads, varied widely in communications (ending up about where it started), and fell, sometimes by as much as 86 percent (steel) in all other industries.

One difficulty in comparing the behavior observed in Argentina with that of Brazil is that the periods under consideration are not comparable in length. Unfortunately, reliable estimates of capital stock prior to 1976 are not available for Argentina. One could compare the five-year periods 1977–1982 (Argentina) and 1970–75 or 1975–79 (Brazil), or one could compare 1977–79 in Argentina with 1975–79 in Brazil, because there is some overlap between the periods. In general, the increase in the use of capital relative to labor in the Argentine SOE sector appears to be less dramatic than that in the Brazilian

Table 5.9.
Capital/Output Ratios[a] (1970 Local Currency Values)

Argentina		1976	1979	1981
Mining		146.6	(14.7)	(25.2)
Steel		0.1	0.2	2.1
Petroleum		2.1	1.9	(1.4)
Communications		15.8	11.4	8.4
Electricity (AE)		90.0	46.0	36.1
Electricity (SG)		5.4	3.4	5.4
Railroads		1.4	41.9	(119.3)

Brazil	1966-8	1970	1975	1979
Mining	2.08	2.12	2.41	4.62
Steel	4.92	2.79	3.54	5.66
Petrochemicals	0.50	1.22	1.46	2.86
Communications	3.61	4.57	6.15	7.08
Railroads	na	2.63	13.58	16.16
Electricity	8.90	9.56	10.63	13.86
Public Enterprises	2.73	3.33	4.06	6.68
Public Enterprises (Excluding Railroads)	na	3.54	3.74	6.50

Note: (a) Output (measured as value-added) and capital in 1970 constant local-currency values.
Sources: Trebat (1983), p. 158; SIGEP.

SOE sector. The exception to this general trend is the energy sector (electric and petroleum industries). Comparing 1977–1982 or 1977–79 in Argentina with 1975–79 in Brazil, indicates that the Argentine increase in capital relative to labor exceeds the rate of increase in Brazil. Argentina would almost appear, perhaps prompted by developments in world oil markets, to be catching up with the Brazilian levels of energy investment.

An examination of capital/output ratios for Argentine SOEs presents enormous difficulties. When output is measured as value-added, the ratios often take on negative values or become exceedingly large. This result is believed to be more a function of accounting difficulties in the high-inflation environment of the late 1970s in Argentina than of any variation of real output. Thus, this study uses an alternative measure; Table 5.10 provides capital/output ratios measured as capital per unit of physical output. With this measure, the decapitalization of the Argentine SOE sector becomes apparent. Electric energy and steel show a steep decline over the period, although SEGBA shows a sudden

Table 5.10.
Alternative Capital/Output Ratios: Capital per Unit of Physical Output, Argentina
(Index Numbers, 1976 = 100)

	YPF	A y EE	YCF	SEGBA	FF AA	ENTEL	SOMISA
Capital Index							
1976	100	100	100	100	100	100	100
1977	60	88	106	93	102	108	95
1978	104	102	82	68	232	136	97
1979	89	83	91	47	221	127	87
1980	101	58	94	48	315	118	86
1981	115	48	181	130	397	172	74
Output (in physical units)							
1976	100	100	100	100	100	100	100
1977	108	111	86	136	77	101	90
1978	113	114	71	142	62	103	118
1979	118	138	118	144	66	107	119
1980	123	141	63	129	69	111	115
1981	123	122	81	168	55	119	82
Capital/Output Ratio							
1977	.55	.79	1.23	.68	1.32	1.07	1.06
1978	.92	.89	1.15	.48	3.74	1.32	.82
1979	.75	.60	.77	.33	3.35	1.19	.72
1980	.82	.41	1.49	.37	4.57	1.06	.75
1981	.93	.39	2.23	1.14	7.22	1.45	.90

Source: (Capital and Output index numbers), SIGEP.

increase in 1981. The increasing capital/labor ratios in these industries combined with the falling capital/output ratios suggest that output was not sacrificed as employment declined. Only the mining and rail industries show an increase in capitalization, and that appears to result mostly from declining output in these industries.

The difficulties in measurement mentioned in the Brazilian case are compounded in the Argentine case. Measurement of capital in the presence of such high rates of inflation is almost impossible. While the use of physical output instead of any price-sensitive output measures helps eliminate distortions, the substantial variation in economic activity may be expected to have a serious impact on capacity utilization.

In view of the differences in the capital endowments of the SOE sectors in these two countries, it is interesting to look at labor productivity in each sector. Following Trebat, value added per worker was calculated for each industry in both countries. The results, reported in Table 5.11, show that, in each in-

Table 5.11.
Productivity: Value Added per Employee (Index Numbers, 1970 = 100)

	Argentina	Brazil	Argentina	Brazil	Argentina	Brazil
	1967		*1970*		*1975*	
Mining	72	58	100	100	79	136
Steel	--	64	100	100	44	178
Petroleum	na	74	100	100	163	259
Communications	124	119	100	100	85	209
Electricity	na	119	100	100	21	125
Railroads	na	53	100	100	53	163
Other Trans- portation	329	--	100	--	131	--
TOTAL:	--	64	--	100	--	334
	1979		*1980*		*1983*	
Mining	-46	124	3	na	77	na
Steel	39	148	26	na	38	na
Petroleum	196	207	28	na	119	na
Communications	132	309	151	na	84	na
Electricity	22	139	27	na	na	na
Railroads	57	307	2	na	40	na
Other Trans- portation	71	--	115	--	120	--
TOTAL:	--	345	--	--	--	--

Sources: Trebat (1983), p. 160; calculations based on data from SIGEP.

dustry, increases in productivity appear to be greater in Brazil than in Argentina.

In Brazil, the largest gains in labor productivity were registered in the petrochemical and steel industries between 1965 and 1975. In the following four years, however, productivity either grew distinctly more slowly or, in some

Table 5.12.
Productivity: Physical Output per Worker, Argentina (Index Numbers, 1966 = 100)

	YPF	YCF	SEGBA	A y EE	FF AA	ENTEL	SOMISA
1966	100	100	100	100	100	100	100
1967	114	144	109	103	99	100	103
1968	140	184	126	115	108	141	89
1969	150	202	132	136	114	180	124
1970	168	249	138	151	107	151	121
1971	170	218	158	161	103	170	128
1972	166	233	163	159	107	249	116
1973	153	153	164	159	109	207	107
1974	139	148	125	157	121	161	100
1975	113	106	109	126	116	121	117
1976	117	122	113	135	113	95	106
1977	142	104	163	166	124	101	100
1978	172	114	188	184	127	157	135
1979	191	197	209	236	139	208	139
1980	209	109	193	250	161	212	137
1981	219	143	224	346	138	251	94
1982	222	168	199	383	130	277	106
1983	212	144	190	413	124	265	136

Source: Calculated from SIGEP data.

cases, declined. Trebat explains this behavior of productivity in the late 1970s as a result of tightened government price controls, increasing excess capacity, and increases in employment. In Argentina, the largest gains were made in petroleum, telecommunications, and other transportation. Some decline in 1979 is noticed in mining and steel, but gains continued to be made in the energy and telecommunications industries. By 1983, productivity growth had slowed considerably, and value added per employee fell to near or below 1975 levels.

Because in the Argentine case this result might well be attributed to the effect of price controls in the presence of high inflation, physical output per employee was calculated. The results are shown in Table 5.12. When a measure of physical output was used, productivity in many of the Argentine industries fell in the mid 1970s but rose again during the last years of the decade. In the 1980s, there were considerable gains in average output per person, especially in YPF, SEGBA, *Agua y Energia Electrica*, and ENTEL. This observation is especially interesting when considered jointly with the value-added measure, where electricity and telecommunications made a poor showing and no Argentine industry matched the performance of its Brazilian counterpart (although YPF came close in 1979). The results of the use of the physical-output measure reinforce the hypothesis that price controls have severely impaired the usefulness of any price-sensitive performance measures such as revenues, value added, or financial profits.

It is thus with some trepidation that data for performance with respect to real rate of return are presented in Table 5.13. The real rate of return is meas-

Table 5.13.
Real Rate of Return in State-Owned Enterprises (Percent)

	Brazil 1966-68	Brazil 1970	Brazil 1975	Argentina 1976[a]
Mining	33.7	31	29	8
Steel	11.3	21	19	3
Petroleum	124.0	62	64	40
Communications	23.5	10	7	3
Electricity (AE)	--	8	6	4
Electricity (SG)	--	--	--	8
Railroads	--	-3	-5	102

	Argentina 1979	Brazil 1979	Argentina 1981
Mining	17	23	-8
Steel	4	11	8
Petroleum	41	29	-80
Communications	4	8	8
Electricity (AE)	4	5	1
Electricity (SG)	13	--	12
Railroads	-6	-3	-5

Note: (a) Electricity entry from 1975 data.
Sources: Trebat, p. 168; data from SIGEP.

ured as value added minus wages as a proportion of capital stock. This broad
measure of profitability is closer to the economist's concept of profit as the
return on capital. It includes net interest payments, rents, and taxes that would
certainly not be included in the standard financial measure of profit. Including
these items in this definition of rate of return for SOEs gives a more accurate
measure of surplus. Since these firms are owned by the state, the allocation of
this surplus reflects a series of political decisions. This effect is perhaps easiest
to see in the case of taxes: because the state is both the owner of capital and
the recipient of tax payments, what would ordinarily be considered an expense
becomes something like a stockholder's dividend.

The real rate of return is measured in terms of value added and capital
stock; it thus suffers from the distortions introduced as a result of price controls and the measurement errors derived from estimating capital stock under
conditions of very high inflation. Therefore, the results do not appear as poor
as one might expect. In general, the rate of return in Brazilian SOEs is higher
than that in the Argentine firms. By 1979, however, the profitability of the Bra-

zilian firms was declining and that of the Argentine firms showed some improvement—especially SEGBA and the mining company YCF. The declining profitability of Brazilian SOEs is consistent with the slowdown of that country's economy. Similarly, the improvement in Argentine SOE performance occurs simultaneously with economic expansion. The improvement in the performance of the Argentine SOEs in 1979 and the slightly poorer performance in 1981 could be the result of the application and subsequent relaxation of the military government's policies to return public-sector firms to profitability.

IV. CONCLUSIONS

The performance of public enterprises in Argentina and Brazil reported here suggests some general lessons that may be learned by examining various measures of public-enterprise activity across industries and countries. While not definitive, the conclusions presented here from the data make clear the need for additional research in this area. Further analysis will undoubtedly be required to clarify the many remaining ambiguities and identify the factors that promote public-enterprise excellence.

At first glance, SOEs, like their counterparts in the private sector, appear to "do better" in a growing economic environment. While not surprising, this conclusion has important implications for policymakers who wish to use SOEs as instruments of macroeconomic policy. In the mixed-economy setting of Argentina and Brazil, it is not apparent that strong SOE growth in isolation could spur economywide expansion. On the contrary, there are some indications that, in periods of slow economic growth, SOEs will accumulate deficits. Unless these deficits can be financed within the firm, the drain on the public coffers may worsen general macroeconomic conditions.

At the same time, a consistent policy towards SOEs does appear to engender better performance. Brazilian SOEs operated under a fairly constant set of policy objectives from 1964 until 1979. In Argentina, the average length of a "policy period" was close to three years, and successive policies varied widely. Under one administration, SOEs would be the preferred policy tool for managing employment problems; in another, they would be an anathema to be "rationalized" or sold. If the Brazilian experience can be generalized, SOEs can apparently both function efficiently and play a significant role in a long-term development strategy.

While Brazilian SOEs' performance is generally superior to that of the Argentine SOEs, it is not clear whether the superior performance is attributable to the prevailing economic climate, the policy environment, some combination of the two (either concurrently or sequentially), or something else entirely. Additional analysis of the data is required, but SOE performance in Argentina appears to have varied more closely with the changing policy environments than with the generally long-term economic stagnation. Policy might thus dominate economic conditions, and the superior results in Brazil may be more strongly associated with the consistency and longevity of Brazilian policy than with general economic conditions. If so, then perhaps SOEs can, in fact, be a leading sector when they are part of a consistent and durable policy to promote economic growth. Although only further investigation will establish if this argument has validity, the idea is an encouraging one for the usefulness of SOEs as instruments of development policy in less-developed countries.

Another lesson that can be derived from the experience of these countries' SOEs involves price controls and inflation—two common phenomena in developing economies. In the Argentine case, the prices of SOE outputs lagged the prevailing rate of inflation. The lag was apparently intentional at first, an attempt to signal to the population the government's lower expected rate of inflation and thus dampen the rise in public expectations. This policy was unsuccessful. Not only did the public soon learn to double or triple the utility rate increase to get a more accurate indication of expected inflation, but SOE prices lost ground they would never be able to regain. After a year at very high rates of inflation (in excess of 100 percent), the rate increase that would have been required to bring the prices in line with operating costs was politically unacceptable. Revenues failed to cover costs, and the data available indicate that subsidies from the Treasury were insufficient. Although the difference was likely covered by increasing debt, the reputation of the firms (and, one supposes, the morale of the managers as well) was damaged.

In Brazil, indexation of almost all prices in the economy became widespread in the 1970s. While there has been some debate in Brazil as to how fairly the indices were calculated, the Trebat data suggest that indexing must have come close to providing full compensation for the goods and services considered in this sample of public enterprises.

The lesson here seems to be that the use of SOE prices as a tool to fight inflation should be avoided. If government officials insist on using SOE prices as an anti-inflation device, the SOEs should be explicitly compensated for revenue losses derived from government-decreed pricing policies. Perhaps some application of the French Contract system would be appropriate in this context.

A final explanation of the difference in SOE performance between the two countries could be the quality of SOE management. In a study of the state-owned electric energy sector in Brazil, Tendler found that highly qualified managerial talent was attracted to the state sector because of (1) the technical nature of the work and the professional challenge that large projects provided and (2) the perceived distance that existed between SOEs and the central government. Managers in this industry believed that the combination of the technical aspects of electricity generation and the organization of firms outside the central government structure allowed them to pursue professional objectives. No data are available on SOE managers in Argentina, but one wonders if the same would hold true. Given the constantly changing political environment there, and the wide swings in public-enterprise policy that resulted, it is difficult to imagine that good managerial talent could be attracted and kept in the public sector. If the sector does attract less technically qualified and more politically motivated managers, this factor could be expected to contribute to poor performance. More research on the motivation and behavior of public-enterprise managers would help clarify this issue.

Finally, the data presented here do not substantiate the idea that SOEs are necessarily inefficient and unprofitable. On the contrary, the data from Brazil suggest that SOEs can be operated efficiently and at a level of profitability that exceeds, in most cases, the opportunity cost of capital. The Argentine data suggest that a poorly designed or frequently changing policy toward SOEs is associated with poor SOE performance. Interestingly, something similar is true of private firms. In a difficult economic environment, firms operating without good strategic planning will, in general, perform poorly. Some evidence shows that many privately owned firms in Argentina did in fact perform poorly in the late 1970s and early 1980s.

Thus, if the reduction of public-sector deficits is the issue, the appropriate question is not the ownership of SOE assets but the management of those assets as part of managing the economy as a whole. Improved SOE performance might serve better as the focus of U.S. policy in the region than the Baker Plan rhetoric of deregulation and privatization. On the basis of the Brazilian experience described here, well-managed SOEs could play an important role in a development strategy that emphasized rapid economic growth. U.S. policy, then, should focus on public asset management as part of an overall regional policy of returning Latin America to economic growth, democratic government, and full participation in international systems of trade and governance.

6

United States Policies and the Labor Sector in Latin America

Russell E. Smith

The performance of labor markets and labor relations systems is central to the process of political and economic development in any society. This chapter discusses policies and programs of the U.S. government that, intentionally or unintentionally, either promote or retard positive outcomes in the labor sector in Latin America.[1] These policies include those that are specifically identified as being related to "labor," including the American Institute for Free Labor Development (AIFLD), the labor attaché program, the internationally recognized worker rights clauses in the United States' trade and foreign investment legislation, and United States' participation in the International Labor Organization (ILO).[2] "Indirect" policies, which are those actions and policies of the United States that indirectly affect the labor sector through the economic performance and the political environment of labor relations, today including policies toward Latin America's external debt and toward political democratization and human rights, are also considered.

Underlying this chapter are three assumptions. The first is that with its complex economic and political ties within the hemisphere, the United States has the de facto equivalent of a policy toward the labor sector in Latin America and that it makes numerous decisions that affect it. The second assumption is that the United States has a national interest in the labor sector in Latin America, at a minimum in the form of having stable, human-rights-respecting democracies as neighbors in the region or in reducing the economic "push" factors behind immigration into United States. The third assumption is that economic and social progress in the last thirty to forty years has made Latin America economically stronger relative to the United States than it was in the past, in spite of the debt crisis.[3] On the political side, Latin Americans have become very sophisticated as a result of the wide swings from left to right and between civilian and military regimes. As a result, the Latin American nations are much more capable of independent action and firm negotiation on a variety of issues. Our discussion will consider broad themes affecting the region rather than providing specific country examples, in part because of the difficulty in doing justice to the diversity which is Latin America.

I. ECONOMICS, POLITICS, AND LABOR IN LATIN AMERICA

The economic and political context within which Latin American labor markets operate has become increasingly complex in the past several decades. In this section we review the major trends which have affected labor in Latin America.

Economic Context: Growth and Adjustment

Latin America has grown in both demographic and economic size relative to the United States. Roughly equal in population in 1960, by 1980 Latin America was about 65 percent larger than the United States. The economies of the two regions grew at about the same rate in the 1950s, while between 1960 and 1980, Latin America grew at roughly twice the rate of the United States. There was in addition a major shift of the population from rural to urban areas, with the share of employment in agriculture falling from fifty percent to around thirty percent, as output and employment in industry grew rapidly.[4]

Growth between 1950 and 1980 took place under a variety of economic policy regimes and under both civilian and military governments. There was substantial reliance on import-substitution industrialization in the early years, later followed by export promotion, frequently of manufactured goods. Both multinational corporations and state firms in domestic economies contributed significantly to the overall successful performance of the period.[5]

From the first oil-shock price increase in 1973 until around 1980 the Latin American countries made heavy use of borrowings of recycled petrodollars to maintain economic growth. Private commercial banks were only too happy to lend, creating the stock of external debt that now hangs over the world financial system.

The output of the Latin American economies declined between 1980 and 1983 under the impact of the second oil shock of 1979, the sharp rise in world interest rates resulting from U.S. monetary and fiscal policies, and the resulting world recession. Despite the recovery of the United States and world economies since 1983, Latin America has stagnated under the weight of the accumulated external debt from the 1970s. External payments difficulties have been aggravated by falling export prices, which have limited foreign exchange earnings gains. Output has not kept up with population growth. The focus on production for export to service the external debt has restricted both internal consumption and investment in productive capacity, with consequent damage to the region's ability to keep up technologically and to produce and compete internationally in the future. The structural adjustment and export-promotion strategy, in spite of its internal human costs, moreover, has not even succeeded as a strategy for servicing the external debt.[6] The banks have had to accept continued rollovers and write-downs of the debt.

Political Context: Authoritarianism versus Democracy

Although most Latin American countries now have civilian constitutional governments, there is no reason to believe that this is a permanent situation. Even under civilian rule, democracy may be only relative, as civilian presidents were often heavy-handed representatives of the oligarchy in systems of limited suffrage, or populist demagogues, either of whom may rule with substantial discretionary power. Similarly, military regimes were often populist and nationalist with significant popular and labor support, as well as bureaucratic-authoritarian or personalistic.[7]

From the mid 1960s to the mid 1970s, beginning in Brazil in 1964 and ending in Argentina in 1976, under the pressures both of legal and extralegal popular demands and of leftist insurgencies, the political pendulum swung almost uniformly to dictatorship across the region. With the continuing basic economic problems of the region, the end of the easy petrodollar credit at the end of the 1970s, and pressures initiated by the Carter administration and continued by the Reagan administration, the military has stepped down in most Latin American countries, despite its retention of substantial control within the framework of elected civilian presidents in several countries.

At present, most Latin American countries have elected or are in the process of electing the successors to the first civilian constitutional presidents in the present cycle. The risk of military takeovers remains. Like the military, civilian rule can be discredited on performance grounds; civilian governments have not been notably successful in resolving the growth, employment, and investment problems. By and large they have balanced the claims of their own citizenry with those of their foreign creditors in a way that neither satisfies the bankers nor allows the basic prerequisites of the countries' future well-being to be met. The political result will be loudly contested elections, with potentially wide shifts toward populist approaches, if not toward left-wing nationalism, and to neoliberalism as well. With no solution to the fundamental problems in sight it becomes possible that crises of government might be resolved temporarily by military interventions.

Labor Markets over Time

Along with the economic transformation of Latin America, there has been a transformation in the labor market.[8] Rapid population growth has led in turn to a rapidly growing labor force with increasing participation rates for women. With the expansion of the primary school system, the labor force has experienced rising educational attainment. A decline in the rate of increase in the labor force is likely in the future, however, as the birth rate declines, permitting a shift in educational priorities toward quality, rather than quantity.

In the same period, agricultural employment has stabilized and there has been a relative shift of employment out of agricultural rural areas and into urban areas. Although industrial employment showed strong growth until 1980, industry was not able to fully absorb the influx and employment has increased in the traditional and modern service sectors, and in the informal sector. The result has been an overall occupational pattern that is dominated by modern manufacturing and modern services, with a substantial traditional service and informal sector in the same urban areas. Although the mix varies from country to country, the general result is the same throughout the region: a modern goods-producing and services-providing economic base alongside an informal sector of small-scale and precarious productive units.

The 1981–83 economic crisis and the stagnation since then have had serious implications for labor markets by exacerbating the unemployment and underemployment.[9] In the 1981–83 crisis, open unemployment rose, with longer duration and incidence, with more underemployment and growth of the informal sector. In the recovery starting in 1983, output growth in formal-sector manufacturing came mostly from productivity gains rather than from new hires. Manufacturing employment in 1986 was still 10 percent less than that of 1980. As a result, the unemployment rate did not fall, the number of discouraged workers increased, and employment in small enterprises in the informal sector grew dramatically. In some countries in the worst days of the crises, employment in the public sector played a clearly countercyclical role. In labor markets, declines in output per capita have been exceeded by declines in average real wages and real wages of the lowest skilled industrial workers. With output declines of 8 or 9 percent per capita, for example, real wages declined in the formal sector as much as 40 percent from 1981 to 1983 or 1984, depending on the occupational grouping and country, with per capita income declines in the informal sector even greater. Combined with massive capital flight, this pattern indicates a significant worsening of the income distribution, as the real losses have been borne most heavily by the economically weakest members of Latin American society.[10]

Labor Relations and Collective Bargaining

Along with the economic, political, and labor-market changes, Latin America has experienced changes in its labor relations system. Traditionally, labor organizations in Latin America have been limited in their coverage, although there are substantial differences in the pattern among and within countries.[11] Unions were initially found only in urban or modern-sector activities outside of agriculture in societies that were traditional and almost feudal in their class relationships. Unions were most likely to exist in transportation and urban services, government and white-collar occupations, and later in manufacturing.

The formal labor relations systems that grew up were centralized, with a major role for government in recognizing unions, regulating their activities, and resolving disputes. In practice, collective bargaining was limited to the larger workplaces, and workers and labor organizations tended to rely on detailed labor codes to establish minimum standards and to govern workplace conditions. The right to strike was closely regulated; mediation and arbitration were often mandatory. The system was heavily politicized in that unions were frequently extensions of political parties with ideological bases which were more interested in politics than in workplace issues. General strikes of a political nature were common. What limited collective bargaining existed at the level of the establishment was frequently characterized by ideological polemic and name-calling.[12]

The long-run trend in labor relations in Latin America is away from the state-run, tripartite labor relations system and toward a more voluntary system of collective bargaining where workers and employer take more responsibility at the establishment level. Several forces have contributed to this process. Urbanization, modernization, and industrialization have created large and complex productive units that cannot be effectively managed by relying on the guidance of underfunded state agencies and legalistic external procedures. In some cases, military takeovers have effectively decapitated the political aspects of the labor movement, thus forcing workers to look for solutions to workplace problems closer to home. The survival of democratically run local unions may in fact provide the basis for the resurgence of union activity when the repression is lifted.[13] Finally, the workers themselves have changed. They are now more educated and more likely to be urban in origin and members of a working-class rather than recent rural migrants. In addition, union leaders and members are much more likely to have benefited from labor education leadership programs.[14]

With the return to democracy in the 1980s, workers and the labor movement are much better prepared and organized to negotiate directly and collectively with their employers. They are also able to put pressure on the formal structures of the old state-centered labor relations system at the workplace level, on the older generation of labor leaders, and on the national political leadership. This more independent and politically aware working class, regardless of ideology, can find its political expression through explicit links to political parties as well as in the workplace or through lobbies. Although explicit linkage to a political party is an idea that is rather alien in the United States, it is the norm in the democracies of Europe.[15]

II. INDIRECT AND DIRECT UNITED STATES LABOR POLICIES

United States policies which affect labor in Latin America may be divided into those general policies which have an indirect effect, and those which are specifically aimed at Latin American labor. Among the former are United States macroeconomic and trade policies. Direct labor policies include those which function through the AFL-CIO's International Affairs Department, and the programs of the U.S. labor attachés in the major embassies.

Indirect Policies

The most important economic policy affecting the labor sector in Latin America is the state of the U.S. economy itself and its rate of growth, which, in turn, affects activity in Latin America through U.S. demand for imports. The U.S. economy, of course, depends on fiscal and monetary policies, interest rates, trade policies and a low exchange rate value of the dollar to promote U.S. exports and protect import-competing industries. Since Latin American currencies are generally pegged to the dollar, a lower dollar helps Latin American exports to third markets without necessarily hurting them in the United States. Independent of economic conditions, the degree of protectionism affects the access of Latin American goods to the United States. Exports affect the labor sector in Latin America through the jobs created by export industries and jobs lost through structural adjustment.

In the financial area, U.S. policies on Latin American debt administered through domestic bank regulation and through economic stabilization and reform programs sponsored by the international organizations like the International Monetary Fund (IMF) and the World Bank, where it is the dominant member, can pressure the Latin American debtors to cede more of their scarce foreign exchange to their international creditor banks than they otherwise would do, in effect exporting capital. The result is the allocation of production away from the optimal mix of domestic consumption and investment in future job-creating productive capacity.[16]

In addition to its negative impact on the labor sector in Latin America, the debt crisis has an adverse impact on the labor sector in the United States. When Latin America is not importing capital goods and food, the United States loses its traditional markets and jobs in the United States. To the extent that Latin America exports to the United States, then U.S. import-competing industries suffer. The labor sector in neither country is better off and only the creditors gain—and that gain may only be in the short run.[17] In all these contacts between countries, there exists the possibility of differing intensities in the willingness to cooperate with a government, various levels of recognition and the associated prestige implied, and the speed with which matters are processed. For example, the United States can award prestige to a new government through its prompt recognition of a new regime, or withhold cooperation on other, seemingly unrelated, bilateral issues, including military aid. Apart from the direct labor policies discussed below, issues relevant to the labor sector include the support of basic political rights that guarantee the open and free environment that workers need to exercise their rights as citizens and that a democratic labor movement needs to function. Support of representative government, free speech, freedom of association and other internationally recognized worker rights, and human rights can be shown by the relative prestige given to democratic versus authoritarian governments. If authoritarian rulers are given full honors as allies and friends, then it is a step backward for a democratic labor relations system and for labor rights.

Direct Labor Policies

Probably the most visible direct United States labor policy is the program of the American Institute for Free Labor Development (AIFLD), a component of the International Affairs Department of the American Federation of Labor and Congress of Industrial Organizations (AFL-CIO) and the AFL-CIO's representative arm in Latin America.[18] The AIFLD program has two main thrusts. The first is labor education for union leaders. Labor education courses provide training to union leaders and organizers on the theory and practice of union management, as well as history, social science, and basic skills where appropriate. Social development and rural development projects are the second thrust of AIFLD programs in Latin America. These projects are designed to provide services and to support and strengthen union organizing activities. Social projects included housing projects in the 1960s and the first half of the 1970s, for a total of 18,048 units, financed with capital from U.S. pension funds, the AFL-CIO Impact Projects program, and the Regional Revolving Loan Fund, financed by the Agency for International Development (AID). The latter two are revolving loan funds available to Latin American unions for small- and medium-sized social projects of up to $50,000. AIFLD's Agrarian Union Development Service has been active in support of peasant organizations in El Salvador and Honduras. As part of the AFL-CIO's own foreign policy apparatus, AIFLD maintains offices and country program directors in most Latin America countries. In addition to maintaining fraternal relations with the anticommunist or noncommunist labor centers (confederations), generally affiliated with the International Confederation of Free Trade Unions (ICFTU), AIFLD provides financial support for the labor education institutes run by those centers and for training by individual unions. About 20,000 students per year participated during the 1960s and 1970s, and about 30,000 per year in the 1980s. Small groups of about twenty students receive advanced training in the Washington, D.C. area. There is also a "union-to-union" program where various U.S. unions, often through the international trade secretariats, assist the Latin American unions in their own industries.[19] AIFLD was founded in the early 1960s as a continuation of labor education efforts of the Organizacion Regional Interamericana del Trabajo (ORIT) and the international trade secretariats in building "free" trade unions, defined as democratic and anticommunist. In the context of the Cold War and the Cuban Revolution, and until the swing to the right in the region was completed in 1976, the urgency of the anticommunist impulse should not be discounted. In the 1970s, the political focus shifted to maintaining the existence of labor organizations in the face of the right-wing military dictatorships that dominated the region. More recently, with the emergence of democratic political systems, AIFLD training increasingly has included political as well as technical skills. Largely funded by the AID, AIFLD was originally a part of the Alliance for Progress. As a development program directed toward organized labor and grassroots groups, AIFLD is a private voluntary organization whose goal is to avoid the distributional inequities of trickle-down approaches to development. In 1987, AIFLD's income was a little under $15 million. Of that, over $13 million came from AID, with $9 million in the form of the general grant, $2.5 million for cooperatives in El Salvador, and $1.5 million for operational program grants (OPGs) or other program in seven Central American or Caribbean countries. AIFLD received another $1.33 million from the National Endowment for Democracy and $230,000 from the AFL-CIO.[20]

AIFLD programs have been politically controversial when associated with other U.S. political initiatives, most recently in Central America and the Caribbean. At a minimum, the controversy resulted from AIFLD's firmly centrist democratic program directed at a hotly contested working class in a region where the political spectrum breaks down into right, center, and left, and where elements of all three have been willing to accept anti-democratic solutions. It was inevitable that a foreign organization in such a conflict-ridden environment would be controversial. The problem was complicated, however, by AIFLD's militant, procapitalist anticommunism in an environment where there could be legitimate democratic and nationalist workers' organizations that are socialist and still independent from Moscow. It is important not to escalate legitimate competition for the right to represent workers in the political and economic arena into an issue of the Cold War, rhetoric of the various groups notwithstanding.[21]

Finally, some of the controversy has centered on alleged AIFLD links to the U.S. intelligence community, specifically to the Central Intelligence Agency (CIA).[22] Informal contacts at several levels may in fact have occurred, for reasons which are not particularly sinister. First of all, both programs were funded by the same government, worked out of the same embassies, and, in the context of the Cold War and the aftermath of McCarthyism, believed they shared the same Communist enemy. Such informal contacts would seem natural at the height of the Cold War conflict until the mid 1970s. At that time, it became apparent that the certain "cure" of a right-wing military dictatorship might turn out to be worse than the not-so-certain dictatorial left-wing disease. National sensitivities in these matters, moreover, became more acute.[23]

Another direct labor policy is the system of labor attachés and labor reporting officers within the Foreign Service. The labor attaché system is under the control of the State Department, but with some input from the Labor Department in the appointment and selection processes. Labor attachés are political officers within an embassy's political section in larger embassies and spend from ten to fifty percent or more of their time on their duties as labor attachés, depending on their overall assignment from their ambassador. In posts without a labor attaché, minimum labor reporting duties are typically performed by a junior political officer.

Labor attachés have a reporting and representational function and make reports on the labor situation, including human rights and worker rights violations, and labor events as they occur. The work involves direct contact with organized labor and government agencies. After review by the regional labor advisors in the departments of State and Labor, the reports become part of the State Department's annual human rights report and also the new Country Reports on Economic Policy and Trade Practices.[24] The information is used by the Labor Department in its role as lead review agency and technical advisor in the worker rights area, including on the interagency committee that reviews Generalized System of Preferences (GSP) eligibility in terms of worker rights issues. Labor attachés may organize informational and training programs and events in conjunction with the United States Information Service (USIS).

Complaints about the low status of labor attachés within the Foreign Service are common. There are few "real" labor attachés, defined as persons who make a career of holding labor attaché positions, particularly at a senior level. Foreign service officers tend to hold the position once, to broaden their experience, although the position may not be seen as a good stepping stone to advancement within the foreign service. There has been some suggestion that the low status of the labor attaché within the United States diplomatic corps has restricted potential contacts with government officials at the upper levels.[25]

An emerging area in United States policies affecting the labor sector in developing countries are the recent, and as yet little-known, labor-rights provisions in U.S. trade and foreign investment legislation. Worker rights clauses link access to the U.S. market with respect for internationally recognized worker rights in a sort of worker rights conditionality. The idea is that if violations of worker rights are the norm, certain trade privileges can be revoked, or sanctions can be applied.[26]

Under current law, trade privileges include access to the United States market since 1983 under the Caribbean Basin Initiative (CBI), since 1984 under the Generalized System of Preferences (GSP), and insurance protection for United States foreign investment under the Overseas Private Investment Corporation (OPIC) since 1985. Sanctions, in contrast to withholding privileges, at present consist of the provision to treat the systematic denial of worker rights as an unreasonable and unfair trade practice under Section 301 of United States trade law since 1988. The 1988 Trade Act also established worker rights as a negotiating objective of the United States in the General Agreement on Tariffs and Trade (GATT), including promotion of respect for worker rights, a review of the relationship of worker rights and existing GATT articles, and adoption, as a principle of GATT, of the position that denial of worker rights should not be a means to gain competitive advantage in international trade.[27]

Internationally recognized worker rights are defined in U.S. law to include: freedom of association; the right to organize and bargain collectively; prohibition of any form of forced or compulsory labor; the establishment of a minimum age for the employment of children; and acceptable conditions of work with respect to minimum wages, hours of work, and occupational safety and health. These worker rights run parallel to conventions adopted by the International Labor Organization and most of its member states. The ILO conventions are not specifically cited in United States law.

The 1988 Trade Act also includes two measures that should improve the quantity and quality of information available to the United States Government on worker rights. One measure requires the government to report annually to the Congress on worker rights in countries with which the United States has an economic or trade relationship as one of eight parts of the Country Reports on Economic Policy and Trade Practices mentioned above. The other measure requires the Secretary of State to conduct an in-depth study as part of the annual reports submitted to Congress on the status of internationally recognized worker rights in foreign countries and to make recommendations about the capacity of the United States Government to report on other countries' respect for such rights.[28]

Although the worker rights program is a program of the Department of State and of the United States Trade Representative, the Department of Labor has specific responsibilities. These responsibilities include review of the worker rights section of the Department of State Human Rights report. In the specific programs, it is the lead agency in the interagency review of worker rights petitions filed under GSP and OPIC. In addition, Congress requires a biannual report on worker rights in Economic Processing Zones (EPZ), or Free Trade Zones, provided they are for export.

The intent of the worker-rights policy initiative is to promote the sharing of the benefits of international trade with workers, in addition to owners and consumers, by limiting access to the U.S. market when the preconditions of such sharing, such as the right to bargain collectively, are not present. The apparent aim of the provision is to provide workers with a better chance to benefit from international trade through the bargaining process and minimum standards set through legislation. This is not an attempt to cancel out the "natural comparative advantage" of developing countries in the areas of lower labor costs, since the standards set are to be appropriate to the level of development of each country. To be certified, countries have to be making progress rather than be at any particular international standard. The standards of freedom of association and collective bargaining are procedural and only require that workers be able to organize and bargain freely, and not necessarily that they achieve all of their bargaining objectives or wages and standards comparable to the United States and Western Europe.

At present, the worker rights provision most in the public eye is that connected with beneficiary status under the GSP program which grants special tariff treatment to many goods from many developing countries subject to a variety of conditions. The GSP program is administered by the GSP Subcommittee of the Interagency Trade Policy Committee chaired by the Office of the U.S. Trade Representative. Interested parties can submit petitions each year by June 1, asking that GSP status be denied to a specific product or country for a variety of reasons, including failure to respect internationally recognized worker rights. Nicaragua, Paraguay, Romania, and Chile have had GSP privileges removed or restricted for worker rights reasons.

The petition process is relatively simple and requires the petitioner to present specific, though not necessarily lengthy, evidence that internationally recognized worker rights are being violated in the country in question. Petitions are often filed by the AFL-CIO and by the human rights community. In spite of the relatively low threshhold for a complaint to be accepted for review by the GSP Subcommittee, petitions are not often accepted, possibly because of a failure to separate worker rights from human rights issues or because the Office of the United States Trade Representative has not applied the worker rights portion of the trade law vigorously.

An important direct labor policy is the intensity, or lack of intensity, of U.S. support for the International Labor Organization (ILO). The ILO is a United Nations–related specialized agency, of which the United States is a highly visible member and in principle the largest financial contributor. The ILO's mandate is to concern itself with labor and social justice issues. ILO programs include an annual meeting of tripartite delegations from member countries made up of government, labor, and employer representatives to discuss labor and employment issues. There is a system of international labor standards conventions on industrial relations and working conditions which have been adopted by a meeting of the ILO and which can be adopted by member countries, after which time they theoretically have the force of law in the adopting country. To support the conventions, there is a technical assistance program to help countries comply with the conventions and a review process to determine whether or not a country is complying in case of a complaint. In the development area, the ILO established the World Employment Programme in 1969 to promote growth and development from the point of view of labor market issues. In support of all areas of ILO activity, there is a substantial research program.[29]

The history of U.S. participation in the ILO has been problematic. The United States has frequently not adopted ILO conventions, both because the issues covered were state issues and because of a general reluctance to do things that might be perceived as giving up sovereignty. The United States has been in conflict over the participation of Eastern-bloc employer and labor representatives, which, it has claimed, are not independent of the government, and the participation of the Palestine Liberation Organization. Under the Reagan administration, the United States was greatly in arrears in its payment of dues (as it was in other United Nations agencies), which greatly hampered the work of the ILO.

III. THE POTENTIAL CONTRIBUTION OF U.S. POLICY

There are a variety of ways in which U.S. policies can contribute to the well-being of the labor sector in Latin America. In the economic area, these actions involve the management of the U.S. economy in ways which further growth, investment, and employment in Latin America. In the political area, this means the encouragement of constitutional regimes, democratic participation, and human rights, including for workers and labor organizations. In the labor area, this means maintenance or active support for specific programs that promote worker rights, collective bargaining, workplace protections, human capital development, and greater understanding of Latin American labor issues in the United States and awareness in Latin America of the importance of labor issues to the United States.

As Latin America's most important trade and investment partner, there are numerous ways in which U.S. economic policies affect Latin American economic welfare in general and that of laborers in particular. At the end of a decade of slow growth or even stagnation, there is little question that major real external debt relief would be a central contribution, since it would ease the external constraint and free foreign exchange for necessary imports and domestic investment.

Macroeconomic policies in the United States itself have profound effects on Latin America. The rise in real interest rates in the United States between the 1970s and the 1980s is one of the major causes of Latin America's external payments problems; Latin America was in effect "crowded out" of world credit markets by the combination of expansionary U.S. fiscal policy and restrictive monetary policy.

On a bilateral level, protectionism in the United States, particularly against rising imports of manufactures, has increased in the past decade. In addition to its negative effects on U.S. consumers, protectionism increases the burden of external adjustment faced by the Latin American economies. At the multilateral level, it is in U.S. interests, as well as those of Latin America, that multilateral organizations like the International Monetary Fund, World Bank, and Inter-American Development Bank renew their primary commitment to economic development and act first and foremost as development agencies and suppliers of capital and not primarily as agencies or allies of the private lenders.

There are a number of potential political contributions to be made by the United States. A decade or more of experience has shown us that the generals are no better managers of economies than civilians; in addition, they cannot be held accountable to their citizens. U.S. support for authoritarian and nondemocratic solutions to Latin America's dilemma creates more problems in the long run than it solves. In this context, U.S. support for human rights can have a strong positive impact on Latin American labor. Because of the relatively humble position of workers and labor organizations in Latin American society, they are more likely to be subjected to human rights abuses while lacking the legal resources to oppose them.

U.S. policies that directly affect labor in Latin America also offer possibilities for constructive contributions. Support for the International Labor Organization would include the prompt payment of dues, ratification of ILO labor standards conventions, and political and financial support for ILO development and training programs such as the World Employment Program and the specialized training missions.

The linking of trade to internationally recognized worker rights is another way in which the United States can help Latin American labor. This would include: active pursuit of worker rights as a negotiating objective in the GATT in accord with the 1988 Trade Act; making worker rights a priority agenda item of the U.S. Trade Representative in its bilateral negotiations with U.S. trading partners as well as in the GSP review process; vigorous implementation of the worker rights provisions in existing U.S. trade and foreign investment law, as well as strengthening and extending the legislation; and developing the information base and capability to evaluate and monitor the worker rights situation in the trading partner countries.

Although extensive use of sanctions would be counterproductive and inefficient, it is important to signal to trading partners that worker rights are important to the United States. Willingness to impose trade sanctions in the case of a substantially worsened worker rights situation in the aftermath of a military takeover or the reestablishment of an authoritarian regime would both further the cause of democracy and of free collective bargaining and labor relations systems.

At an institutional level, a strengthening of the labor attaché program of the Department of State in both prestige and resources would be a positive step. This could include incentives for foreign service officers to make a career of being a labor attaché and more extensive in-service training for labor attachés. A stronger labor attaché program would prove especially useful in signaling a commitment to democracy in Latin America by listening to a broader range of groups in Latin American society.

Another positive step would be continued support of the AFL-CIO's AIFLD program while broadening bilateral labor programs with other program initiatives to include participation by a wider spectrum of U.S. labor professionals, including academics, labor educators, and others not associated with the AFL-CIO staff. Examples would include programs using other labor educators such as those working in labor extension programs at state universities in the United States; direct support to individual union initiatives, or exchanges, through the United States Information Service.

IV. CONCLUSION

This chapter has examined both positive and negative aspects of development in the labor sector in Latin America and in U.S. policies which affect labor in the region. On the positive side is the shift in activity toward the urban formal sector, and human capital development. On the negative side are the economic stagnation of the 1980s, and the relative shift of employment toward the informal sectors and the decline in wages and incomes. Our overall assessment is cautiously optimistic, both in the context of the challenge of redemocratization and the increased decentralization and grassroots nature of the industrial relations system, as well as the increased sophistication of the actors in all areas. There are numerous ways that policies and practices of the U.S. government might affect the functioning of labor markets and labor relations systems in Latin America. Although these are primarily domestic issues within Latin America, the United States can assist Latin America in meeting the challenge it faces in its labor sector.

The support for a democratic decisionmaking process to shape Latin America's future is fundamental. This is not only a political position, but one with far-reaching economic consequences, since there are economic preconditions for a stable democratic political process.

U.S. policies that directly support the labor sector in Latin America are an important component of our support for the democratic process. Although these potential policies are presented as measures which might be adopted, the United States may in fact have little choice in the long run. In spite of current difficulties, Latin America is progressing politically to a point the United States will have to recognize sooner or later. It is to the long-run advantage of the United States to go with the flow and to encourage the process of development, democratization, and worker rights. The security of the United States is enhanced if its closest neighbors, which share histories and political values close to its own, are prosperous and developing economically. The United States should not want to go down in history as having consistently blocked, through a continuing policy of short-run expediency, the realization of its own values in its sister republics.

NOTES

1. The term "labor sector" used here is meant to include all those who work for a living as employees, or as small scale self-employed. It therefore would include the popular sector as a whole and the informal sector as well as unionized and nonunionized formal-sector workers.

2. Concern for the impact of U.S. policy on the labor sector, broadly defined, and especially on worker rights, has a parallel on the human rights area. For a discussion of the complexity of the policy apparatus, including both the executive and legislative branches, and points of leverage (and lack thereof) of the United States relative to Latin America in the context of human rights policy in the 1970s, see Schoultz (1981).

3. Latin America's progress and maturation in the postwar period are presented in great detail by Lowenthal (1987). He argues that Latin America has developed enough socially and politically to successfully implement a program of democratic reform such as that of the Alliance for Progress (Lowenthal, 1987; p. 24).

4. For more detailed discussions of the period, see Lowenthal (1987; pp. 8–14) and Banco Interamericano de Desarrollo (1987; pp. 81–85).

5. The roles both of multinational enterprises and state enterprises have been the subjects of much controversy in Latin America. One of the ironies of the debate on state firms and structural adjustment, and the frequent call for privatization as a solution, is that Brazil, the major debtor that has most successfully reoriented itself toward an export strategy, was able to do so because of a major public-sector investment program in the 1970s in which state firms played major roles. See, in this regard, Castro e Souza (1985).

6. The deliberations of the International Labour Organisation on the human costs of stabilization and structural adjustment are reported in ILO (1988).

7. For discussion of patterns of Latin American politics and relations with the United States, including U.S. support for military takeovers in the 1970s, see Gaspar (1978).

8. For a discussion of the long-run evolution of labor markets in Latin America, see BID (1987).

9. BID (1987), PREALC (1987), A. Marshall (1987).

10. For more detailed discussion of wage and income performance, see World Bank (1986) and PREALC (1987).

11. In spite of the most general characterizations given here, the labor movements and industrial relations systems in Latin America are very diverse and have rich histories. For a current and comprehensive standard reference on labor relations and on the labor movements in the Latin American countries, see Greenfield and Maram (1987).

12. The basic literature on labor relations, society, and politics in Latin America in the 1950s and 1960s includes Alexander (1965), Form and Blum (1965), and Alba (1968).

13. For this argument, see Freedom House (1982; p. 99).

14. Many of these programs have been sponsored by institutes organized by the national labor movements with the encouragement of various international organizations. For a discussion of the role of labor education in forming leadership in Latin American labor movements, see Robert J. Alexander, "The Latin American Labor Leader," in Form and Blum (1965; pp. 77–78) and AIFLD (1987).

15. For discussions of the future of industrial relations in Latin America in the areas of unions, management, employment security, and the role of the state, see Relations Industrielles (1989).

16. Programs that give singular priority to servicing the external debt, or to structural adjustment such as the privatization of state firms can have serious consequences for the well-being of the labor sector. With regard to the labor sector difficulties that can result from an IMF-sponsored stabilization program, see Schechter (1985). For the labor implications of privatization, see Accolla (1989).

17. Marshall (1988; pp. 181–186) reports that United States exports to Latin America fell 26 percent between 1981 and 1986 and that most of job losses linked to trade with developing countries have been due to lost exports. A total of 650,000 jobs were lost due to lost exports to the Third World and another 1.1 million were lost because of the failure of trade to grow in the 1980s, with a third of the total, 600,000, attributable to lost exports to Argentina, Brazil, Mexico, and Venezuela.

18. This discussion is drawn in part from Schoultz (1981; pp. 333–340), who presents a thorough, scholarly, and somewhat critical treatment of AIFLD, including

budget figures and a review of the various controversies, and from AIFLD's own dec-ade-by-decade account of itself in AIFLD (1987). See, also, Doherty (1988).

19. An international trade secretariat (ITS) is an industry-based international con-federation of national unions. For further information, see Bendiner (1987) and Wind-muller (1969).

20. Budget figures are from AFL-CIO (1987, No. 182), which has similar figures for AIFLD's sister institutes, the African-American Labor Center (AALC), founded in 1964, with a total income of about $5.5 million, the Asian-American Free Labor In-stitute (AAFLI), founded in 1968, with a total income of about $6.3 million, and the Free Trade Union Institute (FTUI), founded in 1977 and working mostly in Europe, with a total income of around $1.6 million, none of which appears to come from AID.

21. For a detailed and generally critical literature that links AIFLD to some of the more controversial anticommunist or counter-revolutionary aspects of United States foreign policy, see Cantor and Schor (1987), Kwitny (1986), NACLA (1988), and Weinrub and Bollinger (1987). For discussions of the labor history of the earlier years with a somewhat more conservative flavor, see Alba (1968) and Alexander (1965). For a defense of corporate contributions to AIFLD in the early years, and of business lead-ers on the board of directors, see Godson (1982).

22. These allegations have been made most explicitly in Agee (1975).

23. For a discussion of the context of the Cold War and McCarthyism, see Alexander and Hammond (1975; pp. 39–41) and of informal contact in the field, see Schoultz (1981; p. 340).

24. For the first issue of the Country Reports on Economic Policy and Trade Prac-tices, see U.S. Congress (1989).

25. Some of these issues are not new. Concern about the low status of labor attachés and the deterioration of the State Department's labor function in Latin America was voiced in 1975 by Alexander and Hammond (1975; pp. 67–71).

26. For a discussion of the history and rationale of the recent effort to link worker rights to trade, see Cavanagh, et al. (1988). For a discussion of earlier efforts in Europe and the United States, and for a rationale for why worker rights clauses properly go in trade agreements under the purview of the General Agreement on Tariffs and Trade (GATT) and not exclusively under the ILO, see Charnovitz (1987).

27. Public Law 100-418, Sec. 1101(b)(14), August 23, 1988.

28. Public Law 100-418, Sec. 2207, August 23, 1988.

29. For a discussion of the ILO from its origins through the establishment of the World Employment Programme, see Morse (1969). For an understanding of the work of the World Employment Program, see International Labor Office (1977) and (1988).

7

Debt Servicing and Its Impact on
Financial Markets in Latin America

John H. Welch

Finding a clear statement of U.S. economic policies toward Latin America which goes beyond rather broad generality is a difficult task. Two broad objectives, however, are clear: strong support for financial liberalization and maintenance of the servicing of public and private external debt. This chapter investigates the interaction of these two policies, arguing that emphasis on debt servicing compromises the chances of successful financial liberalization, due to the internal strains which servicing the external debt places on the financial system.

With strong U.S. support, both bilaterally and through multilateral channels, a number of Latin American countries have implemented financial liberalization policies in the past two decades. The most extensive programs were those in the Southern Cone countries of Argentina, Chile, and especially Uruguay (Diaz Alejandro, 1985; Felix, 1986; Corbo, de Melo, and Tybout, 1986; Tybout, 1986). In Brazil a more gradual path was followed, with a higher level of state intervention (Welch, 1989). Mexico had a well-established policy of financial nonintervention, supplemented by public sector institutions, until the early 1980s, when capital flight led to nationalization of the banking system and controls on capital movements in the balance of payments (Maxfield, 1988).

In the past two decades Latin American capital markets have played two successive roles. From the late 1960s until 1982 they absorbed and allocated massive inflows of foreign capital; after 1982 they were called upon to effect a large transfer abroad. Financial liberalization occurred mainly during the first period. After 1982 the negative resource transfer put a heavy strain on Latin American capital markets, which has been manifested in high inflation rates, capital flight, economic stagnation, and financial market inefficiency.

The main argument of this chapter is that movement toward more "efficient" (in the microeconomic sense) financial market policies is not compatible with a massive transfer of resources out of the country. It is in this sense that U.S. economic policy objectives in Latin America may not be consistent. The external transfer of resources, which implies in turn an internal transfer from the private to the public sector has either led to significant capital flight and a shrinking financial system, or alternatively has led to increasingly oligopolistic and inefficient financial systems, due to barriers to entry and formal indexation arrangements. Future financial market development crucially depends upon a reduction in the net resource transfer from Latin America to the rest of the world.

The chapter is organized as follows. The first section briefly examines the financial liberalization and development attempts of the 1960s and 1970s in a number of Latin American countries. Section II outlines some basic relationships which arise from the transfer problem and their relevance for domestic financial markets. In Section III these relationships are considered in the context of a number of Latin American countries. The chapter concludes with a discussion of the main findings.

I. FINANCIAL LIBERALIZATION AND GROWTH IN LATIN AMERICA

In the 1960s a number of Latin American countries began to place a new emphasis on improving the efficiency of their financial markets, which were increasingly viewed as key sectors in the development process. This view was reinforced by a number of studies of the role of financial development in growth, among them Goldsmith (1969), McKinnon (1973), and Shaw (1973). The thrust of the new approach was to "liberate" financial markets through the freeing of interest rates, reduction of credit subsidies, the relaxation of restrictions on capital flows, and the maintenance of "rational" exchange rate policies. The new approach was based on the related perceptions that financial market deepening is a necessary condition for economic growth and that future development could not be financed simply by increases in the level of foreign debt.

The Principal Elements of Financial Liberalization

The most pervasive reforms were undertaken in the Southern Cone, particularly in Uruguay, experiences which are documented by Felix (1986); Diaz-Alejandro (1985), Cavallo and Petrei (1983); Corbo, de Melo, and Tybout (1986); Calvo (1986); and Tybout (1986) and only briefly noted here. Less extensive reforms were undertaken in Peru under the second Belaunde government (1980–84), despite the problems which had appeared in the Southern Cone countries (Palmer, 1984; Schydlowsky, 1986; and Beckerman, 1987). Another modest financial liberalization was undertaken in Colombia during the 1974–78 Lopez administration (Reveis and Perez, 1986).

Most of these neoliberal financial liberalization attempts were undertaken during a period of large capital inflows, mainly in the form of multinational bank lending. Whether the liberalization attempts were a cause or an effect of the Latin American countries' new ability to borrow in international capital markets, it was implicitly assumed that free and "unrepressed" financial markets were necessary to allocate these capital resources efficiently. Typical liberalization programs combined a reduction of trade barriers, an opening of the capital account, the freeing of interest rates, reduction of barrier to entry by new financial institutions, and the encouragement of "innovation" in financial markets.

Although there were important differences in the sequences and the degree to which these combinations of policies were implemented, the short-term problems which they encountered were surprisingly similar in all the liberalizing Latin American economies. All had difficulty in allocating overabundant capital efficiently, a problem which was manifested by the "overlending" which took place, increasing the riskiness of the financial sector loan portfolio. Adverse movements in the terms of trade and the rise in real interest rates after 1982 subsequently revealed the vulnerability of these financial structures. In each of the Southern Cone countries, the central banks intervened to monetize nonperforming loans. Both Uruguay and Chile weathered the crisis, although at a high cost and with significant capital flight. In Argentina "financial repression" returned, with the reinstatement of 100 percent required reserve ratios and a closing of the capital account.[1]

Brazil and Mexico pursued paths to financial development that differed from the Southern Cone countries. In Brazil financial reforms began in the 1960s, with the creation of indexed assets and policies which permitted positive real interest rates (Welch, 1989). In Mexico financial development in the 1960s and 1970s was undertaken by private sector "multiple banks" relatively free of government regulation (Glade, 1984; Maxfield, 1988).

The design of the Brazilian reforms was partly inspired by U.S. experience, in that institutions were intended to specialize in respective parts of the financial market. In actuality, the market functioned more along European lines, due to the high degree of conglomeration in the 1970s, partially promoted by government policy. Despite this, a degree of segmentation remained in the Brazilian system.

Capital market reforms after 1964 were implemented primarily through three laws. The Housing Finance System (SFH), with its central institution, the National Housing Bank (BNH), was created in 1964 by Law 4380. The "Bank Reform Act," embodied in Law 4595 in 1964, created the Banco Central (BCB), replacing the weaker Superintendency of Money and Credit (SUMOC) and redefining the government-owned Banco do Brasil's role as a monetary authority. Other parts of the law expanded the functions and programs of the National Development Bank (BNDE) and established the National Monetary Council (CMN) to coordinate monetary and financial policy.

The third important law, the "Capital Markets Law," (Law 4728) in 1965 created "open capital companies" and provided firms with fiscal incentives to issue common stock.

In the late 1960s and early 1970s additional resources for both financial and equity markets were provided by the increase in forced savings from social security-type taxes. Inflationary threats to financial development were mitigated by the widespread use of Adjustable National Treasury Bonds (ORTNs), which were inflation-indexed bonds created in 1964. Finally, external borrowing was facilitated by the Central Bank's Resolution 63, which allowed commercial and investment banks to contract foreign loans for relending in domestic financial markets. The nonmonetary sectors of Brazilian financial markets consequently grew rapidly. In 1963 they provided only 13.7 percent of loans to the private sector; by 1985 62.5 percent of loans came from nonmonetary sectors (Welch, 1989).

One explicit goal of financial policy in the post-1964 period was the promotion of conglomeration in order to place the banking system on a sounder base. Brazilian authorities believed that there were economies of scale which could be exploited by larger institutions, thus reducing operating costs. Downward rigidity of real interest rates in the 1964–67 recession was attributed to the inefficient financial structure inherited from the preceding inflationary period, and conglomeration was consequently viewed as a way to decrease the real cost of capital over the longer run. In reality, however, there is no evidence that this occurred (Welch, 1989). The emergence of large conglomerates was encouraged by tight control of the number of new bank charters for commercial banks and other financial institutions.[2]

Uruguayan policymakers pursued a parallel policy of "strengthening" financial markets through conglomeration, implemented in part through a large number of bankruptcies among financial institutions in the 1950s and 1960s (Spiller and Favaro, 1984; Hanson and De Melo, 1985). The reforms of 1977 opened the banking sector in Uruguay not only to external loans but also to direct foreign investment in the financial sector to a greater degree than in most Latin American economies.

The Mexican experience was distinctly different from the preceding ones. Mexico moved from a relatively unregulated financial market to increasing government intervention, culminating in the nationalization of the banking sector in 1982 (Maxfield, 1982; Glade, 1984). The increased internationalization of the financial sector, combined with flawed macroeconomic and exchange rate policy, the fall in oil prices in the early 1980s, and the increase in U.S. interest rates, led to increased dollarization and capital flight. In an effort to prevent further losses in reserves, the government intervened in 1982. The Mexican case is idiosyncratic in that of the countries considered here it is the only one which had a longstanding laissez faire policy with respect to financial markets, which was reversed after the 1982 moratorium and nationalization.

Why did the neoliberal programs of financial market opening impose such stress on financial markets and on their economies? Much of the blame in the

Southern Cone economies can certainly be placed on the attempt to manipulate inflationary expectations through the exchange rate.[3] An even more fundamental flaw in the neoliberal arguments is the implicit assumption that debt and equity are perfect substitutes, so that firms are indifferent between financing projects using debt or equity. There is good reason to believe that this is not an appropriate assumption, particularly in developing countries. First, the differential tax treatment of deductible interest payments and nondeductible dividends creates a bias against equity issue. Second, the ability of a firm to distribute the risk of bankruptcy by stock issue may lead the market to see a stock issue as a negative signal about the firm's quality (Greenwald, Stiglitz, and Weiss, 1984), leading good firms to expand operations by debt finance while poor ones expand through stock issue, making the cost of equity financing higher and possibly prohibitive. Finally, in a firm with decentralized ownership though equities, monitoring of management is a "public good" which may not be produced at the optimal level. There will thus be underinvestment in the monitoring of managers, making equity investment less attractive than debt (Stiglitz, 1985).

When these potential problems exist, as they undoubtedly do in Latin America, capital liberalization will favor financial markets over stock markets. It is therefore not surprising that stock markets in the Latin American countries play a relatively limited role in the financing of economic activity, despite the efforts which have been made to stimulate such markets, most notably in Brazil. This financial market weakness reinforces the supply-side effect of credit rationing, since the high cost of equity makes stock issue inviable as an alternative source of capital. Capital market liberalization may increase the supply of credit, but interest rates do not decline significantly as there is credit rationing due to adverse selection (Stiglitz and Weiss, 1981). If banks impose high collateral requirements, perhaps in the form of compensating balances, they will tend to make riskier loans, as safer borrowers are rationed out of the market by higher interest rates. An increase in resources available to the banking system then causes "overlending" to risky borrowers, eventually threatening the solvency of the banking system. Explicit or implicit deposit insurance will tend to exacerbate this tendency, due to moral hazard. The recent financial market liberalization experiences of Argentina and Chile suggest that there is a strong possibility for a decrease in the stability of the financial system due to liberalization. Regulatory improvements and convergence should be clearly articulated when capital market integration is undertaken.

Individual Country Experiences

One can group the Latin American financial market experiences into two broad categories: (1) those like Argentina before 1982, Chile, Uruguay, Colombia, Peru, and Venezuela, which attempted to liberalize their financial markets and (2) countries like Brazil, Bolivia, and Argentina after 1982 which

Table 7.1.
Value Added by the Financial Sector (as a Percentage of GDP)

	1960	1970	1980	1984	1985	1986	1987
Argentina	7.4	6.7	7.9	6.7	6.9	7.0	7.1
Bolivia	11.3	12.2	15.1	13.0	13.3	14.0	14.2
Brazil	16.4	18.8	14.2	16.5	16.6	16.3	16.3
Chile	12.4	14.5	16.6	16.3	15.6	15.6	15.4
Colombia	5.5	14.8	14.6	24.9	24.9	24.8	24.7
Ecuador	16.0	10.0	8.6	8.4	8.3	8.2	8.7
Mexico	8.8	9.0	7.5	8.5	8.6	9.3	9.5
Peru	8.9	8.3	8.2	8.4	8.6	8.6	8.3
Uruguay	13.2	6.7	5.3	6.3	6.4	6.0	5.8
Venezuela	10.0	14.0	14.0	16.2	15.3	15.0	15.3

Source: Inter-American Development Bank (1988), *Economic Development and Social Progress in Latin America.*

undertook financial development programs which paralleled "import substitution" trade strategies, in that they provided a high degree of protection to existing domestic financial institutions. In this section we will try to assess the overall effects of these two types of strategies.

The size of financial markets scaled by Gross Domestic Product (GDP) varies widely among Latin American countries.

Table 7.1 shows value added from the financial sector as a percentage of GDP between 1960 and 1987 for ten Latin American economies, including all of the larger ones. Table 7.2 shows the average of M2 and total credit to GDP for these ten countries during the 1981–86 period. In recent years the highest

Table 7.2.
Average Financial Market Size: 1981–86

	M2/GDP	Credit/GDP
Argentina	15.1	56.7
Bolivia	18.2	21.0
Brazil	11.8	28.9
Chile	28.0	66.5
Colombia	21.2	22.0
Ecuador	21.2	28.0
Mexico	29.5	39.6
Peru	26.8	25.5
Uruguay	47.0	72.9
Venezuela	41.1	28.5

Source: International Monetary Fund (1989), *International Financial Statistics.*

Table 7.3.
Financial Efficiency Index: I (M2/Value Added by Financial Sector)

	1984	1985	1986	1987	Average
Argentina	1.64	1.59	2.36	--	1.86
Bolivia	1.21	0.21	0.34	--	0.59
Brazil	0.71	0.86	--	--	0.79
Chile	1.80	--	--	--	1.80
Colombia	0.84	0.80	--	--	0.82
Ecuador	2.48	2.41	2.43	2.56	2.47
Mexico	3.41	3.05	2.95	--	3.14
Peru	3.38	3.22	--	--	3.30
Uruguay	7.16	7.69	8.20	7.12	7.54
Venezuela	2.46	2.56	2.94	2.31	2.64

Sources: International Monetary Fund (1989); *International Financial Statistics*; Inter-American Development Bank (1988), *Economic Development and Social Progress in Latin America.*

value-added shares were in Colombia, Brazil, Bolivia, Chile, and Venezuela, while the lowest were in Argentina and Uruguay. Comparison with Table 7.1 suggests that relatively large value added does not necessarily imply a large financial sector "output," where the latter is defined either as M2/GNP or the ratio of total credit to GDP.

As a crude measure of the "efficiency" of different countries' financial sectors, Tables 7.3 and 7.4 present respectively measures of the ratio of M2 and of total credit to financial sector value added. Although there are a number of

Table 7.4.
Financial Efficiency Index: II (Total Credit/Value Added by Financial Sector)

	1984	1985	1986	1987	Average
Argentina	8.19	6.14	5.60	--	6.61
Bolivia	1.77	0.38	0.29	--	0.81
Brazil	1.67	1.84	--	--	1.75
Chile	4.82	--	--	--	4.82
Colombia	1.04	0.98	--	--	1.01
Ecuador	3.81	3.61	3.53	--	3.65
Mexico	4.13	4.36	4.75	--	4.41
Peru	3.34	2.28	--	--	2.81
Uruguay	13.08	11.66	10.55	--	11.76
Venezuela	1.72	1.48	1.92	1.67	1.70

Sources: International Monetary Fund (1989): *International Financial Statistics*; Inter-American Development Bank (1988), *Economic Development and Social Progress in Latin America.*

extraneous factors which could potentially affect either the numerator or the denominator of either ratio, comparisons between countries are interesting. By either index Uruguay stands out as producing a large volume of finance in relation to the value added in the financial sector, while Bolivia, Venezuela, and Brazil show a relatively low level of total credit in relation to financial sector value added.

Despite their lack of precision, these data suggest that if a country can weather the short-term adverse effects of an extensive financial liberalization, it may succeed in developing a relatively efficient financial system, as appears to have occurred in Uruguay. The prospects for the success of financial reforms depend on inflation rates, the public sector's financial activity, and on the net transfer of resources abroad, a topic which we address in the following section.

II. THE TRANSFER PROBLEM

The liberalizing tendencies in Latin American financial market policies occurred primarily during a period of large net capital inflows. With the Mexican moratorium in 1982 and the ensuing collapse of voluntary lending to most Latin American nations, these countries were forced to effect a net transfer of resources abroad. In terms of their balances of payments, large current account deficits which had been financed by capital inflows before 1982 had to be eliminated or even reversed, as capital inflows ceased and creditors insisted on maintenance of debt servicing.

In countries in which the public sector is ultimately responsible for the majority of foreign debt servicing and is financed by a small tax base, much of the external resource transfer implies a corresponding internal resource transfer from the private sector, a net exporter, to the public sector, a net debtor. In the absence of adequate tax financing of the public sector expenditure for debt servicing, this necessarily occurs through financial markets. Governments can either transfer resources to themselves by taxing the reserves of the banking system via an "inflation tax" or, if there is an active market for government securities, by issuing government debt.

The monetary consequences of the internal transfer problem have been higher inflation rates and lower investment in most Latin American countries. In this section we formalize some of these relationships in order to analyze the effect of the transfer problem.

Basic national accounting rules imply that GDP equals domestic absorption plus the current account exclusive of factor service payments, or

$$y = \text{GDP} = A + (X^* - N^*) \tag{1}$$

where A is domestic absorption and $(X^* - N^*)$ is the surplus on the merchandise trade and nonfactor services accounts. The value of the resources transferred abroad equals the excess of domestic production over domestic absorption, or by (1)

$$y - A = (X^* - N^*) \tag{2}$$

The surplus on current account, $(X - N)$, differs from the trade balance and nonfactor service account by net interest payment on foreign debt and net profit remittances, or

$$(X - N) = (X^* - N^*) - i^*ED^* - PR \tag{3}$$

where E is the exchange rate, D^* the value of the foreign debt in foreign currency terms, and PR the rate of net profit remittance. Finally, the basic national income accounting identity shows that the current account surplus equals net public plus private saving, or

$$(X - N) = (T - G) + (S - I) \tag{4}$$

In a Latin American context (4) has implied that the end of the current account deficit must have been financed by either a rise in the public sector surplus, $T - G$, or by a rise in net private saving, $S - I$. As the former effect has been small, and savings response low, most of the adjustment has been made through a sharp fall in investment, I. This private sector "surplus," however, must be transferred to the public sector, and this transfer necessarily involves financial markets. Equations (3) and (4) can be combined to yield

$$(X^* - N^*) = (T - G) + (S - I) + i^*ED^* + PR \tag{5}$$

The public sector deficit is equal to the noninterest deficit, d, plus interest payments on foreign and domestic debt, or

$$(G - T) = d + i^*EDg^* + iB \tag{6}$$

where Dg^* is the foreign debt payable by the public sector, i^* the average interest rate on foreign debt, B the stock of domestic public sector debt in the hands of the public, and i the nominal interest rate on domestic public debt.

Increases in the monetary base occur on the asset side of the central banks accounts due to increases in domestic credit extended by the central bank, C, and the increase in central bank foreign reserves, R, so that

$$M = C + ER \text{ or } C = M - ER \tag{7}$$

Public sector deficits can be financed by expanding the domestic component of the monetary base, C, by issuing new domestic government debt, B, or by increasing the government's foreign debt outstanding,

$$C + B = d + i^*EDg^* + iB - EDg^* \tag{8}$$

Combining equations (7) and (8) yields

$$M + B = d + i^*EDg^* + iB + eR - EDg^* \tag{9}$$

By definition, the change in official reserves in the balance of payments equals the current account and capital account surpluses (ignoring errors and omissions and foreign direct investment), or

$$ER = (X - N) + EDg^*$$
$$= (X^* - N^*) - i^*EDg^* - PR + EDg^* \tag{10}$$

Substituting equation (10) into (9) yields

$$M + B = d - i^*E(D^* - Dg^*) + iB$$
$$+ (X^* - N^*) - PR + E(D^* - Dg^*) \tag{11}$$

If the foreign transfer problem is "solved," in the sense that the balance of payments is in equilibrium with no new voluntary lending, the ER = 0 and M = C. In this case equation (7) holds, and may be rewritten to reflect the fact that increases in the monetary base occur only due to increases in the domestic component, or

$$M + B = d + i^*EDg^* + iB \tag{12}$$

Rewriting equation (12) in real terms yields

$$M/P + B/P = d^* + i^*(Dg^*/P) + i(B/P) \tag{13}$$

If m = M/P, then

$$m = M/P + pm \tag{14}$$

and

$$b = B/P + pb \tag{15}$$

where p is the continuous time rate of inflation. Substituting equations (14) and (15) into equation (13) yields

$$m + b = d^* + i^*dg^* + (i - p)b - pm \tag{16}$$

Equation (16) has a straightforward interpretation. The real increase in the government's internal obligations, equivalent to the internal transfer effected through the financial system, will increase in proportion to the real nonfinancial deficit, d^* and the financial public sector deficit i^*dg^*. The real internal transfer will be smaller, the higher is the inflation rate or the monetary base.[4]

There are a number of policy implications of equation (16). If governments can no longer borrow in foreign markets (i.e., $EDg^* = 0$), the higher the stock of foreign debt or the interest rates on that debt for which the government is responsible, then the larger must be the increase in the total internal debt (m + b) for a given nonfinancial deficit d^*. The higher the stock of internal debt or the higher the interest rate on internal debt, moreover, the larger will be the increase in domestic government obligations outstanding. If the country does not have a viable internal market for government debt, the increase in government obligations must be made mainly through increases in the domestic component of the monetary base.

III. THE EXTERNAL RESOURCE TRANSFER, INFLATION, AND FINANCIAL MARKETS

The preceding discussion has shown how the transfer problem is related to inflation and the size of the existing public debt. In this section we will examine some of the relationships between the resource transfer, inflation, and financial "efficiency," in the sense used earlier.

The External Transfer

All Latin American countries began transferring significant amounts of resources abroad after 1981. Table 7.5 summarizes the annual resource transfer from selected Latin American countries between 1981 and 1986.[5] Venezuela is clearly the country in the group for which the resource transfer was greatest in the period, averaging almost 9 percent of GDP. Resource transfers were also high from Argentina, Ecuador, and Mexico, and only slightly lower as a percentage of GDP from Bolivia, Brazil, Peru and Uruguay. It should be noted that the estimate for Bolivia understates the burden, since the inflation stabilization plan of 1985 entailed large amounts of new international lending. The hyperinflation suffered by Bolivia between 1984 and 1985 was largely due to Bolivia's inability to effect a net resource transfer, given its lack of domestic capital market financing of the internal resource transfer (Sachs and Morales,

Table 7.5.
Average Annual Resource Transfer

Argentina	4.45	Ecuador	4.35
Bolivia	2.77	Mexico	4.68
Brazil	3.13	Peru	2.25
Chile	1.73	Uruguay	2.90
Colombia	-0.55	Venezuela	8.88

Note: Measured as the merchandise trade account surplus of the balance of payments as a percent of GDP.
Source: International Monetary Fund; *International Financial Statistics.*

1988). Of the ten Latin American economies considered here, Chile and Colombia showed the lowest levels of resource transfer during the 1981–86 period.

Resource Transfer, Inflation, and Financial Sector Efficiency

It was shown in the preceding section that if the government is responsible for a large portion of the foreign debt but is limited in its ability to tax its citizens, then financial markets may suffer in transferring financial resources from the private sector to the public sector. If the government ability to borrow using interest-bearing government debt instruments, moreover, is small due to the lack of a domestic market, the transfer will be effected through expansion of the monetary base, diminishing the value of the existing high powered money stock. This will hurt financial institutions in a number of ways.

First, if financial institutions cannot recapture some of the "inflation tax," as in Argentina, the profitability of the institution will suffer. Second, if these institutions are allowed to benefit from inflation by intermediating the issuance of interest-bearing public debt with funds obtained through demand deposits, they will tend to misallocate investment resources toward capturing these "free" funds. This may involve a number of inefficiencies, among them the opening of an excessive number of agencies or the creation of redundant services, as in Brazil. Finally, as inflation rises, financial markets will tend to become less liquid unless a domestic constant purchasing power financial asset can be marketed, as in Brazil, Mexico, Colombia, and Peru. If residents lose confidence in domestic financial institutions and instruments, the financial market will shrink due to "dollarization" and capital flight, as has occurred in Argentina and Bolivia.

In earlier sections we have presented measures which might be interpreted as rough estimates of financial market size, defined as M2/Value-added or Credit/Value-added, as well as corresponding estimates of the resource transfer as a percentage of GDP. Comparison of the two measures shows that there is no strong relationship between financial efficiency and the resource transfer.

Several countries with a relatively high level of "efficiency" and more "liber-alized" financial markets (Uruguay, Chile, Argentina, and Mexico) transferred roughly similar percentages of GDP as did economies with more restricted fi-nancial markets like Brazil and Bolivia. Both Colombia and Venezuela appear relatively "inefficient" by both our measures, but vary significantly and in op-posite directions from the other economies in terms of resource transfer.[6]

There is a similar variety among countries in the relation between financial market efficiency and inflation. Several countries with relatively efficient finan-cial markets, among them Uruguay, Chile, and Argentina, had widely different average inflation rates, as did the financially less efficient economies like Ven-ezuela, Colombia, and most of all, Bolivia.[7]

Our earlier discussion suggested that the strains imposed by the resource transfer on the financial system might be manifested in the inflation rate. Our cross-country data for the post-1981 period provides some weak support for this position. Although there is a mildly positive relationship between infla-tion and the resource transfer, especially if one notes that Venezuela's inflation rate has increased sharply in recent years, the relation is not strongly signifi-cant. There is, however, a clear and statistically significant positive relation-ship between government deficits and inflation.[8]

A brief comparison of the experiences of Brazil and Argentina provides some further insight into the problems which the external and internal transfer process creates for domestic financial markets. After the 1982 crisis, Brazil quickly "solved" the external transfer problem through an IMF-type stabili-zation policy which generated a record merchandise trade surplus but also produced a sharp inflationary acceleration (Welch, Primo Braga, and Andre, 1987). As Brazil's public sector is responsible for around 80 percent of its total outstanding foreign debt, the necessity of meeting foreign debt service created a large fiscal burden which tax receipts could not cover. The government has had to borrow heavily by issuing inflation indexed government debt at rela-tively high interest rates in order to service this debt. In addition, some of the financing has been provided by increases in the monetary base.

Not only was inflation indexing necessary to affect the internal transfer, but government paper became increasingly liquid over the period. Financial insti-tutions were able to "capture" some of the inflation tax by intermediating via repurchase agreements in the "overnight" market between final borrowers and the government. In addition, they could capture some of the inflation tax by financing asset positions with "free" funds from sources such as demand deposits, and the tax float (Welch, 1989).[9] The existence of inflation indexing not only allowed the Brazilian government to transfer resources to itself by borrowing, but also kept individuals transacting in domestic assets rather than foreign ones. This arrangement allowed banks to profit from the internal transfer process at the same time that it increased the influence of financial institutions on the Banco Central's monetary policies. Not only did the effi-ciency of the financial sector suffer, but the existence of financial asset indexation also created additional inflation feedback mechanisms (Beckerman, 1979; Baer and Beckerman, 1980; Baer and Welch, 1987).

Argentina faced very similar problems. Although it did not experience such a dramatic turnaround in its balance of payments as Brazil, the internal transfer problem was acute. Argentina, unlike Brazil, never successfully launched a domestic constant purchasing power asset, so that Argentines preferred to hold foreign currency denominated assets. As a result, Argentina's internal transfer relied more on inflationary finance than did Brazil's. The financial sector suffered greatly due to the fact that the main tax base for this transfer was the reserves of the banking system (Aguirre and Feldman, 1987). In part to appease the banks, a complex system of Central Bank intermediation has evolved in which the Central Bank pays high interest rates on some forms of reserve deposits and lends at the rediscount window at below market rates. The losses incurred by the Central Bank in its intermediation activities is sometimes referred to as the "quasi-fiscal" deficit. In spite of these measures, financial intermediaries in Argentina have had a poor profit performance since 1982.

IV. CONCLUSIONS

This chapter has examined the implications for Latin American financial markets of financial liberalization on the one hand, and service of the foreign debt on the other, both of them centerpieces of U.S. economic policy in the region in the recent past. Liberalization attempts in the Southern Cone countries of Argentina, Chile, and Uruguay caused severe financial instability and fragility in spite of the microeconomic improvements presumably attainable by "getting prices right." Substantial improvements in financial sector productive efficiency were gained by those countries which were able to weather the macroeconomic problems of financial sector liberalization. Recent studies have suggested, moreover, that allocative efficiency improved in those countries which undertook these types of policies (Pretrei and Tybout, 1985; Galvez and Tybout, 1985; de Melo, Pascale, and Tybout, 1985).

The main obstacle to further financial sector improvement, however, is no longer the possibility of destabilizing capital inflows, but the implied internal transfer problem due to the external transfer problem. A situation in which the private sector must transfer resources to the public sector through financial markets after generating trade surpluses is not sustainable in the medium or long run. Improvements in the financial system, moreover, will be hindered by a combination of the inflation tax "collection" and internal debt issue, as has been the case in Brazil and Argentina. Only when the burden of the external debt is substantially reduced will advance in the Latin American financial sectors be possible.

NOTES

I would like to thank the Oakland University School of Business Administration and the University of North Texas for supporting this research. I would also like to thank Sylvia Maxfield for helpful comments on an earlier draft.

1. There has been much recent work on the timing of policies in a liberalization program. Among them are Edwards and Van Wijnbergen (1986, 1987) and McKinnon (1985), who conclude that trade liberalization should precede capital account liberalization.

2. Brazil's control of bank charters increased bank concentration after 1967 and had important additional incentive effects on the banking system. First, it led to a secondary market in bank charters, promoted by monetary authorities, which became a source of profit for inefficient banks. Second, due to the asymmetrical treatment of the indexation of the assets and liabilities of banks in receivership in an inflationary context, it became profitable to file for reorganization under Central Bank intervention, in effect transferring the costs to depositors.

3. There is now a large literature on the effects of these exchange rate policies. Among the analyses of some of the features of these programs is Diaz-Alejandro (1985) and Felix (1986).

4. The level and growth of both the real monetary base and the real debt outstanding are determined by the public's behavior. These behavioral relationships typically posit a negative effect of the inflation rate on real money demand, so that there will be an inflation rate which is compatible with a given resource transfer, a relationship analyzed by Dornbusch and Fischer (1986).

5. The merchandise trade balance is used here as a proxy for the resource transfer. As this omits nonfactor services, which have been negative in this period for many Latin American economies, our estimates are probably underestimates of the true resource transfer to the rest of the world.

6. A formal statistical test for a linear relationship between efficiency and resource transfer was not significant.

7. A test for any linear relationship between efficiency and inflation was not significant.

8. This relationship is significant at the 1 percent level. It should be remembered, however, that increasing government deficits in Latin America are as much a consequence as a cause of higher inflation.

9. The tax float arose from receipts collected by banks but not yet disbursed to the government.

8

U.S. Policies and the Prospects for Latin American Economic Integration

Carlos Alberto Primo Braga

The 1980s have been characterized by many asymmetries north and south of the Rio Grande. One of the longest periods of economic expansion in U.S. history contrasts with the so-called "lost decade" in Latin America. The thrust of trade policies has also deviated from those of the United States, which has moved toward a more protectionist regime, while major Latin American countries have initiated efforts at trade liberalization. There is, however, an area of convergence in terms of economic strategy both in the United States and in Latin America. This centers on a renewed interest in regional integration projects.

This chapter explores the reasons behind the new appeal of "minilateralism."[1] It begins with a review of the impact of U.S. policies on Latin American regional trade in the first half of the 1980s. The second section examines the history of Latin American integration attempts and the reasons why "minilateralism" is again fashionable all over the continent. The chapter ends with a brief analysis of the prospects for Latin American economic integration in the near future.

I. LATIN AMERICAN ECONOMIC INTEGRATION AND REAGANOMICS[2]

The economic developments of the early 1980s were not kind to the existing integration programs in Latin America. As the foreign debt crisis evolved, intraregional trade plummeted, as is clearly shown in Table 8.1.[3]

The importance of external shocks in the debt crisis cannot be overemphasized. The significant increase in real interest rates, the slowdown of the OECD economies and the deterioration of regional terms of trade had a dramatic negative impact on the balance of payments of Latin American countries in the early 1980s. These developments are in part explained by the United States' unorthodox mix of macroeconomic policies during the first years of the Rea-

Table 8.1.
Latin America and Caribbean: Exports and Regional Integration Programs
(Billion Dollars, FOB)

	1960	1965	1970	1975	1980	1985[a]	1986[a]
Latin American Association for Integration							
Total Exports	7.3	9.4	13.8	29.6	78.1	89.1	69.9
Exports to Latin America	--	--	1.6	5.0	12.9	9.1	9.1
Exports to Latin America/ Total (percent)	--	--	12%	17%	17%	10%	13%
Intrazonal Trade	0.6	0.8	1.3	4.0	10.9	7.1	7.7
Andean Group[b]							
Total Exports	3.6	4.3	5.4	12.9	29.3	25.7	18.5
Exports to Latin America	--	--	0.6	2.1	4.8	3.0	2.4
Exports to Latin America/ Total (percent)	--	--	11%	16%	17%	12%	13%
Intrazonal Trade	0.0	0.1	0.1	0.5	1.2	0.7	0.7
Central American Common Market							
Total Exports	0.4	0.8	1.1	2.3	4.4	3.5	4.0
Exports to Latin America	--	--	0.3	0.7	1.3	0.7	0.6
Exports to Latin America/ Total (percent)	--	--	28%	28%	28%	19%	15%
Intrazonal Trade	0.3	0.1	0.3	0.5	1.1	0.5	0.4
Caribbean Community[c]							
Total Exports	0.5	0.8	1.0	3.0	5.5	3.3	2.5
Exports to Latin America	--	--	0.6	0.3	0.6	0.3	0.2
Exports to Latin America/ Total (percent)	--	--	6%	9%	11%	10%	8%
Intrazonal Trade	--	--	--	0.2	0.4	0.3	0.1

Table 8.1.
(continued)

	1960	1965	1970	1975	1980	1985[a]	1986[a]
Latin America and Caribbean[d]							
Total Exports	8.5	11.5	15.2	36.2	89.6	97.4	77.7
Intraregional Trade	0.8	1.3	2.0	6.0	14.9	10.1	9.9
Intraregional/ Total Trade (percent)	9%	11%	13%	17%	17%	10%	13%

Note: (a) Estimates; (b) Does not include Chile; (c) Only Barbados, Guyana, Jamaica, and Trinidad and Tobago were considered; (d) Includes only eleven countries from LAIA, five from CACM, four from CARICOM, Panama, Dominican Republic and Haiti.
Source: ECLA (1988).

gan administration. Tight monetary policy coupled with fiscal expansion in the United States explain much of the historically abnormal behavior of real interest rates in the 1980s.

It is important to note, however, that U.S. policies could only have the harmful impact they had in an international monetary system which was not working properly. The roots of the ongoing crisis can be traced back to the rupture of the Bretton Woods system in 1971. Since then, the world economy has been living with a "non-system" in which the proliferation of exchange rate regimes and growing international capital mobility have eroded the discipline that the system was supposed to impose on its participants. Negative real interest rates in the 1970s, which provided a strong incentive to overborrowing by the less developed countries (LDCs), and their dramatic upswing in the early 1980s are at the core of the foreign debt crisis. Domestic errors, among them public sector mismanagement, currency overvaluation, and policy-induced capital flight, magnified Latin American countries' economic disequilibria, setting the stage for the painful adjustment programs of the 1980s.

The spark for the crisis was the announcement in August 1982 that Mexico would not be able to comply with its service obligations on foreign debt. From the second semester of 1982 on, Latin America began to experience a negative net transfer (disbursements of external loans minus interest and amortization payments on foreign debt) in its external accounts. With the sudden interruption of voluntary private lending, Latin American countries initiated orthodox stabilization programs, centered on the control of domestic absorption and on real depreciation of the domestic currency. Some countries also adopted debt-led commercial policies: export incentives coupled with import restrictions.

As a consequence, Latin America began to generate significant balance-of-trade surpluses from 1983 on. Despite this dramatic transfer of real resources to the rest of the world, the region continued to experience an increase in its external debt. In other words, the regional surplus in the balance of goods and nonfactor services remained smaller than the deficit in the factor services balance (interest, profits and dividends). Latin America's total foreign debt would only begin to diminish in nominal terms by 1988 when debt relief initiatives, such as debt-equity swaps, exit bonds and buy-backs, became significant.

The evolution of Latin American total and intraregional exports during the 1980s is of particular interest in this context. Intraregional exports as a proportion of total exports decreased from 16.6 percent in 1980 to 12.8 percent by 1986 (ECLA, 1988). Such a development was related to the adjustment pattern followed by Latin American countries in response to the foreign debt crisis. As local markets contracted in response to domestic absorption control, intraregional exports were squeezed in nominal terms. The overvalued dollar, which distorted international trade flows, moreover, tended to magnify the relative importance of the U.S. market for Latin American exports. As a consequence, intraregional exports also fell as a proportion of total Latin American exports.

In sum, U.S. economic policies in the first half of the 1980s had a negative impact on existing Latin American minilateral arrangements. The increase in real interest rates directly affected the financial position of the countries of the region. The interest rate shock also played an important role in the OECD economic slowdown, besides causing appreciation of the dollar. These side effects compounded the financial shock, since they curtailed the dynamism of Latin American exports and contributed to the deterioration of the terms of trade of the region.[4] As the foreign exchange constraint became binding, Latin American countries reoriented their trade efforts in the direction of the industrialized economies, particularly the United States, in an attempt to generate surpluses in hard currency.

This reorientation, allied with beggar-thy-neighbor trade policies, hampered intraregional trade in Latin America. In the next section we discuss the recent revival in interest in economic integration programs as well as some previous integration attempts.

II. REGIONAL INTEGRATION: OLD AND NEW ATTEMPTS

The goal of economic and political integration in Latin America is as old as the independent history of the region. Simón Bolívar, for instance, was a strong supporter of political unity among the former Spanish colonies. All attempts toward regional unity during the nineteenth century, however, even those based on rather limited concepts of political unification, did not last long.[5] After World War II, interest in regional integration reappeared, although the focus was no longer on political unity but instead on the economic potential of a common market. This new approach reflected not only experience with the failures of political unity attempts, but also the search for a new style of economic development for the region.

This search was very much influenced in turn by the ongoing theoretical debate about the role of international trade as an engine of growth. The United States was at that time committed to the design of a neoliberal multilateral trade system, with global trade liberalization as its goal and the General Agreement on Tariffs and Trade (GATT) as its cornerstone. In most LDCs, however, there was a strong belief that trade liberalization achieved via reciprocal negotiations would not be mutually beneficial for the center and the periphery of the capitalist world. In this view, trade liberalization would not help the developing world since it was assumed that the terms of trade for primary products exporters tended to be secularly declining. LDC trade policies should favor resource transfer from the export sector to import-substituting activities. Import substitution (IS) would not only foster economic growth via industrialization and its positive externalities, but would also tend to reverse the terms of trade decline for LDCs. Accordingly, LDCs should be granted the right to protect their domestic industries and should not be expected to fully reciprocate trade concessions granted by developed countries.

The United Nations Economic Commission for Latin America (UN-ECLA), under the leadership of the Argentine economist Raul Prebisch, became the main source of institutional support for IS industrialization as the proper development strategy for the countries of the region. The growth potential via IS was obviously much larger for countries like Brazil, Mexico, and Argentina than for the smaller Latin American countries. In all cases, however, the basic procedure was the same: trade barriers and exchange rate overvaluation made IS activities relatively more profitable than export activities. The relative smallness of national markets was recognized as a major problem for successful IS industrialization in that it constrained the capacity of local firms to exploit economies of scale. To address this problem, economists from ECLA supported regional integration.[6]

The First Integration Attempts

The interest in regional integration in Latin America in the 1950s was not a mere by-product of ECLA's influence on policymaking in the region. The example of the creation of the European Economic Community (EEC) in 1957, under the Treaty of Rome, also had a "demonstration effect."[7] The implicit threat of a wave of discriminatory arrangements, outside GATT's discipline, inspired defensive reactions in other parts of the world. In Latin America, this effect was magnified by concern with the declining trend in intraregional trade in the second half of the 1950s. According to Dell (1966), exports of Latin American countries to one another fell from US$ 770 million in 1955 to US$ 570 million in 1961.

This trend in reality reflected the anti-export bias of the inward-oriented development strategies which were being implemented by the countries of the region. It was interpreted, however, as evidence of the need to revive bilateral arrangements and to promote regional integration.

In 1958, discussions were initiated in the Southern Cone, reflecting the interests of Argentina, Brazil, Chile, and Uruguay in expanding intraregional trade. Initially, the project envisaged the consolidation of several bilateral preferential treaties, covering trade in primary commodities among these countries. It rapidly evolved, however, into a proposal for a free-trade area encompassing most of Latin America. The signing of the Treaty of Montevideo in February 1960 marked the birth of the Latin American Free Trade Association (LAFTA, *Asociación Latinoamericana de Libre Comercio*/ALALC).[8] It is important to point out that LAFTA did not follow ECLA's ambitious proposals for regional integration. The agreement, for instance, did not explicitly promote economic coordination among its members. In fact, as Tussie (1987) notes, the design of LAFTA was significantly influenced by the orthodox approach to economic integration, based on Viner's classical distinction between trade creation and trade diversion. In short, there was a clear compromise between the discipline imposed by Article XXIV of GATT and ECLA's emphasis on regional complementarity as an instrument to intensify IS industrialization.

Article XXIV sets forth the basic conditions under which the formation of a customs union or a free-trade area (FTA) is consistent with GATT rules. Among these conditions, several are of particular interest (GATT, 1986):

a) the integration process should not bring on the whole a higher level of restrictions to trade between the constituent territories and other GATT contracting parties vis-á-vis those levels which prevailed prior to the agreement;

b) interim agreements should result in the formation of a customs union or of a free-trade area within a specified period;

c) trade barriers should be eliminated on substantially all the trade between the constituent territories.

As Long (1987) and Patterson (1989) note, Article XXIV has usually been interpreted in such a way as to allow a considerable flexibility for the contracting parties. This flexibility, or pragmatism, at GATT level simply reflected the recognition that a strict adherence to its discipline would probably lead to the disruption of the General Agreement. Ever since this point was made clear by the creation of the EEC, every economic integration arrangement for which the GATT has been formally notified has been evaluated in a manner sufficiently ambiguous to avoid any final conclusion with respect to its eligibility under the GATT article. Despite this ambiguity, Article XXIV is an important benchmark not only for normative reasons, but also because it reflected U.S. attitudes toward economic integration attempts in the late 1950s.

The Treaty of Montevideo paid formal attention to GATT's concerns. Tariff negotiations were to proceed on a two-track format (the so-called national and common lists) aiming at the complete elimination of tariffs on intraregional trade after a transition period of twelve years. Offers based on the "national list" were to be negotiated yearly on a most-favored-nation (MFN) basis. Concessions were to be discussed product by product (they could be withdrawn later if adequate compensation was provided), but each participant was to make a yearly reduction of its average tariff against imports from LAFTA members of no less than 8 percent in relation to the weighted average tariff faced by nonmember countries. Every three years, a common list was to be negotiated; in each round 25 percent of the items entering intraregional trade were to be covered. The products included in the common list were not to face any restrictions in intraregional trade and these concessions would be binding.[9]

There were, however, aspects of the treaty which did not conform precisely to GATT discipline. LAFTA, for instance, adopted the concept of special and differential (S&D) treatment for its least developed members. This concept, which would only be incorporated to the GATT in the Kennedy Round (1964–67), allowed departures from full reciprocity.[10] Industrial complementarity among the participants was also an explicit goal, as defended by ECLA. In this context, the treaty clearly downplayed the potential costs of trade diversion, a major concern at GATT level. The so-called industrial complementarity agreements (typically bilateral negotiations focusing on intra-industry trade) were supposed to be negotiated on a MFN basis, but this requirement was already waived by 1964. As a result, these agreements became a source of discriminatory trade practices. Other major departures from Article XXIV appeared in the implementation of the agreement. As the first round of negotiations for the establishment of the common list collapsed, the period contemplated by the member countries for the creation of a free-trade area was first extended (from 1972 to 1980) and later, when this new deadline also became unattainable, LAFTA was replaced by a new integration arrangement, the Latin American Association for Integration (LAIA, *Asociación Latinoamericana de Integración*/ALADI). As a result of this failure, the goal of full liberalization in substantially all intraregional trade became a distant mirage.

LAFTA was not the only regional integration scheme established in Latin America in the early 1960s. In December 1960, the Central American Common Market (CACM, *Mercado Comun Centroamericano*/MCCA) was created.[11] One of its main objectives was the organization of a customs union in Central America in a five-year period. The CACM project was closer to ECLA's ideas concerning regional integration than was that of LAFTA. The CACM promoted across-the-board elimination of tariffs in intraregional trade (with the exception of goods considered to be of strategic importance) together with regional planning of investment. This approach reflected ECLA's concern with regional imbalances which could be magnified by the process of integration. In order to "bribe" the least developed countries of the region into the customs union, CACM strategists suggested that these countries should be favored in the future allocation of industrial investment. In short, the CACM program envisaged a much higher degree of economic coordination among its members than did LAFTA. CACM also subscribed to the concepts of S&D and industrial complementarity. It went a step further in the direction of ECLA's recommendations, moreover, to the extent that it emphasized regional planning.

Despite these differences both programs (LAFTA and CACM) evolved along similar paths. After some progress in the initial years, when concessions basically consolidated already existing bilateral arrangements (covering items which were traditionally important for intraregional trade), the programs stalled. As negotiations began to address items for which trade creation could be significant (particularly manufactured products), inefficient domestic producers voiced their opposition to the integration process. In the case of LAFTA, as the difficulty of working out negotiating packages along inter-industry lines evolved, intra-industry agreements became frequent. These agreements, however, required a degree of industrial maturity which was only found in the most advanced economies of the region. The resulting perception that the benefits of intraregional trade liberalization were not evenly distributed among member countries added to the complexity of the negotiations. In the case of the CACM, the level of conflict increased when inter-governmental agreement became necessary for the allocation of industrial investments in the region. In theory, according to the S&D rhetoric of the agreement, the least developed member countries should be favored in this process. In practice, this was not only resisted by other member countries, but also was difficult to implement given the important role of foreign capital in industrial investment in Central America.[12]

U.S. trade policies throughout this period stressed multilateralism and non-discrimination (that is, unconditional MFN treatment) as defined by GATT, as was noted above.[13] The United States opposed ECLA's proposals for regional integration, arguing that they had a high potential for trade diversion. The influence of this opposition to Latin American integration attempts, however, seems to have been more one of form than of substance. The Treaty of Montevideo, for instance, was drafted taking into account the principles embodied in GATT's Article XXIV. Its implementation, however, clearly revealed the inherent conflict between GATT discipline and the discriminatory character typical of the protectionist regimes which prevailed in Latin America. The waiver of MFN treatment for industrial complementarity agreements in 1964 was a natural development in this context. Over time, moreover, several other measures reinforced the slide of the system into a discriminatory path.

The creation of the Andean Group (*Grupo Andino*) in 1969 can be interpreted as another example of this trend.[14] The Andean Group was a response of middle-sized economies to the perception that LAFTA was moving too slowly and that it basically benefited the larger economies (Argentina, Brazil, and Mexico) of Latin America. The Cartagena Agreement, which was drafted in a period of growing economic nationalism, had as its main objective the paving of the way for regional autonomous development.[15] Like the CACM program, it stressed industrial planning at regional level and a supranational decisionmaking process. It was, however, even more ambitious to the extent that it also had integration objectives in noneconomic areas (such as education, cultural affairs, and labor relations). Its goals in terms of intraregional trade liberalization were to be promoted by mandatory tariff reductions at a 10 percent yearly rate. After ten years this process would establish a free-trade area. In a parallel movement, harmonization efforts among member countries' trade policies would set the stage for the future creation of a customs union. It should be noted, moreover, that the Andean Group adopted a series of measures to control foreign investments and to accelerate technological transfers, which were clearly antagonistic to foreign capital.

In sum, U.S. efforts to influence the shape of early integration attempts in Latin America were not very successful. In the case of LAFTA, the initial "commitment" to GATT discipline did not last long. The CACM and the Andean Group were from their very beginning at odds with this discipline. This is hardly surprising, however, since no minilateral agreement can immediately override the basic character of the trade policies of its participants. The direct impact of U.S. emphasis on nondiscriminatory trade practices upon Latin American integration programs hence was at best marginal.

The poor economic records of these programs basically reflected endogenous restrictions. First and foremost was the anti-export bias of the development strategies followed by most Latin American countries. Second, conflicts of interest among the participants, a clear indication of the low priority given to regional integration by many governments, often created insurmountable problems. A third restriction was the political and economic instability of the region. The "soccer war" between El Salvador and Honduras in 1969, for instance, magnified the problems that the CACM already faced. The dramatic reorientation of economic policies in Chile, following the overthrow of Salvador Allende in 1973, culminated with Chile's withdrawal from the Andean Group in 1976. The Southern Cone experiments in trade liberalization of the late 1970s accelerated the process of deterioration of LAFTA. As Chile, Argentina, and Uruguay pursued unilateral tariff reductions, the margins of preference which benefited imports from other LAFTA members were rapidly eroded and LAFTA's economic significance suffered an additional blow.[16]

The New Face of Minilateralism

All Latin American integration schemes were in disarray by the end of the 1970s. None of them had delivered the original promises of economic integration. In the case of the CACM, non-economic developments, particularly the

Sandinista Revolution in Nicaragua, had all but destroyed the scheme. Against this background, major revisions of these arrangements began to be implemented.

For LAFTA, the revision was inevitable given the existing deadline for the creation of a free-trade area in 1980. As noted above, the solution was to replace LAFTA for a new and more pragmatic agreement. LAIA was a clear step in the direction of preferential bilateralism. The new Treaty of Montevideo, signed in August 1980, emphasized the role of bilateral and subregional agreements as the main instruments of economic integration. Trade concessions negotiated via these agreements would not be bound by unconditional MFN treatment. This new approach was a direct reaction to a common criticism of LAFTA: the proposition that unconditional MFN had hindered the integration process and stimulated free-rider behavior among member countries. It was also influenced by the relative dynamism of the industrial complementarity agreements. This dynamism, essentially a consequence of the interest of multinational corporations in intra-industry trade in the region, was interpreted as an indication of the benefits of abandoning unconditional MFN treatment.

The creation of LAIA occurred at a moment characterized by major changes in the world macroeconomic environment. The failure of previous regional integration attempts in Latin America may be basically explained in terms of the fragility of the economies involved and by the antitrade bias of the development strategies pursued by most countries of the region after World War II. The exogenous shocks of the early 1980s, however, came to magnify the crisis of the existing regional integration schemes. It is ironic that Reaganomics was more efficient than explicit U.S. hostility to minilateral arrangements in influencing Latin American regional integration programs.

The crisis in intraregional trade, however, stimulated the search for alternatives to reverse this process.[17] At the same time, the renewed interest within the First World in minilateral schemes also generated a "demonstration effect." One could even say that the rebirth of minilateralism in Latin America in the second half of the 1980s was fostered by forces similar to the ones that in the late 1950s led to the first wave of regional integration programs. Even at the ideological level there are some similarities. The first round of export pessimism was tied to the idea of declining terms of trade of primary products, following Prebisch's argument, and led to recommendations in favor of ISI. The antitrade bias of such policies was recognized, but regional integration was then offered as the appropriate response. In the 1980s, a new school of export pessimists evolved.[18] According to this school the "new protectionism" in the First World, with its growing emphasis on nontariff barriers, would hinder the chances of success of outward-oriented programs, based on the dynamism of North-South trade under the multilateral trade system. The potential of minilateralism and South-South trade should consequently be explored as an alternative.

There is, however, a major difference in the power of the "demonstration effect" of the 1980s and the experience of the 1950s. It is true that in both circumstances, European countries have played an important role: in the 1950s with the Treaty of Rome, today with the project of European integration in 1992. But the position of the United States with respect to minilateralism has changed dramatically. The open hostility of the past has been substituted by a much more pragmatic approach, which some authors have even identified as a clear trend back to bilateralism.[19] The turning point for U.S. attitudes appears to have occurred at the 1982 GATT Ministerial Meeting, when the U.S. effort to launch a new multilateral round of negotiations centered on the so-called "new themes" (services, trade-related aspects of intellectual property rights, trade-related aspects of investment measures, and high-technology trade) was defeated.[20] As Schott (1989) notes, after this setback the United States began to pursue a dual-track strategy with respect to trade liberalization. Although it maintained the rhetoric in favor of the multilateral approach (an effort which finally led to the Uruguay Round), the United States also began to pursue bilateral trade agreements with some of its major economic (Canada) and political (Israel) partners.

The architects of the new American strategy have made a determined effort to present it as a tactical device to foster trade liberalization and eventually to strengthen the multilateral system. William E. Brock, the former U.S. Trade Representative, for instance, stated in September 1984 that:

Without any diminution in its adherence to or support for the GATT, the United States is proceeding with various groups of countries or individual countries to explore trade liberalization on a basis less comprehensive than GATT. . . . The reasoning behind these efforts is that additional trade-creating, GATT-consistent liberalization measures should not be postponed while some of the more inward-looking contracting parties contemplate their own economic malaise. (Brock [1985: 38])

Minilateralism, in other words, is presented as a more efficient way to address trade liberalization among like-minded nations, avoiding the "free-rider" and the "convoy" problems which plague multilateral negotiations.[21] It is also true that these agreements have allowed the United States to break new ground in terms of international cooperation, especially in establishing rules for trade in services. Yet, as I have pointed out elsewhere (Primo Braga, 1989b), the movement toward bloc formation is definitely a movement toward discrimination. By becoming a frequent user of GATT's Article XXIV, the United States favors vested interests and the consequent fragmentation of the world trade system. The negative impact of such a strategy will be directly proportional to the magnitude of the trade diversion associated with these agreements. Even if trade creation dominates trade diversion in the case of U.S. minilateral arrangements, defensive reaction of those countries affected by trade diversion may create additional incentives for bloc formation. Furthermore, as

Whalley (1988: 175) has observed, the basic message conveyed to the rest of the world "is that the United States, the pillar of the GATT system, has gone bilateral with its largest trading partner."

III. THE IMPACT OF THE NEW MINILATERALISM IN LATIN AMERICA

An important implication of the new minilateralism for Latin American countries is the possibility of free-trade area negotiations between Latin American countries and the United States.[22] For the United States, the natural candidates for minilateral initiatives are Mexico and the Caribbean Basin countries. From the point of view of this chapter, however, the main question is to what extent the new minilateralism will foster successful regional integration attempts in Latin America.

The most important minilateral experiment in Latin America today is the Argentina-Brazil Economic Integration Program (ABEIP).[23] Beginning in July 1986, Brazil and Argentina signed several protocols dealing with sectoral trade, the formation of binational companies, and other programs of bilateral cooperation, among them joint high-technology and economic research and coordinated nuclear policies. At the core of the ABEIP is Protocol No. 1, which defines a "universe" of capital goods to be considered for reciprocal trade liberalization. A "common list" (a subset of the "universe") was established and tariffs and nontariff barriers (NTBs) for these products were abolished, starting in 1987.[24] The common list is expected to correspond to 50 percent of the so-called universe by 1990. Several mechanisms to assure "dynamic equilibrium," defined as an imbalance not superior to 10 percent in bilateral trade over a four-month period, were also introduced. These included the possibility of a "fast-track" expansion of the common list and the use of bilateral funds to finance investments in the capital-goods industry of the country in deficit. This protocol also established that the level of protection against third-country imports of goods in the common list should be similar in Brazil and in Argentina.

Baumann and Lerda (1987) have pointed out that the ABEIP is essentially a sectoral customs union in capital goods. This kind of approach toward economic integration does not conform to GATT discipline as spelled out by Article XXIV. The "Enabling Clause" of November 1979, however, provides for differential treatment in the case of regional agreements among LDCs.[25] To say that the ABEIP is formally GATT-consistent under the "Enabling Clause," however, does not say much about its economic consistency. There are no reliable estimates on the impact of the ABEIP in terms of trade creation and trade diversion. The potential for trade diversion is significant since the barriers against imports from third countries remain high in both Brazil and in Argentina. Furthermore, as the cost structures of both countries in capital goods are not internationally competitive, the welfare gains per unit of trade creation will tend to be small, while the costs per unit of trade diversion will tend to be large. There may be, however, other considerations outside the conventional trade creation/trade diversion calculus which favor the ABEIP on economic grounds. Less distorted patterns of consumption, economies of scale and a more efficient allocation of resources in R&D are some of the potential benefits that may result from the agreement. In any case, economic stabilization in both countries is a necessary prior condition for meaningful economic integration.[26]

The ABEIP trade concessions are being made under the Montevideo Treaty rules, which gave origin to the LAIA. Brazil and Argentina appear willing to extend these bilateral preferential agreements to other Latin American countries in the future. Uruguay has in fact already joined the process. This sectoral approach to economic integration with limited partnership is probably the easiest way to proceed in the case of economies in which there is no strong political support for comprehensive trade liberalization. Nonetheless, the new minilateralism can be a highly inefficient strategy for LDCs, if it is not pursued in parallel with a broader program of trade liberalization.

In summary, the new minilateralism does not offer a revolutionary path for economic integration in Latin America. In reality, it will probably foster disintegration to the extent that Mexico and the Caribbean Basin countries will tend to be attracted by preferential deals with the United States. For the most developed economies in the region, the new minilateralism may provide an attractive option for the pursuit of intra-industry specialization. Its potential costs, however, should not be ignored.

IV. CONCLUSION

U.S. policies have influenced Latin American regional integration attempts in many ways. In the past, when the United States was a staunch supporter of the multilateral approach, the influence was more in form than in substance. Despite U.S. efforts to discourage discriminatory trade practices, Latin American countries were attracted by minilateralism as a natural complement to their inward-oriented development strategies. In the 1980s, despite U.S. rhetoric in favor of the GATT system, its perceived slide toward bilateralism has fostered a renewed interest in bloc formation in the region.

The future of the new minilateralism in Latin America will depend both on exogenous and endogenous variables. It is quite clear that any attempt to deepen regional integration efforts in Latin America will first require the successful implementation of stabilization programs in the region. Stabilization is a necessary condition because macroeconomic instability not only constrains the role of the public sector in the process by hampering its investment and financing capacities, but also distorts the private calculus required for appropriate trade decisions. Macroeconomic stabilization, however, is not a sufficient condition for effective regional integration programs. If these programs are implemented amid high levels of protection against nonparticipants, the potential for trade diversion is very high. In such a scenario, the new minilateralism will probably add another chapter to the history of failures in regional integration attempts.

It is important to recognize that an open and growing multilateral trade system is the best antidote against the lure of discriminatory trade arrangements. The present U.S. dual-track approach is inconsistent, since it sends the wrong signals to LDCs and may foster bloc formation around the world. The higher the level of discrimination in these trade arrangements, the greater is the likely damage to the world trade system. The best scenario for the new minilateralism in Latin America would thus be one combining the long-run dynamic benefits of economic integration at regional level with a global movement toward trade liberalization. In this context, the successful completion of the Uruguay Round would be a major step in the right direction.

NOTES

1. For simplicity, the term multilateralism is used as synonomous with GATT. As Jackson (1987) has noted, one can envision a multilateral system which does not depend on the most-favored-nation (MFN) principle or on the institution of GATT. Minilateralism, in turn, is used here as a general concept covering regional and other non-multilateral arrangements, linking the bilateral agreements of two or more countries. On this point, see also Diebold (1988).

2. This section follows Primo Braga (1989a and 1989b).

3. The Caribbean Community (CARICOM) was established by the English-speaking countries of the region in 1973 as a substitute for the Caribbean Free Trade Area. Its central element is the Caribbean Common Market. Although data on CARICOM is presented in Table 8.1, this regional arrangement is not examined in this study.

4. On this topic see Dornbusch (1986).

5. A good summary of the history of regional integration attempts in Latin American is given by Mace (1988).

6. See, for example, ECLA (1959).

7. This point is also made by Tussie (1987).

8. Mace (1988) notes that LAFTA embraced "all the Spanish-speaking countries of South America (except Bolivia and Venezuela, who joined later), Brazil, and Mexico."

9. Further details are given in Versiani (1987).

10. The S&D debate at the GATT level is discussed in Wolf (1987) and in Martone and Primo Braga (1988).

11. The original CACM participants were Costa Rica, El Salvador, Guatemala, Honduras, and Nicaragua.

12. See Mace (1988).

13. This position was maintained despite congressional ambivalence towards GATT, an issue examined by Jackson (1987).

14. Bolivia, Chile, Colombia, Ecuador, and Peru were the original members. Venezuela joined in 1973. Further details are given in Wonnacott and Lutz (1989).

15. On this subject see Milenky (1971).

16. For details see Tussie (1987).

17. Our focus in this section is on the "umbrella" character of the LAIA (Tussie, 1987) and on the most important bilateral trade arrangement made under it, the Argentina-Brazil Economic Integration Program. It should be noted, however, that the Cartagena Agreement was amended in 1987 in an effort to reactivate subregional trade. Attempts to revitalize economic integration in Central are also being implemneted under the recent Constituent Treaty on the Central American Parliament. For a discussion, see IADB (1988).

18. These two schools of "export pessimism" are discussed by Bhagwati (1986).

19. See, for example, Schott (1989) and Jackson (1987).

20. A brief description of the clash in Geneva in 1982 as well as the negotiations which finally led to the Uruguay Round is given in Primo Braga (1989c).

21. Wonnacott and Lutz (1989) explain these problems in the following way: "During a multilateral negotiation, when concessions are to be extended to all parties, there is a political incentive to hold back, keeping one's own tariff barriers up while hoping to get the advantages of other countries' tariff cuts. The only way to avoid free-riding is to make cuts only when every participant is willing to do so. In this case, the least willing participant determines the pace of negotiations; the speed of the convoy moving toward freer trade is limited by the speed of the slowest ship."

22. Fritsch (1989) has analyzed the difficulties for LDCs engaging in comprehensive FTA negotiations with the United States.

23. The description of the ABEIP presented here relies extensively on Martone and Primo Braga (1988). For a more detailed analysis of the ABEIP, see Baumann and Lerda (1987).

24. Baumann (1988) notes that the common list "concentrates in machine tools for metalwork, machinery for the food industry and for beverage production, machinery for leather and footwear industries and equipment for the agricultural sector." The common list originally included 140 items (LAIA classification), representing 320 products. Seventy-four more items (representing 126 additional products) were added to the list in June 1987 (IADB, 1988).

25. Details on the "enabling clause" are given in Long (1987).

26. This issue is discussed by Primo Braga and Fasano (1988).

Bibliography

Accolla, Peter. "Caught in the Middle: A Special Study of Privatization in Latin America and its Impact on Workers and Their Unions." U.S. Department of Labor, Bureau of International Labor Affairs, November 1988.(Mimeograph.)

Agee, Phillip. *Inside the Company: CIA Diary.* New York: Stonehill, 1975.

Aguirre, Ubaldo, and Ernesto Feldman. "The Argentine Financial Sector." In Richard Portes and Alexandre Swoboda, eds., *Threats to International Financial Stability.* New York: Cambridge University Press, 1987.

Alba, Victor. *Politics and the Labor Movement in Latin America.* Stanford: Stanford University Press, 1968.

Alexander, Robert J. *Organized Labor in Latin America.* New York: The Free Press, 1965.

Alexander, Robert J., and Henry S. Hammond. "Report on United States Government Labor Programs in Latin America." Washington, D.C.: U.S. AID, August 1975.(Mimeograph.)

American Federation of Labor and Congress of Industrial Organizations (AFL-CIO). *The AFL-CIO Abroad.* Publication No. 182. Washington, D.C.: AFL-CIO, August 1987.

American Federation of Labor and Congress of Industrial Organizations (AFL-CIO). *The AFL-CIO's Foreign Policy.* Publication No. 181. Washington, D.C.: AFL-CIO, August 1987.

American Institute for Free Labor Development (AIFLD). *Twenty-Five Years of Solidarity with Latin American Workers.* Washington, D.C.: 1987.

Baer, Werner. "The Resurgence of Inflation in Brazil, 1974–86." *World Development* 15, no. 3 (1987): 1007–1034.

Baer, Werner. *The Brazilian Economy: Growth and Development.* 3rd ed. New York: Praeger, 1989.

Baer, Werner, and Paul Beckerman. "The Trouble with Index-Linking: Reflections on the Recent Brazilian Experience." *World Development* 2, nos. 10–11 (1980).

Baer, Werner, and John H. Welch. "The Resurgence of Inflation in Latin America." Special edition of *World Development* 15, no. 8 (1987).

Banco Interamericano de Desarrollo. *Progreso Economico y Social en America Latina: Tema Especial: Fuerza de Trabajo y Empleo.* Washington, D.C.: Banco Interamericano de Desarrollo, 1987.

Baumann, Renato. "Brazil-Argentina Economic Integration: A Partial Approach." Paper presented at the panel "Economic Crisis and Prospects for a Brazil-Argentina Common Market." New Orleans, Latin American Studies Association XIV International Congress, 1988. (Mimeograph.)

Baumann, Renato and Juan C. Lerda. "A Integração Econômica entre Brasil, Argentina e Uruguai: Que Tipo de Integração se Pretende?" In R. Baumann and J. C. Lerda, eds., *Brasil-Argentina-Uruguai: A integração em Debate.* São Paulo: Editora Marco Zero, 1987.

Beckerman, Paul. "Inflation and Dollar Accounts in Peru's Banking System, 1978–84" *World Development* 15, no. 3 (1987): 1087–1106.

Beckerman, Paul. "Ativos Financeiros Indexados e o Mecanismo de Realimentação Inflacionária no Brasil," *Pesquisa e Planejamento Econômico* 9, no. 2 (1979).

Bendiner, Burton. *International Labour Affairs: The World Trade Unions and the Multinational Corporations.* Oxford: Clarendon, 1987.

Bhagwati, Jagdish N. "Export Promoting Trading Strategy: Issues and Evidence." (World Bank Discussion Paper). Washington, D.C., 1986.

Brock, William E. "U.S. Trade Policy Toward Developing Countries." In E. H. Preeg, ed., Hard Bargaining Ahead: U.S. Trade Policy and Developing Countries. Washington, D.C.: Overseas Development Council, 1985.

Calcagno, Alfred, and Amalia Martinez. *La Evolución de la Estrategía de los Bancos Acreedores.* Buenos Aires: Ministerio del Relaciones Exteriores y Culto, Centro de Economia Internacional, 1988.

Calvo, Guillermo A. "Fractured Liberalism under Martinez de Hoz." In Pedro Aspe Armella, Rudiger Dornbusch, and Maurice Obstfeld, eds., *Financial Policies and the World Capital Market: The Problem of Latin American Countries.* Chicago: University of Chicago Press, 1983.

Cantor, Daniel, and Juliet Schor. *Tunnel Vision: Labor, the World Economy, and Central America.* Boston, MA: South End Press, 1987.

Carrizosa, Mauricio, and Antonio Urdinela. "El endeudamiento privada interna in Colombia, 1975–85." *Revista de la CEPAL* 32 (August 1987): 27–53.

Casar, María Amparo, and Wilson Peres. *El estado empresario en Mexico: Agotamiento o Renovación?* Mexico: Sigeo Ventiuno Editores, 1988.

Caskey, John. "The IMF and Concerted Lending in Latin American Debt Restructurings: A Formal Analysis." *Journal of International Money and Finance* 8 (March 1989): 105–120.

Castro, Antonio Barros de, and Francisco Eduardo Pires de Souza. *A economia brasileira em marcha forçada.* Rio de Janeiro: Paz e Terra, 1985.

Cavanagh, John, et al. *Trade's Hidden Costs: Worker Rights in a Changing World Economy.* Washington, D.C.: International Labor Rights Education and Research Fund, 1988.

Charnovitz, Steve. "The Influence of International Labour Standards on the World Trading Regime: A Historical Overview." *International Labour Review* 126, no. 5 (September–October 1987).

Corbo, Vittorio, and Jaime de Melo, eds., "Liberalization with Stabilization in the Southern Cone of Latin America." Special edition of *World Development* 13, no. 8 (1985).

Corbo, Vittorio, Jaime de Melo, and James Tybout. "What Went Wrong in the Southern Cone?" *Economic Development and Cultural Change* 34, no. 3 (1986).

Dell, S. *A Latin American Common Market?* London: Oxford University Press, 1966.

Diaz-Alejandro, Carlos. "Goodbye Financial Repression, Hello Financial Crash." *Journal of Development Economics* 19, 1985.

Diebold, William, Jr. "The History and the Issues." In William Diebold Jr., ed., *Bilateralism, Multilateralism and Canada in U.S. Trade Policy*. The Council on Foreign Relations Series on International Trade. Cambridge, Mass.: Ballinger Publishing Company, 1988.

Doherty, William C., Jr. "Labor and the Alliance." In L. Ronald Scheman, ed., *The Alliance for Progress*. New York: Praeger, 1988.

Dornbusch, Rudiger. "The Effects of OECD Macroeconomic Policies on Non-Oil Developing Countries: A Review." World Bank Staff Working Paper 793. Washington, D.C., 1986.

Dornbusch, Rudiger, and Stanley Fischer. "Stopping Hyperinflations Past and Present." *Welwirtschaftliches Archiv* 122, April 1986.

Echenique, José Piñera. *Privatization in Chile*. La Jolla: University of California at San Diego, Institute of the Americas, May 1988.

ECLA. *The Latin American Common Market*. Mexico, United Nations Economic Commission for Latin America, 1959.

ECLA. "Potencialidades y Limitaciones de la Integracion y Cooperacion." Notas Sobre La Economia y el Desarrollo 465, July 1988.

The Economist 26 (November 1988): 112.

Edwards, Sebastian. "On the Timing and Speed of Economic Liberalization in Developing Countries." In Michael Connally and Claudio Gonzales-Vega, eds., *Economic Reform and Stabilization in Latin America*. New York: Praeger, 1987.

Edwards, Sebastian, and Sweder Van Wijnbergen. "The Welfare Effects of Trade and Capital Market Liberalization." *International Economic Review* 27, no. 1 (1986).

Errazuriz, Enrique. "Capitalización de la Deuda Externa y Desnacionalización de la Economía Chilena." Santiago: Academia de Humanismo Cristiano Programa de Economía del Trabajo, Documento de Trabajo no. 57, Agosto 1987.

Escamilla, Juan Perez. *La Venta de Empresas del Sector Público, 1983–1988*. Mexico: Secretaria de Hacienda, 1988.

Felix, David. "Income Distribution and the Quality of Life in Latin America: Patterns, Trends, and Policy Implications." *Latin American Research Review* 18, no. 2 (1983): 3–33.

Felix, David. "Solving Latin America's Debt Crisis." *Challenge* 28 (November/December 1985):44–51.

Felix, David. "On Financial Blowups and Authoritarian Regimes in Latin America." In Jonathan Hartlyn and Samuel A. Morley, eds., *Latin American Political Economy: Financial Crisis and Political Change*. Boulder: Westview Press, 1986.

Felix, David, and Juana Sanchez. "Capital Flight Aspects of the Latin American Debt Crisis." In Peter Gray, ed., *The Modern International Environment*, Greenwich, Connecticut, JAI Press. 1989.

Ffrench-Davis, Ricardo. "Debt and Growth in Chile: Trends and Prospects." In David Felix, ed., *Debt and Transfiguration: Prospects for Latin America's Economic Revival*. New York: M.E. Sharpe, 1990.

Form, William H., and Albert A. Blum. *Industrial Relations and Social Change in Latin America*. Gainesville: University of Florida Press, 1965.

Foxley, Alejandro. "Towards a Free Market Economy; Chile 1974–1979." *Journal of Development Economics* 10 (1982): 3–29.

Fraga, Javier Gonzalez. "Privatization in Argentina." La Jolla: University of California at San Diego, Institute of the Americas, May 1988. (Mimeograph.)

Freedom House. "Worker Freedoms in Latin America." In Raymond D. Gastil, ed., *Freedom in the World: Political Rights and Civil Liberties*. Westport: Greenwood, 1982.

Fritsch, Winston. "The New Minilateralism and Developing Countries." In J. J. Schott, ed., *Free Trade Areas and U.S. Trade Policies*. Washington, D.C.: Institute for International Economics, 1989.

FUNCEP. *Estatização e Privatização, Os Limites da Intervenção do Estado*. São Paulo, 1987.

Fundación de Investigaciones Económicas Latinoamericanos. *El Fracao del Estatismo*. Buenos Aires: Sudamericana/Planeta, 1987.

Gallegos, Armando. Mapa Económico Financiero dela Actividad Empresarial del Estado Peruano. Lima: ESAN, 1985.

Galvez, Julio, and James Tybout. "Microeconomic Adjustments in Chile during 1977–1981: The Importance of Being a Grupo." *World Development* 13, no. 8 (1985).

Gaspar, Edward. *United States–Latin America: A Special Relationship*. AEI-Hoover policy studies 26. Washington, D.C.: American Enterprise Institute, 1974.

GATT. *The Text of the General Agreement on Tariffs and Trade*. Geneva: GATT, 1986.

Glade, William P. *The Latin American Economies*. New York: American Book, 1969.

Glade, William P. "Mexico: Party-Led Development." In Robert Wesson, ed., *Politics, Policies and Development in Latin America*, 1984.

Godson, Roy. "Corporate Unionism: An Erroneous and Misleading Theory of American Labor's International Involvement." *Labor Studies Journal*, Winter 1982.

Goldsmith, Raymond. *Financial Structure and Development*. New Haven: Yale University Press, 1969.

Greenfield, Gerald Michael, and Sheldon L. Maram. *Latin American Labor Organizations*. Westport, CT: Greenwood, 1987.

Greenwald, Bruce, Joseph E. Stiglitz, and Andrew Weiss. "Informational Imperfections in the Capital Market and Macroeconomic Fluctuations." *American Economic Review*, May 1984.

Guttentag, Jack M., and Richard Herring. "Accounting for Losses on Sovereign Debt: Implications for New Lending." *Princeton Essays in International Finance* no. 172. Princeton U. Press, 1989.

Hachette, Dominique, and Rolf Luders. *Aspects of the Privatization Process: The Case of Chile, 1974–82*. Washington D.C.: the World Bank, 1987.

Hachette, Dominique. *Aspects of Privatization: the Case of Chile 1974–85*. Washington, D.C.: the World Bank, April 1988.

Hanson, James, and Jaime de Melo. "External Shocks, Financial Reforms, and Stabilization Attempts in Uruguay during 1974–1983." *World Development* 13, no. 8 (1985).

Inter-American Development Bank. *Economic and Social Progress in Latin America*. Washington, D.C., various years.

International Labour Office. *Bibliography of Published Research of the World Employment Programme*. 7th ed. *International Labour Bibliography* no. 4. Geneva: ILO, 1988.

International Labour Office. *Employment, Growth, and Basic Needs: A One-World Problem.* New York: Praeger, for the Overseas Development Council, 1977.

International Labour Organisation. *High-Level Meeting on Employment and Structural Adjustment.* Geneva, 23–25, November 1987: Report of the meeting. Geneva: International Labour Office, 1988.

International Monetary Fund. *IMF Survey,* various issues.

Jackson, John H. "Multilateral and Bilateral Negotiating Approaches for the Conduct of U.S. Trade Policies." In R. M. Stern, ed., *U.S. Trade Policies in a Changing World Economy.* Cambridge, Ma.: The MIT Press, 1987.

Jones, Hywel. *An Introduction to Modern Theories of Growth.* New York, 1975.

Kapstein, Ethan. "Privatization in Brazil." La Jolla: University of California at San Diego, Institute of the Americas, May 1988.(Mimeograph.)

Kwitny, Jonathan. *Endless Enemies: The Making of an Unfriendly World.* New York: Viking Penguin, 1986.

Le Fort, Guillermo R. "Financial Crisis in Developing Countries and Structural Weaknesses of the Financial System." *IMF Working Paper* WP/89/33, 1989.

Long, Olivier. *Law and Its Limitations in the GATT Multilateral Trade System.* Dordrecht: Martinus Nijhoff Publishers, 1987.

Losoviz, Horacio A. "Empresas Publicas en Argentina, Realidad y Nuevas Políticas." Buenos Aires: Ministerio de Obras y Servicios Públicos, 1988. (Mimeograph.)

Lowenthal, Abraham F. *Partners in Conflict: The United States and Latin America.* Baltimore and London: Johns Hopkins University Press, 1987.

Mace, Gordon. "Regional Integration in Latin America: A Long and Winding Road." *International Journal* 43 (Summer 1988): 404–427.

Marcel, Mario. *La Privatización de Empresas Públicas en Chile 1985–88.* Santiago: CIEPLAN, Notas Tecnicas 125, January 1989.

Marshall, Adriana. "Non-Standard Employment Practices in Latin America." Discussion Paper of the Labour Market Programme of the International Institute for Labour Studies. Geneva: 1987.

Marshall, Jorge, and Felipe Montt. "Privatization in Chile." Santiago: March 1987. (Mimeograph.)

Marshall, Ray, and Richard Perlman. *An Anthology of Labor Economics: Readings and Commentary.* New York: John Wiley & Sons, 1972.

Marshall, Ray. "Jobs: The Shifting Structure of Global Employment." In John W. Sewell, et al., eds., *Growth, Exports, and Jobs in a Changing World Economy: Agenda 1988.* New Brunswick (USA): Transaction Books, 1988.

Martone, Celso, and C. A. Primo Braga. "Brazil and the Uruguay Round." Paper presented at the conference "The Multilateral Trade Negotiations and the Developing Countries," Washington D.C., September 15–16, 1988, The Rockefeller Foundation and the Institute for International Economics. (Mimeograph.)

Massad, Carlos, and Roberto Zahler. "Otro angulo de la crisis latinoamericano: la deuda interna." *Revista de la CEPAL* 32, August 1987.

Massad, Carlos, and Roberto Zahler, eds. *Deuda Interna y Estabilidad Financiera* Vol. 1–Vol. 2. Buenos Aires: Grupo Editor Latinoamericano, 1988.

Maxfield, Sylvia. "Losing Command of the Heights: The Politics of Mexican Financial Policy." Yale University, 1988.

McKinnon, Ronald I. *Money and Capital in Economic Development.* Washington, D.C: The Brookings Institution, 1973.

Mead, Walter Russell. *Mortal Splendor: The American Empire in Transition*. Boston: Houghton Mifflin, 1987.

Melo, Jaime de, Ricardo Pascale, and James Tybout. "Microeconomic Adjustments in Uruguay during 1973–1981: The Interplay of Real and Financial Shocks." *World Development* 13, no. 8 (1985).

Melo, Jaime de. "The Order of Economic Liberalization: Lessons from Chile and Argentina." In Karl Brunner and Alan Meltzer, eds., "Economic Policy in a World of Change." *Carnegie-Rochester Series on Public Policy* 17. Amsterdam: North Holland Publishing, 1982.

Melo, Jaime de. "How to Manage a Repressed Economy." In Armin Gutowski, A. A. Arnaudo, and Hans-Eckart Scharrer, eds., *Financing Problems of Developing Countries*. London: MacMillan, 1985.

Melo, Jaime de. *Financial Liberalization and Economic Development: A Reassessment of Interest Rate Policies in Asia and Latin America*. San Francisco: International Center for Economic Growth, 1988.

Milenky, Edward S. "From Integration to Developmental Nationalism: The Andean Group 1965–1971." *Inter-American Economic Affairs* 25 (Winter 1971): 77–92.

Morgan Guaranty Trust. *World Financial Markets*, March 1989.

Morse, David A. *The Origin and Evolution of the I.L.O. and its Role in the World Community*. Ithaca: New York School of Industrial and Labor Relations, 1969.

NACLA. *Report on the Americas* 22, no. 2 (March/April 1988).

NACLA. "Neither Pure nor Simple: The AFL-CIO and Latin America." *NACLA Report on the Americas* 22, no. 3 (May/June 1988): 13–40.

New York Times, July 20, 1989.

Nogueira Batista, Paulo, Jr. "Formação de capital e Transferências." Working paper, Fundação Getúlio Vargas, Rio de Janeiro, 1986.

Onandi, D., and L. Viana. "El deficit parafiscal: un analisis de la experiencia Uruguayana." Paper presented to CEMLA, Seminario: Efectos Monetarios de la Politica Fiscal, Brasilia, August 1987.

Palmer, David Scott. "Peru: Military and Civilian Political Economy." In Robert Wesson, ed., *Politics, Policies, and Development in Latin America*. Stanford, Hoover Institution Press, 1984.

Patterson, Gardner. Implications for the GATT and the World Trading System." In J. J. Schott, ed., *Free Trade Areas and U.S. Trade Policy*. Washington, D.C.: Institute for International Economics, 1989.

Petrei, A. Humberto, and James Tybout. "Microeconomic Adjustments in Argentina during 1976–1981: The Importance of Changing Levels of Financial Subsidies." *World Development* 13, no. 8 (1985).

Piekarz, Julio A. "El deficit fiscal del Banco Central." Paper presented to the Centro de Estudios Monetarios para America Latina (CEMLA), Seminario: Efectos Monetarios de la Politica Fiscal, Brasilia, August 1987.

PREALC. *Adjustment and Social Debt: A Structural Approach*. Geneva: International Labour Office, 1987.

Primo Braga, Carlos A. "Promoting Mutual Growth: U.S. and Latin American Trade. in *A New Framework for Global Growth in the 1990s*. Hearings before the Subcommittee on International Economic Policy and Trade of the Committee on

Foreign Affairs, U.S. House of Representatives. Washington, D.C., U.S. Government Printing Office, 1989a.

Primo Braga, Carlos A. "U.S.–Latin American Trade: Challenges for the 1990s." *Economic Impact* 67 (1989b): 51–55.

Primo Braga, Carlos A. "The Economics of Intellectual Property Rights and the GATT: A View from the South." *Vanderbilt Journal of Transnational Law* 22, no. 2 (1989c): 243–264.

Primo Braga, Carlos A. and Ugo Fasano Filho. "Monetary Reform and Trade in Brazil and Argentina." Paper presented at the panel "Economic Crisis and Prospects for a Brazil-Argentina Common Market." New Orleans, Latin American Studies Association XIV International Congress, 1988. (Mimeograph.)

Ramos, Joseph. *Neoconservative Economics in the Southern Cone of Latin America, 1973–1983.* Baltimore: Johns Hopkins University Press, 1986.

Reisen, Helmut, and Axel Van Trotsenburg. "Developing Country Debt: The Budgetary and Transfer Problem." Paris: OECD, 1988.

Relations Industrielles/Industrial Relations 44, no. 1 (Winter 1989).

Reveis, Edgar, and Maria Jose Perez. "Colombia: Moderate Economic Growth, Political Stability and Social Welfare." In Jonathan Hartlyn and Samuel A. Morley, eds., *Latin American Political Economy: Financial Crisis and Political Change.* Boulder: Westview Press, 1986.

Reyes Heroles, Jesus. "Operaciones cuasi-fiscales' in un contexto de estabilizacion: un apunte sobre la experiencia de Mexico in 1986–87." Paper presented to CEMLA, Seminario: Efectos Monetarios de la Politica Fiscal, Brasilia, August 1987.

Richie, Martha F. "The American Institute for Free Labor Development." *Monthly Labor Review* 88(9) (Sept. 1965): 1049–1055.

Robinson, Donald. "Bill Doherty's Blue-Collar Freedom Fighters." *Reader's Digest* (September 1985): 141–144.

Robinson, Joan. "The Production Function and the Theory of Capital." *Review of Economic Studies* (1953/1954): 88–106.

Sachs, Jeffrey. "Bolivia: 1952–1986." *Country Study* no. 6. San Francisco: International Center for Economic Growth, 1988.

Saez, Raul. "La Privatización de la Compañía de Aceros del Pacífico (CAP)." Materiales para Discusion no. 180. Santiago: Centro de Estudios del Desarrollo, 1987.

Saraiva, Enrique. "The Brazilian Privatization Program." Rio de Janeiro: Fundação Getúlio Vargas, Inter-American School of Public Administration, 1988. (Mimeograph.)

Saulniers, Alfred H. "Public Enterprises in Latin America: Their Origins and Importance." *International Review of Administrative Sciences* 51, no. 4 (1985): 329–448.

Saulniers, Alfred H. *Public Enterprises in Peru: Public Sector Growth and Reform.* Boulder, Colorado: Westview Press, 1988.

Schechter, Henry B. "IMF Conditionality and the International Economy: A U.S. Labor Perspective." In Robert J. Myers, ed., *The Political Morality of the International Monetary Fund, Ethics and Foreign Policy* Vol.3. New Brunswick: Transaction, 1985.

Scheetz, Thomas. "Public Sector Expenditures and Financial Crisis in Chile." *World Development* 15, no. 8 (1987): 1053–1075.

Schott, Jeffrey J. "More Free Trade Areas." In J. J. Schott, ed., *Free Trade Areas and U.S. Trade Policies*. Washington, D.C.: Institute for International Economics, 1989.

Schoultz, Lars. *Human Rights and United States Policy toward Latin America*. Princeton: Princeton University Press, 1981.

Schydlowsky, Daniel M. "The Tragedy of Lost Opportunity in Peru." In Jonathan Hartlyn and Samuel A. Morley, eds., *Latin American Political Economy: Financial Crisis and Political Change*. Boulder: Westview Press, 1986.

Selowsky, Marcelo, and Hermann C. van der Tak. "Economic Growth and External Debt." *World Development* (September 1986): 1107–1124.

Shaw, Edward, S. *Financial Deepening in Economic Development*. New York: Oxford University Press, 1973.

Sheahan, John. *Patterns of Development in Latin America*. Princeton, N. J.: Princeton University Press, 1987.

Simonsen, Mario Henrique. "Os Rumos da Dívida Externa." *Conjuntura Econômica*, March 1984.

Spiller, Pablo T., and Edgardo Favaro. "The Effects of Entry on Oligopolistic Interaction: the Uruguayan Banking Sector." *Rand Journal of Economics* 15, no. 2 (1984).

Stiglitz, Joseph, and Andrew Weiss. "Credit Rationing in Markets with Imperfect Information." *American Economic Review*, June 1981.

Stiglitz, Joseph. "Credit Markets and the Control of Capital." *Journal of Money, Credit and Banking* 17, no. 2 (1985).

Superintendecia de Bancos e Instituciones Financieras. "Comparaciones de Patrones Internacionales de Resultados, Chile, E.E.U.U." *Información Financiera*, October 1982.

Tendler, Judith. *The Electric Power Industry in Brazil*. Cambridge, MA: Harvard University Press, 1968.

Trebat, Thomas J. *Brazil's State-Owned Enterprises: A Case Study of the State as Entrepreneur*. New York: Cambridge University Press, 1983.

Trebat, Thomas J. "An Evaluation of the Economic Performance of Public Enterprises in Brazil " Ph.D. dissertation, Vanderbilt University, 1978.

Tussie, Diana. *The Less Developed Countries and the World Trading System: A Challenge to the GATT*. New York: St. Martin's Press, 1987.

Tybout, James. "A Firm Level Chronicle of Financial Crisis in the Southern Cone." *Journal of Development Economics* 24 (1986).

Ugalde, Alberto J. *Las Empresas Publicas en la Argentina*. Buenos Aires: Ediciones El Cronista Comercial, 1984.

U.N. Economic Commission for Latin America and the Caribbean. *Economic Panorama of Latin America*, 1988.

U.S. Congress. Country Reports on Economic Policy and Trade Practices. Report submitted to the Committee on Foreign Affairs, Committee on Ways and Means of the U.S. House of Representatives and Committee on Foreign Relations, Committee on Finance of the U.S. Senate by the Department of State in accordance with Section 2202 of the Omnibus Trade and Competitiveness Act of 1988. Joint Committee Print. 101st Cong., 1st Sess., 1989.

U.S. Department of Commerce. *Survey of Current Business,* various issues.

Vera, Oscar. "The Political Economy of Privatization in Mexico." La Jolla: University of California at San Diego, Institute of the Americas, May 1988. (Mimeograph.)

Versiani, Flávio R. "A Experiência Latino-Americana de Integração e os Novos Acordos Brasil-Argentina-Uruguai." In R. Baumann and J.C. Lerda, eds., *Brasil-Argentina-Uruguai: A Integração em Debate.* São Paulo: Editora Zero, 1987.

Wall Street Journal, May 10, 1989. *Wall Street Journal,* July 25, 1989. Webb, Richard. "Deuda interna y ajuste financiero in el Peru." *Revista de la CEPAL* 32 (August 1987): 55–74.

Weinrub, Al, and William Bollinger. *The AFL-CIO in Central America: A Look at the American Institute for Free Labor Development.* Oakland, CA: Labor Network on Central America, 1987.

Welch, John H., Carlos A. Primo Braga, and Paulo T. A. Andre. "Brazilian Public Sector Disequilibrium." *World Development* 15, no. 8 (1985).

Welch, John H. *Capital Markets in the Development Process: The Case of Brazil.* Pittsburgh: University of Pittsburgh Press, 1989.

Werneck, Rogerio L.F. "The Uneasy Steps of Privatization in Brazil." La Jolla: University of California at San Diego, Institute of the Americas, May 1988. (Mimeograph.)

Whalley, John. "Comments." In J. J. Schott and M. G. Smith, eds., *The Canada–United States Free Trade Agreement: The Global Impact.* Washington, D.C.: Institute for International Economics, 1988.

Windmuller, John P. "Labor Internationals: A Survey of Contemporary International Trade Union Organizations." Bulletin 61, April 1969, New York State School of Industrial and Labor Relations, Cornell University, Ithaca, New York.

Wolf, Martin. "Differential and More Favorable Treatment of Developing Countries and the International Trading System." *The World Bank Economic Review* 1 (September 1987): 647–668.

Wonnacott, Paul, and Mark Lutz. "Is There a Case for Free Trade Areas? In J. J. Schott, ed., *Free Trade Areas and U.S. Trade Policy.* Washington, D.C.: Institute for International Economics, 1989.

World Bank. *Poverty in Latin America: The Impact of Depression.* Washington, D.C.: The World Bank, 1986.

World Bank. *World Debt Tables.* Washington, D.C.: The World Bank, various years.

Zahler, Roberto. "Recent Southern Cone Liberalization Reforms and Stabilization Policies: The Chilean Case, 1974–82." *CEPAL Review,* 1984.

Author Index

Accolla, Peter, 135
Agee, Phillip, 136
Aguirre, Ubaldo, 150
American Institute for Free Labor
    Development, 135–136
Alba, Victor, 135–136
Alexander, Robert J., 135–136
André, Paulo T., 149

Baer, Werner, 30, 149
Banco Interamericano de Desarrollo. *See*
    Inter-American Development Bank
Baumann, Renato, 164, 167
Beckerman, Paul, 30, 138, 149
Bendiner, Burton, 136
Bhagwati, Jagdish, 167
Blum, Albert A., 135
Bollinger, William, 136
Brock, William E., 163

Calcagno, Alfred, 6, 10, 37
Calvo, Guillermo A., 138
Cantor, Daniel, 136
Carrizosa, Mauricio, 38
Casar, María Amparo, 96
Caskey, John, 37
Castro, Antonio B., 135
Cavallo, Domingo, 138
Cavanagh, John, 136
Charnovitz, Steve, 136
Corbo, Vittorio, 137–138

Dell, Sidney, 157

Diaz Alejandro, Carlos, 137–138, 151
Diebold, William, Jr., 166
Doherty, William C., Jr., 136
Dornbusch, Rudiger, 151, 166

Echenique, José Piñera, 96
Economic Commission for Latin
    America, 155–156, 166
Economist, 53
Edwards, Sebastian, 151
Errazuriz, Enrique, 96
Escamilla, Juan Perez, 96

Fasano, Ugo, 167
Favaro, Edgardo, 140
Feldman, Ernesto, 150
Felix, David, 35, 37, 137–138, 151
Ffrench-Davis, Ricardo, 18
Fischer, Stanley, 151
Form, William H., 135
Foxley, Alejandro, 96
Fraga, Javier Gonzalez, 96
Freedom House, 135
Fritsch, Winston, 167
Fundación de Investigaciones
    Económicas Latinoamericanos, 96

Gallegos, Armando, 95
Galvez, Julio, 150
Gaspar, Edward, 135
Glade, William, 139, 140
Godson, Roy, 136
Goldsmith, Raymond, 138

Greenfield, Gerald M., 135
Greenwald, Bruce, 141
Guttentag, Jack M., 37

Hachette, Dominique, 81, 96
Hammond, Henry S., 136
Hanson, James, 140
Herring, Richard, 37

IMF *International Financial Statistics*, 142, 143, 147
IMF *Survey*, 6, 38, 103
Inter-American Development Bank, 13, 17–18, 32–33, 41–42, 53, 135, 142–143, 167
International Labor Organization, 135–136

Jackson, John H., 166–167
Jones, Hywel, 57

Kapstein, Ethan, 96
Kwitny, Jonathan, 136

Le Fort, Guillermo R., 36, 38
Lerda, Juan C., 164, 167
Long, Olivier, 158, 167
Losoviz, Horacio A., 96
Lowenthal, Abraham F., 134–135
Luders, Rolf, 81, 96
Lutz, Mark, 166–167

Mace, Gordon, 166
Maram, Sheldon L., 135
Marcel, Mario, 96
Marshall, Adriana, 135
Marshall, Jorge, 96
Marshall, Ray, 135
Martinez, Amalia, 6, 10, 37
Martone, Celso, 166–167
Massad, Carlos, 30–31, 33, 38
Maxfield, Sylvia, 137, 139, 140
McKinnon, Ronald, 138, 151
Melo, Jaime de, 137–138, 140, 150
Milenky, Edward S., 167
Montt, Felipe, 96
Morales, Juan Antonio, 148
Morgan Guaranty Trust, 6

Morse, David A., 136

NACLA, 37, 136
New York Times, 14
Nogueira Batista Jr., Paulo, 55, 57

Onandi, D., 32

Palmer, David S., 138
Pascale, Ricardo, 150
Patterson, Gardner, 158
Peres, Wilson, 96
Perez, Maria José, 138
Petrei, A. Humberto, 138, 150
Piekarz, Julio A., 31, 32
Primo Braga, Carlos, 149, 163, 166, 167

Ramos, Joseph, 96
Reisen, Helmut, 31, 34
Relations Industrielles, 135
Reveis, Edgar, 138
Reyes Heroles, Jesus, 31

Sachs, Jeffrey, 148
Saez, Raul, 96
Sanchez, Juana, 37
Saravia, Enrique, 96
Saulniers, Alfred H., 76, 95
Schechter, Henry B., 135
Scheetz, Thomas, 29
Schor, Juliet, 136
Schott, Jeffrey J., 163, 167
Schoultz, Lars, 134–136
Schydlowsky, Daniel M., 138
Selowsky, Marcelo, 55
Shaw, Edward, 138
Sheahan, John, 4
Simonsen, Mario H., 56
Souza, Francisco E. Pires de, 135
Spiller, Pablo, 140
Stiglitz, Joseph, 141

Tendler, Judith, 118
Trebat, Thomas, 99, 102–103, 105–109, 111–116, 118
Tussie, Diana, 158, 166–167
Tybout, James, 137–138, 150

Ugalde, Alberto J., 99
Urdinela, Antonio, 38
U.S. Congress, 136
U.S. Department of Commerce 40–43, 46–48
U.S. Federal Reserve Bulletin, 21

van der Tak, Hermann C., 55
Van Trotsenburg, Axel, 31, 34
Van Wijnbergen, Willy, 151
Vera, Oscar, 96
Versiani, Flávio R., 166
Viana, L., 32

Wall Street Journal, 6
Weinrub, Al, 136
Weiss, Andrew, 141
Welch, John H., 137, 139–140, 149
Werneck, Rogerio L. F., 96
Whalley, John, 164
Windmuller, John P., 136
Wolf, Martin, 166
Wonnacott, Paul, 166–167
World Bank, 11–13, 19, 21, 107, 135

Zahler, Roberto, 30–31, 33, 38

Subject Index

Adjustment burden, 51, 102, 132, 145

Adjustment programs, 40–41, 155–156

Adverse selection, 141

Alfonsin, Raul, 88, 91, 101. *See also* Argentina

Allende, Salvador, 77, 78, 79, 80, 161. *See also* Chile

Alliance for Progress, 1, 128, 134

American Institute for Free Labor Development (AIFLD), 121, 127–28, 135–136

Andean Group, 160–161. *See also* Regional trade

Argentina

    Alfonsin government, foreign support, 91

    Banco de la Nación, 90

    Banco Nacional de Desarrollo, 88

    Caja Nacional de Ahorro y Seguros, 88

    capital account, 139

    capital flight, 46, 148

    capital formation, 62

    capital stock, 111

    capital use, 110–113

    commercial policy, 161, 164

    dollarization, 148

    domestic investment, 106

    economic growth, 53, 78, 99, 102

    economic policies, 91, 99–102, 110, 117–119, 149

    external debt, 9, 14, 20, 25, 37, 63, 74

financial development, 31, 141, 143, 150

financial intermediaries, 150

financial liberalization, 9, 29, 137, 141, 150

financial market efficiency, 149

fiscal deficit, 32, 33

foreign currency holdings, 150

import substitution, 157

industrial production, 105, 115

inflation, 17, 100, 102, 112, 115

inflation tax, 31, 148, 150

Interministerial Commission for Privatization, 88

Interministerial Committee on Public Enterprises, 90

internal debt creation, 150

internal market, 78

internal transfer problem, 149, 150

intra-regional trade, 158, 161, 164, 165, 167

labor force, 108

mining industry, 102, 111–113, 117

Ministry of Defense, 90

mixed enterprises, 90

net factor-service payments, 63

Plan Austral, 92

Plan Primavera, 92

political climate, 51, 88–89, 100, 110, 123

private debt, 29

private enterprise profitability, 119

privatization, 87–92

Argentina (continued)
  public enterprises, 89–92, 99–102,
    105–107, 109–119
  public sector, 92, 106–108
  quasi-fiscal deficit, 32–33
  railroads, 105
  real interest rate, 34
  resource transfer, 148
  secondary debt market, 53
  Sindicatura General de Empresas
    Publicas (SIGEP), 90, 102
  Subsecretariat of Privatization, 93
  trade liberalization, 25, 91
  U.S. exports to, 135
Argentina-Brazil Economic Integration
  Program (ABEIP), 164, 165, 167
Asociación Latinoamericana de
  Integración (ALADI), 159
Asociación Latinoamericana de Libre
  Comercio (ALALC), 158
Austerity programs, 25, 52. See also
  Restructuring programs

Bailout lending, 9–10, 37. See also Debt
  relief, External borrowing and debt
Baker Plan
  assumptions, 5, 55–56, 72
  bank lending, 6, 11, 56
  deregulation, 119
  financial liberalization, 56
  internal adjustment, 56
  privatization, 56, 119
  results, 56–59, 71
  rhetoric, 119
  trade liberalization, 56
Bank creditors, 123
Bank lending, international, 139. See
  also External borrowing and debt
Banking system
  incentive effects on, 151
  overlending, 141
  reserves, 144, 150
  solvency, 141
Bankruptcy risk, 141
Bilateral cooperation, 164
Bilateral funds, 164
Bilateral trade arrangements, 133, 158–
  167

Bolivia
  capital flight, 148
  capital formation, 62
  domestic capital market, 148
  external saving flows, 63
  financial development, 141, 143, 144
  financial market efficiency, 149
  inflation, 148
  intra-regional trade, 166
  privatization, 76
  resource transfer, 148
Brady Plan. See also Debt relief
  bank role, 12
  capital flight, 8, 20
  consequences, 27
  debt relief, 5–7, 20–21
  financial liberalization, 27
  Mexican agreement, 14
  origins, 5–6
  problems, 8, 27
  strategy, 12–15
Brazil
  "Bank Reform Act" (Law 4595), 139
  Adjustable National Treasury Bonds
    (ORTN's), 140
  balance of payments, 149
  Banco Central (BCB), 139, 149
  Banco do Brasil, 139
  bank charters, 140, 151
  banking system, 140, 151
  BNDES (Banco de Nacional de
    Desenvolvimento Econmico e
    Social), 84–87, 90, 139
  "Brazilian Miracle," 99, 101
  capital flight, 30
  capital formation, 62
  capital goods, 41, 110
  capital market, 84, 89, 139
  Capital Markets Law (Law 4728),
    140
  capital use, 110–113
  Central Bank intermediation, 150
  commercial banks, 140, 149
  commercial policy, 164
  debt burden, 31
  debt crisis, 99
  direct investment incentives, 101
  domestic market, 83
  economic growth, 15, 23–25, 53, 102

economic policies, 83–84, 98–102, 117–119, 139–140, 149
electricity sector, 109, 118
equity markets, 140
exports, 50, 53
external debt, 20, 25, 30, 37, 63, 101, 140
external transfer problem, 149
financial asset indexation, 149
financial development, 137–144, 148–150
financial vs. direct foreign investment, 45
fiscal incentives, 140
Housing Finance System (SFH), 139
IMF-type stabilization policy, 149
import substitution, 157
indexation 30, 118, 148–149
industrial production, 105
inflation, 17, 101
inflation tax, 150
infrastructure, 110
Inter-Ministerial Council on Privatization, 86
internal debt, 29–30, 34, 150
internal market, 78
internal transfer problem, 149–150
intra-regional trade, 158, 161, 164–167
investment, 15, 41, 77, 110
investment banks, 140
mining industry, 102, 105
monetary authority, 139
monetary correction, 30
National Housing Bank (BNH), 84, 139
National Monetary Council (CMN), 139
net factor-service payments, 63
"overnight" market, 149
political climate, 51, 82, 87, 99, 110, 123
price controls, 85
private enterprises, 86
private sector loans, 140
privatization
    decentralization, 84
    largest enterprises, 86

origins, 82–83, 86
political climate, 87
"of private sector," 83
procedures, 86–87
receivership, 83
resistance to, 82
role of BNDES, 87
"semi-privatization," 84
support, 83, 86, 88, 96
public enterprises, 76, 83–87, 97–99, 101–102, 105–110, 112, 114–119
public sector
    decision process, 87
    external debt, 149
    financing, 86
    investment, 107, 135
railroads, 105
real cost of capital, 140
real interest rate, 34, 139, 140
real wages, 52, 101
reprivatization, 83
Resolution 63, Central Bank, 140
resource transfer, 148
Sarney government, 82
Second National Development Plan, 101
secondary debt market, 53
Secretariat for Public Enterprise Control (SEST), 85
Special Commission for Privatization, 86
trade liberalization, 25
trade surplus, 149
U.S. exports to, 135
Bretton Woods system, 155
Brock, William E., 163
Buybacks, 156. See also Debt-equity swaps, Debt relief

Capital account liberalization, 138–139, 141, 151
Capital, equity market as source of, 141
Capital flight
    causes, 35, 36, 77
    consequences, 37, 47
    dollarization, 148
    effects, 33
    financed by U.S. banks, 46

Capital flight (continued)
    in U.S. capital account with Latin
        America, 45
    income distribution, 35
    internal transfer, 138
    obstacle to reforms, 35
    policy-induced, 155
    real interest rates, 34
    reduction in tax base, 31
    resource transfer, 137
Capital flows, private, 98
Capital formation, decline after 1982,
    61, 62
Capital goods, 126, 164
Capital inflows, 144, 150
Capital markets
    development, 137
    integration, 141
    resource transfer, 137
Capital repatriation, 8, 20, 35, 36
Capital-output ratio, 57
Caribbean Basin trade, 129, 164–166.
    See also Regional trade
Cartagena Agreement, 161, 167
Carter administration, 123
Central American Common Market
    (CACM), 159–161, 166
Central Bank intervention, 151
Central Intelligence Agency (CIA), 128
Chile
    adjustment burden, 18
    Andean group, 161
    bad bank loans, 31
    Banco Continental, 82
    bilateral government lending to, 18
    borrowing requirements, 25
    capital flight, 46, 139
    capital formation, 62
    capital market, 89
    "Chicago Boys," 18, 77
    commercial policy, 80, 161
    CORFO (Corporación de Fomento),
        79–80, 82, 87, 90
    Credit Lyonnais, interest in Banco
        Continental, 82
    debt ratio, 31
    debt restructuring, 18
    debt service, 18, 31

    deregulation, 77, 80
    economic growth, 15, 24–25, 78
    economic policies, 77, 78, 80–81, 161
    external debt, 6, 9, 20, 25, 29, 63, 74
    financial development, 79, 143
    financial liberalization, 9, 29, 137,
        141, 150
    financial market efficiency, 149
    GSP privileges, 131
    IDB lending, 19
    income distribution, 78
    inflation, 18
    internal market, 78
    intra-regional trade, 158, 166
    lending from multilateral institutions,
        18
    net factor-service payments, 63
    Pinochet government, 18–19, 37
    private bank lending to, 18
    private debt, 29
    private foreign asset holdings, 37
    privatization, 77–79, 81–82, 88, 95–
        96
    public enterprises, 80–82, 95
    public sector, 78–79, 81
    quasi-fiscal deficit, 32
    reprivatization, 83
    resource transfer, 15, 148
    "social question," 79
    "success story," 18, 37
    trade liberalization, 25, 77
Colombia
    capital account liberalization, 38
    debt service, 38
    financial development, 143, 148
    financial liberalization, 138, 141
    financial market efficiency, 149
    indexation, 148
    internal market, 78
    intra-regional trade, 166
    Lopez administration, 138
    net factor-service payments, 63
    privatization, 76
    resource transfer, 148
Commercial banks. See also External
    borrowing and debt
    capital positions, 72
    capital-asset ratio, 8–10
    collateral requirements, 141

continued lending, 56
debt write-offs, 5
IMF-concerted lending, 6
lending resistance, 6, 56, 72
lending to Chile, 18
loan reserves, 8
loan write-offs, 56
Mexican nationalization, 92, 94
new lending, 6
potential insolvency, 9
Commercial policies, 139, 155. *See also*
by country
Common market, Latin America, 157
Costa Rica, 75, 166
Credit subsidies, 138
Creditor countries
asset reporting, 37
courts, 8
"creditor club," 5–9, 14, 25
income transfer public to private
creditors, 44
insistence on debt service, 39
net transfer to, 45
policies, 5, 6, 8, 27, 33, 36, 37
Crowding out, 6, 85, 132
Cuba, 75–76, 78, 127
Currency substitution, 35
Current account
counterpart to savings balance, 50
financing of deficit, 144–45
financing of Latin American, 49
national accounts, 144
surplus countries, 8, 13–14, 39
Customs union, 158–161, 164

Debt and equity substitution, 141
Debt burden. *See also* External
borrowing and debt
consequences, 71, 150
distribution, 20
growth rate, 55
origins, 44
private liabilities, 31
stabilizing, 56
U.S. interest, 52
Debt crisis. *See also* External borrowing
and debt
antecedents, 47–49, 77

consequences, 55, 62
evolution, 71
external shocks, 153
forced adjustment, 41
import reduction, 42
intra-regional trade, 153
labor impact, 126
and Latin American growth, 121
origins, 35, 155
proposed solutions, 37
response, 156
shift in U.S. policy, 5
worsening in 1982, 40, 45
Debt issue, as source of public finance,
144, 146
Debt moratorium
alternative to liberalization, 56, 72
Mexico, 14, 144
pressures for, 35
Debt relief
Brady plan, 5–7, 14
market mechanisms, 52
impact on total debt, 156
Debt service
burden, 74
compatibility with recovery, 20
creditor insistence, 52, 144
creditor optimism, 5
effect on capital formation, 3, 56
financial market impact, 137
financing, 23, 25, 30, 50, 74
fiscal burden, 149
interruptions, 6
limitation, 36
moratorium, 72
official, 44
Paris Club reductions, 44
private, 44
public sector role, 144
ratio to exports, 25
U.S. insistence, 3, 14, 39
U.S. share, 41
Debt write-offs, 6–9, 12, 14, 21–24, 27,
123
Debt-equity and debt-debt swaps, 6, 9,
18, 45, 58, 80, 82, 156
Debt-GDP ratio, 25, 67, 69–71, 73
Debt-stabilizing real growth rate, 55, 57,
60–61, 71

Deposit insurance, effect on overlending, 141

Direct investment, 39, 44–45, 47–49, 146. *See also by country*

Dollarization, informal sector growth, 35

Domestic absorption, 144–145, 155–156

Domestic capital market liberalization, 141

Domestic consumption, impact of debt servicing, 126

Domestic credit, 97, 145

Domestic financial institutions, 142, 148

Domestic financial markets. *See also by country*
  fragility, 36
  Latin America, 138, 140
  liberalization, 8
  limitation on government borrowing, 148
  prospects for liberalization, 36
  transfer problem, 149

Domestic investment, effect of debt relief, 132

Domestic producers, opposition to integration, 160

Domestic saving, 50, 56, 61, 71

Dominican Republic, privatization, 76

Economic Commission for Latin America (ECLA), 157–160

Economic integration, 153, 156, 158, 161–162, 164–166

Economic Processing Zones (EPZ), 130

Ecuador, 62–63, 148, 166

Effective tax base, 31

El Salvador, 75–76, 127–128, 161, 166

Equity financing, costs, 141

Equity investment, relative to debt, 45, 141

Escrow account, 36, 37

European Economic Community (EEC), 157

Exchange rate. *See also by country*
  "rational" policies in financial liberalization, 138
  dollar overvaluation, 156
  Latin America, real effective, 41

overvaluation, 46, 155, 157
  proliferation of regimes, 155
  realism, 2, 8
  role in debt swaps, 6
  role in inflationary expectations, 80
  subsidies, 6, 31

Exit bonds, 6, 156

Export diversification, 42

Export elasticities, 22, 25

Export incentives, 155

Export prices, 122

External constraint on economic growth, 132

External borrowing and debt
  boom before 1982, 29
  borrower behavior, 23
  capital flight, 20
  collateralization, 36
  consequences, 122
  creditors, 56, 71–72
  debt buy-backs, 6, 8
  effect of relief, 132
  effect of write-off, 24
  effect on internal debt, 147
  exports and servicing, 122–123
  illiquidity versus insolvency, 9
  increase after 1982, 156
  interest payment, 145
  interest rate, 145
  legal obligation, 74
  limitations, 138
  minimum for growth, 25
  nominal decline after 1988, 156
  non-dollar denominated, 11
  origins, 122
  overhang, 35
  private, 9
  public sector, 145, 148–149
  ratio to GDP, 69
  ratio to total exports, 55
  requirements for recovery, 20
  service, 135, 137, 150, 155
  US policies, 121, 126
  value in foreign currency, 145
  write-off effect, 23

External resource transfer, 138, 144, 147, 149

External saving, 55, 57–58, 60–61, 63, 67, 69, 72–73
External shocks, role in debt crisis, 153
External transfer problem, 150, 155
Exxon, staffing compared to Pemex, 94

Federal Reserve, 9–10
Financial institutions, inflation tax and, 148
Financial liberalization, 8, 35–36, 137–140, 144, 150
Financial markets. *See also by country*
  capital account liberalization, 141
  deepening, 138
  demand deposits, 148–149
  development, 138–139, 150
  efficiency, 137–138, 140, 143–144, 148–149
  liberalization, 138
  liquidity, 148
  non-monetary sectors, 140
  relative to GDP, 142
  repression, 29, 139
  reserve deposits, 150
  resource transfer, 138, 149–150
  risk, 139
  size, 148
  specialization, 139
  transfer problem, 144, 147–148
  value added, 142, 143
Financial shock, post-1982, 156
Fiscal deficit
  causes, 31
  debt write-down effect, 35
  effect on domestic financial markets, 33
  effect on public investment, 35
  fiscal "overstretching," 31
  motive for privatization, 76
  off-budget items, 31
Fiscal forgiveness, 82
Fiscal restructuring, 87. *See also* Adjustment programs, Restructuring programs
Foreign capital allocation, 137
  antagonism to, 161
  as financing source, 101
  Central America, 160

  political resistance to, 98
Foreign exchange constraint, 22, 156
Free-trade area (FTA), 158–159, 161–162, 164

General Agreement on Tariffs and Trade (GATT), "Enabling Clause," 164, 167
1982 Ministerial Meeting, 163
  Article XXIV, 158, 160, 163
  customs union, 158
  discipline, 157, 159, 160, 161, 164
  free-trade area, 158
  Kennedy Round, 159
  Mexican entrance, 93
  most favored nation (MFN) treatment, 160, 166
  multilateralism, 166
  notification, 158
  trade diversion, 159
  trade liberalization, 163
  Treaty of Montevideo, 159
  United States policies, 129, 133, 157, 163, 164, 166
  violation of rules, 39, 51
  worker rights, 129, 136
Generalized System of Preferences (GSP), 129–131, 133
Gramm-Rudman constraints, 20
Grupo Andino, 160. *See also* Regional trade
Guatemala, 75, 166

Harrod-Domar growth model, 57–61
Honduras, 75, 127, 161, 166
Human capital development, 132, 134
Human rights, 121, 127, 129–134
Hyperinflation, 18, 35, 90

Import elasticities, 22, 25
Import restrictions, 50, 155
Import substitution, 41, 142, 157
Incentives
  banking system, 151
  investment, 101
  overborrowing, 155
  trade negotiations, 167
  trading blocs, 164
Income distribution, 35, 78, 82, 124

Incremental capital-output ratio (ICOR),
    55, 57, 60–61, 71, 73
Indexation
    debt takeovers, 31
    financial assets, 139–140, 151
    financial system effects, 138
    internal transfer, 149
Inflation. See also by country
    Bolivian stabilization plan, 148
    effect of trade surplus, 149
    effect on
        capital measurement, 113
        financial markets, 148
        public enterprises, 118
        real money demand, 151
        receivership, 151
    expectations, 118, 141
    feedback mechanisms, 149
    finance source, 150
    financial development, 140
    financial market efficiency, 149
    financial reform, 144
    government deficits, 149
    indexation, 149
    public enterprise pricing, 118
    relation to financial efficiency, 151
    relation to government deficits, 151
    resource transfer, 137, 147, 149
    transfer problem, 144, 147, 148
Inflation tax 31, 144, 148–150
Informal sector, 4, 15, 35, 124, 134
Infrastructure
    maintenance, 31, 35, 76
    public enterprises, 98
    public investment, 101
Inter-American Development Bank
    (IDB), 19, 45, 51, 132
Interbank deposits, 9
Interest payments and rates. See also
    External borrowing and debt
    after second oil shock, 122
    capital market liberalization, 141
    capitalization, 18
    effect on external debt, 55
    financial liberalization, 138–139
    rationing of borrowers, 141
    subsidized, 31
    tax treatment, 141

    uncertainty, 45
    United States, 140
    world trend in 1980s, 44, 51
Internal debt
    financing of deficit, 147
    indexed, 149
    market, 147–148
Internal transfer
    burden on domestic financial
        markets, 149
    counterpart to external transfer, 138
    equivalence to real deficit, 147
    monetary consequences, 144
    property rights, 30
    role of inflation, 149
International banking community, 49–
    50. See also Creditor countries
International capital mobility, 155
International financial markets, 9, 20, 37,
    56, 139
International Labor Organization (ILO)
    development and training programs,
        133
    international labor standards
        conventions, 130–131
    labor representatives, 131
    labor standards conventions, 133
    U.S. participation, 121
    U.S. support, 131
    World Employment Programme, 131,
        136
International Monetary Fund (IMF)
    conditionality, 8
    debt-reduction programs, 13
    estimation of off-budget losses, 32
    facilitation of debt write-offs, 8
    financial liberalization, 36
    lending packages, 6, 9, 14
    lending policies, 132
    stabilization programs, 52, 97,
        135
    support for trade surplus, 50
    US influence, 126
International Trade Secretariat (ITS),
    127, 136
Intra-regional exports, 156. See also
    Regional trade
Investment-GDP ratio, 22, 52

Jamaica, 75–76
Japan
current account surplus, 8
economic growth, 44
financial assistance, 13–14, 20
industrial policy, 83
model of export growth, 83

Labor attaché program, 121, 126, 128–129, 133, 136
Labor force, 123–124
Labor markets, 122–124, 135
Labor relations, 121, 124–125, 128, 132, 135, 161
Labor support for military regimes, 123
Labor use, public enterprises, 110–112
Labor-rights provisions, U.S. trade policy, 129
Latin American intra-regional exports, 156. *See also* Regional trade
Latin American labor migration, 2, 35
Latin American Association for Integration (LAIA), 159, 162, 165, 167
Latin American Free Trade Association (LAFTA), 158, 159, 160, 161, 162, 166
Lending syndicates, 9–10
Liberalization programs, 5, 139, 151
LIBOR (London Interbank Offered Rate), 44
Liquidity squeeze, 10
Loan contracts, 7–8, 12
Loan risk, collateral requirements, 141
"Lost Decade," 15, 20, 22–23, 153

Macroeconomic environment, 162, 165
Malvinas (Falkland) War, 88, 100
Market access, United States, 129–130
Market discounts, 6, 9
Market liberalization, 6, 8, 14–15, 17, 20, 25, 35–37, 75
Martinez de Hoz, José, 88, 100
Mercado Comun Centroamericano (MCCA). *See* Central American Common Market

Mexico
Banco de Mexico, share in Aeromexico, 94
banking sector, 140
banking system nationalization, 137
bilateral lending to, 20
capital flight, 46, 137, 140
capital formation, 62
capital market, 89, 137
De la Madrid administration, 92–93
debt moratorium, 8, 14, 140, 144
dollarization, 140
Echeverria administration, 78
economic growth, 53
entrance into GATT, 93
exchange rate policy, 140
exports, 50, 53
external debt, 6, 14, 20, 25, 31, 63, 155
financial development, 139, 140
financial non-intervention, 137
fiscal deficit, 31
import substitution, 157
indexation, 148
inflation, 18
internal debt, 34
internal market, 78
intra-regional trade, 161, 166
investment, 77
liberalization, 20
Lopez Portillo administration, 78, 92
macroeconomic policies, 140
Mining Development Commission divestitures, 94
Ministry of Tourism divestitures, 94
multilateral lending to, 20
"multiple banks," 139
Nacional Financiera, 94–95
net factor-service payments, 63
primary budget, 31
privatization, 92–96
public enterprises, 76, 78, 92–94
real wages, 52, 93
regional trade, 164, 165
reserves, 140
resource transfer, 148
restructuring programs, 14
Salinas administration, 93

Mexico (continued)
　secondary debt market, 53
　"semi-privatization," 94
　trade liberalization, 25, 93, 95
　trade surplus, 20
　U.S. exports to, 135
　U.S. policy towards, 14, 20
"Minilateralism," 153, 161–166
Monetary base, 145–149, 151
Moral hazard, 141
Moral obligation, 74
Most-favored-nation (MFN) treatment,
　159–160, 162, 166
Motley, Langhorne, 37
Mulford, David, 13
Multilateral institutions, 8, 14, 18–20,
　45, 51, 132. See also IDB, IMF and
　World Bank
Multilateral trade, 157, 162–163, 166–
　167
Multilateralism, 160, 166
Multinational banks, 45, 48
Multinational corporations, 135, 162

"national list," 159
Nationalism, 6, 98, 123, 161
Net external liabilities-GDP ratio, 55–
　60, 69
Net resource transfer, 51, 138. See also
　Resource transfer
Nicaragua, 76, 131, 162, 166
Non-deductible dividends, tax
　treatment, 141
Non-interest deficit, public sector, 145
Non-performing loans, 33
Non-tariff barriers (NTBs), 42, 162, 164
Non-traditional exports, 42, 53, 83
Non-U.S. creditors, 41

Official creditors, 8
Official financing, 8
Oil shock, 1, 49, 85, 122
Oligopoly, 82, 138
OPEC surplus, 45. See also Petrodollars
Organizacion Regional Interamericana
　del Trabajo (ORIT), 127
Overseas Private Investment Corporation
　(OPIC), 129–130

Paraguay, GSP privileges, 131
Parastatals. See Public enterprises
Paris Club, debt negotiation, 14, 44. See
　also Brady Plan, External borrowing
　and debt
Peronism, 89, 100–101, 109–110. See
　also Argentina
Peru
　Belaunde administration, 138
　capital formation, 62
　dollarization, 29
　economic policies, 30, 76
　exception to liberalization trend, 76
　external debt, 14, 63
　financial liberalization, 141
　Garcia administration, 76
　indexation, 148
　inflation, 18
　insolvency, 29
　internal debt, 29
　intra-regional trade, 166
　political context, 76
　public enterprises, 76, 95
　public sector expansion, 78
　reforms 1980–84, 138
　resource transfer, 148
Petrodollars 48–49, 122–123
Positive externalities, in
　industrialization, 157
Prebisch, Raul, 157
Primary budget, 31. See also Fiscal
　deficit
Private sector
　"surplus," 145
　capital flows to, 98
　economic environment, 117
　internal transfer, 138
　investment, 106
　relation to government, 98
　resource transfer, 144, 148, 150
Privatization. See also by country
　business pressure, 35
　consequences, 75, 135
　creditor interest, 73
　deregulation, 76
　effect on capital formation, 77
　labor impact, 135
　motivations, 17, 97, 135
　objectives, 76–77

origins, 75
"retreat of the state," 76
"semi-privatization," 85
simulated privatization, 80, 85, 93, 95
stabilization programs, 97
structural adjustment, 95
world wide trend, 94
Profit remittances, 145
Public enterprises. *See also by country*
capital use, 110, 113
deficits, 97, 117, 119
efficiency, 119
employment, 102, 108, 117
financial performance, 101
history, 98
investment, 102, 106–108
labor productivity, 113–114
macroeconomic policies, 117
management, 79, 118–119
performance, 97, 117–119
pricing, 118
privatization, 76
profits or return on capital, 116
role, 97–98, 135
semi-privatization, 80
Public Law, 100–118, 136
Public sector. *See also by country*
control, 71
deficit, 50
employment and wages, 31, 100, 124
expenditure growth, 50
external debt and financing, 50, 144–145
financial deficit, 147
internal transfer, 138
management, 119, 155
resource absorption, 75
resource transfer, 148, 150
saving, 56
stabilization programs, 97, 165

"Quasi-fiscal" deficit, 32–33, 150. *See also* Fiscal deficit

Reagan administration, 19, 37, 123, 131, 153, 162. *See also* U.S. policies

Real depreciation or devaluation, 41–42, 50, 52, 155
Real interest rate
capital repatriation, 35
economies with excess capacity, 34
effect of financial liberalization, 29
external debt growth, 60
negative, 31, 155
rise in 1980s, 39, 132, 153, 155–156
risk premium, 36
world, 139
Real investment, decline after 1982, 15
Real wage, declines in 1980s, 15, 35, 52, 124
Real-resource burden, 56
Regional trade, 153, 156–159, 162
Reprivatization, 79, 81, 83, 84, 88, 90, 92. *See also* Privatization
Rescue efforts, 31, 33. *See also* Debt write-offs, External borrowing and debt
Reserves, 56, 58, 98
Resource transfer
after 1982, 137
external, 144, 147
financial efficiency, 148–149
impact on investment, 15
inflation, 151
internal, 144, 148
overstatement, 20
real resource transfer, 39, 156
share of GDP, 148
trade balance as proxy, 151
trade policy, 157
Restructuring programs, 5–8, 15–20, 27, 77, 94. *See also* Adjustment programs, U.S. policies
Risk, overlending, 141
Risk premium, 36, 77
Romania, GSP privileges, 131

Sandinista Revolution, 75, 162. *See also* Nicaragua
Secondary market for debt, 6, 52–53
Section 301, 1988 Trade Act, 129
"Semi-privatization," 80, 92, 94. *See also* Privatization

Simulation models
    borrowing requirements, 22, 27
    debt-stabilizing growth, 67–70
South-South trade, 162
Southern Cone. *See also* Argentina,
    Chile, and Uruguay
    central bank policy, 139
    exchange rate policy, 141
    financial disasters, 36
    financial liberalization, 137, 138
    intra-regional trade, 158
    liberalization attempts, 150
    non-performing loans, 139
    rade liberalization, 161
State-owned Enterprises (SOEs). *See*
    Public Enterprises
Stock markets, effect of capital account
    liberalization, 141
Structural adjustment. *See also*
    Restructuring
    Baker Plan, 56
    costs, 122, 126, 135
    creditor support, 72
    debt moratorium, 72
    multilateral institution loans, 8
    privatization, 77

Tariff barriers, 42, 167
Tax base, 35, 144, 150
Tax evasion, 35
Terms of trade
    adverse movements, 139
    alternative assumptions, 22
    effect on export earnings, 22
    effect on external debt, 55
    effect on GDP growth, 73
    Latin American, 37, 153, 156
    primary product exporters, 157, 162
Trade creation, trade diversion, 158–165
Trade liberalization. *See also by country*
    borrowing needs, 25
    capital goods, 164
    comprehensive, 165
    "convoy" problem, 163
    effect of debt burden, 52

    effects on LDCs, 157
    failure, 159
    "free-rider" problem, 163
    GATT-consistent, 163
    global, 157, 166
    intra-regional, 160, 161
    Latin America, 153
    real depreciation, 2
    reciprocal, 157, 164
    regional, 163
    Southern Cone, 161
    timing, 151
    U.S. policy, 163
Trade surplus
    creditor insistence, 50
    import reduction vs. export
        expansion, 50
    Latin America after 1982, 52,
        156
    Latin American with U.S., 41
    ratio to interest payments, 10
    requirement for new lending, 49
    sustainability, 150
Transfer payments, 73
Treaty of Montevideo, 158–160, 162,
    165
Treaty of Rome, 157, 163
Two-gap model, 22

Unemployment
    compensation or relief, 80
    in Harrod-Domar model, 68–71, 73
    1981-83 crisis, 124
    open and underemployment, 124
Unions in Latin America
    "free," 127
    financing, 127
    leadership, 127
    origins, 124
    political context, 125
    recognition, 125
    U.S. affiliations, 127
United States
    balance of payments, profit
        remittances, 44
    bank lending to Latin America, 45,
        47, 49

bank regulation, 126
banking community, 49
bilateral aid or lending, 1, 20
capital account with Latin America, 45–49
creditors, 44
current account, effect of Latin American adjustment on, 40
Department of Labor, 128–130
Department of State, 129–130, 133
exports to Latin America, 135
financial experience, 139
financial intermediation, 45
foreign investment legislation, 129
intelligence community, 128
interest groups, 52
interest rates, 44, 140
labor policies, 121, 127, 134
market for Latin American exports, 156
money-center banks, 37
net bank lending, 46
1988 Trade Act, 129
policies
   adjustment program, 1
   bridge loans, 51
   capital flight, 2
   economic policies, 39, 44, 49, 51, 119, 122, 126, 132, 137, 150, 153, 155–156
   financial liberalization, 2, 4
   pressure on current account surplus countries, 13–14
   Mexico, 14
   trade policy, 1, 39, 126, 129, 153, 160–161, 163, 165–166
protection, 132
Trade Representative, 130–131, 133, 163
United States Information Service (USIS), 129, 133
Uruguay
   banking sector, 140
   capital flight, 139
   economic growth, 78
   economic policies, 140
   external borrowing, 140

financial development, 140, 143–144
financial liberalization, 137, 138, 141, 150
financial market efficiency, 149
fiscal deficit, 32–33
foreign investment in financial sector, 140
intra-regional trade, 158
privatization, 76
quasi-fiscal deficit, 32–33
regional trade, 165
resource transfer, 148
trade policy, 161
Uruguay Round 163, 166–167

Variable interest rate loans, 45. See also External borrowing and debt
Venezuela
   capital flight, 46
   capital formation, 62
   external debt, 20, 63
   financial development, 143–144, 148
   financial liberalization, 141
   financial market efficiency, 149
   inflation, 18, 149
   internal market, 78
   intra-regional trade, 166
   privatization, 76
   public enterprises, 76
   esource transfer, 147
   U.S. exports to, 135
Voluntary lending
   Brady plan, 8
   collapse in 1982, 29, 144, 155
   in balance of payments, 146
   restoration, 9

Western Europe, 44, 130
Worker rights, 121, 127, 129–134, 136. See also Labor relations, Unions in Latin America
World Bank. See also Multilateral institutions
   conditionality, 8

World Bank (continued)
    debt-reduction programs, 13
    facilitation of debt write-offs, 8
    lending policies, 14, 132
    U.S. influence, 45, 51, 126

Write-offs. *See* Debt Write-offs

X-efficiency, 15, 17, 35

Yen appreciation, 11

Contributors

WERNER BAER is Professor of Economics at the University of Illinois, where he has taught since 1974. He taught at Yale University and Vanderbilt University after receiving his Ph.D. from Harvard University. He specializes in economic development and Latin American economics. The third edition of his book *The Brazilian Economy: Growth and Development* was published by Praeger in 1989.

PAUL BECKERMAN is an economist at the World Bank. He previously taught at the University of Illinois, Boston University, and Fordham University after receiving his Ph.D. at Princeton University. He has also served on the staff of the Federal Reserve Bank of New York and has studied the economies of Argentina, Bolivia, and Brazil.

MELISSA H. BIRCH is Associate Professor at the Darden School of Business of the University of Virginia. Her principal research focus is on public sector management in developing countries, especially in Latin America. She received her Ph.D. from the University of Illinois.

JOHN CASKEY is Assistant Professor of Economics at Swarthmore College in Swarthmore, Pennsylvania. He received his Ph.D. from Harvard University. His primary research interest is the functioning of domestic and international credit markets.

DONALD V. COES is Professor of International Management and Associate Director of the Latin American Institute at the University of New Mexico and Associate Professor of Economics at the University of Illinois.

DAVID FELIX is Professor of Economics Emeritus, Washington University, St. Louis. He is the author of numerous studies of Latin American economies, with a special emphasis on industrialization, inflation, and external debt. He is the editor of *Debt and Transfiguration: Prospects for Latin America's Economic Revival,* to be published in 1990.

WILLIAM GLADE is currently Associate Director of the United States Information Agency in charge of the Bureau of Educational and Cultural Affairs. He is on leave from the University of Texas at Austin where he is Professor of Economics. He is the author of *The Latin American Economies* and numerous articles.

CARLOS ALBERTO PRIMO BRAGA is Assistant Professor of Economics at the Universidade de São Paulo in São Paulo, Brazil. In 1988 and 1989 he was a Visiting Professor of Economics at the School for Advanced International Studies of the Johns Hopkins University in Washington, D.C. He received his Ph.D. from the University of Illinois. Most of his recent research has been on Brazilian trade issues.

RUSSELL E. SMITH is Associate Professor of Economics at Washburn University. He received his Ph.D. at the University of Illinois. He has studied wage determination, inflation, indexation, and labor relations in Latin America, and has conducted research on these topics in Argentina and Brazil.

JOHN H. WELCH is Assistant Professor of Economics at the University of North Texas. His study of Brazilian financial markets, *Capital Markets in the Development Process: The Case of Brazil*, will be published in 1990. He received his doctoral degree from the University of Illinois.